D0557925

NEW YORK REVIEW BOOKS
CLASSICS

MONSIEUR PROUST

CÉLESTE ALBARET (1892–1984) was born into a peasant family in the mountainous region of Lozère, France. In 1913, she married Odilon Albaret, a Parisian chauffeur, whose clients included Marcel Proust. Odilon suggested that his new wife, who was lonely in the big city and at a loss for something to do, run errands for Proust, and before long Céleste found herself employed as the writer's full-time (indeed round-the-clock) housekeeper, secretary, and nurse, filling those roles until his death in 1922. In later years, Céleste ran a small hotel in Paris with her husband and daughter, and after Odilon's death in 1960, she became the caretaker of the Musée Ravel in the town of Montfort l'Amaury. *Monsieur Proust* was published in 1972. In recognition of her decade-long service to Proust, Céleste Albaret was made a commander of the French Order of Arts and Letters. She died of emphysema at the age of 92.

ANDRÉ ACIMAN teaches comparative literature at the City University Graduate Center in New York. He is the author of the memoir *Out of Egypt* and of *False Papers*, a collection of essays.

MONSIEUR PROUST

CÉLESTE ALBARET

As told to

GEORGES BELMONT

Translated from the French by

BARBARA BRAY

Foreword by

ANDRÉ ACIMAN

NEW YORK REVIEW BOOKS

New York

This is a New York Review Book
Published by The New York Review of Books
435 Hudson Street, New York, NY 10014
www.nyrb.com

Photographic credits: Céleste Albaret 1, 2, 3, 4, 5, 6, 7, 8, 9, 11, 13, 19, 29, 30, 35, 36, 37, 54, 55, 57; Paris-Match 10; Mante-Proust 14, 17, 20, 24, 25, 31; Bibliothèque National de France 16, 21, 28, 33, 34, 38, 39, 40, 41, 42, 43, 46, 50, 53, 56; Lapad-Viollet 18; René Jacques 22; Jean-Louis Vaudoyer 23, 26; Roget-Viollet 32; Princesse Bibesco 48, 49; Duc de Grammont 51. All other photographs are in private collections.

Library of Congress Cataloging-in-Publication Data
Albaret, Céleste.
  [Monsieur Proust. English]
  Monsieur Proust / Céleste Albaret ; as told to Georges Belmont ;
translated from the French by Barbara Bray ; foreword by André Aciman.
      p. cm.
Originally published: London : Collins : Harvill Press, 1976.
Includes index.
  ISBN 1-59017-059-8 (pbk. : alk. paper)
  1. Proust, Marcel, 1871–1922. 2. Albaret, Céleste. 3. Novelists,
French—20th century—Biography. 4. Domestics—France—Biography.
I. Belmont, Georges. II. Title.
  PQ2631.R63Z461613 2003
  843'.912—dc22

                            2003017246

ISBN 978-1-59017-059-5

Printed in the United States of America on acid-free paper.
10 9 8 7 6

CONTENTS

FOREWORD

In April of 1984 both *The New York Times* and *Le Monde* ran obituaries announcing the death of Céleste Albaret. News of the ninety-two-year-old Frenchwoman's death brought woeful reminders to literary communities on both sides of the Atlantic that an era had indeed come to an end. Céleste Albaret was not only one of the very few remaining individuals who had actually known Marcel Proust, but, in her capacity as his housekeeper from 1913 to his very dying day in 1922, she had become the writer's most trusted conduit to the world beyond his reclusive, cork-lined bedroom. From the tireless and sprightly gal Friday and Jeeves-of-all-trades—she was his errand girl, cook, seamstress, secretary, nurse, chambermaid, and cut-and-paste genius whose handiwork is the focal point of any exhibit devoted to Proust manuscripts—she had become his staunchest confidante. "It will be your beautiful little hands that close my eyes," he would say to her. Elsewhere she scolds him, "[There's] no reason for always talking about dying. . . . You'll live longer than I will." Monsieur Proust was not the sort to trust his eyes, much less his body, to anyone. Nor was Céleste the sort to quip with her perennially fastidious employer. Between them hovered a middle mist that neither would have dared cross and which stayed in place by something they both had an inexhaustible amount of—tact:

We were both orphans—he with his parents dead and his friends scattered, and I with my parents dead, my family far away, and my husband in the army. So we created our own sort of intimacy, though for him it was chiefly an atmosphere within which to work, while I forgot about my own tasks and could see nothing but a magic circle.

One needed to be resourceful, quick-witted, and have more than a strong backbone to serve an ailing workaholic like Proust. But even that was not enough. One had to be as dutiful, as scrupulous, and as selfless as a mother. Céleste anticipated every one of his needs. He grew to expect that she would do no less. They spoke in silences, exchanging secrets and pleasantries, confident that both would never for a moment forget their place. Monsieur Proust did not need reminding that he was the boss. Céleste was too self-effacing to presume that he gave her a second thought. If over the years they developed a certain affection, neither would ever have dared call it love. But love it must have been. Not the love of a servant or of a master, nor the love of equals, but of people who are thrown together in one apartment and who, to their complete surprise, discover that they have achieved a degree of intimacy without ever finding the other unbearable.

Céleste stole in and out of Monsieur Proust's day-to-day life, ministering to his tiniest whims: his very hot coffee, his croissant, his second double-boiled coffee, his mounds of dirty towels, his handkerchiefs, his asthma attacks, his fumigations for his asthma attacks, his hand-delivered messages, especially after he had the telephone removed from his home. Sometimes he went hours, even days without ringing for her in the kitchen. Sometimes he would go out very late and return just before dawn, which meant she'd have to wait up for him; Monsieur Proust never carried house keys.

Life in his employ became one unending vigil. Waiting for him to wake up. Waiting for him to come back. Waiting for him to feel better. Waiting for him to leave the apartment in order for her to air his bedroom or perform heavy-duty work, which, in other circumstances, might prove too noisy and disturb the world's latest riser. Waiting. Waiting. Waiting.

To keep up with Monsieur Proust, Céleste learned to mold her life to his. She kept his hours. She turned night into day and day into night. The curtains that draped all of his windows kept the sunlight out, but they also threw time off course.

Sometimes, when he would come back very late at night, Monsieur Proust just wanted to talk. He would ask Céleste to step into the living room or into his bedroom and there he would unfold the events of the evening and unburden himself of his thoughts. Theirs was, and would always remain, a *ménage à un* in which she was allowed to play the part of the fly on the wall:

> I almost can see M. Proust sitting on the end of his bed in the faint light of the room, telling stories and imitating one person after the other, with delight or sudden sadness, I realize I was the privileged spectator of the most beautiful theater in the world, and I understand why he enjoyed it too. His bringing home the drama of the outside world and unfolding it before me was an attempt to hold back time, to stop it from fleeing and taking his characters with it.

There is something almost magical in seeing these two noctambulists, who couldn't have been more different, doing the one thing both had grown to love together: gossip.

He urged her to keep a diary. "Better still, Céleste: you write it and I shall make comments on it as you go along." In this Proust was probably hoping to emulate in yet another way his model

Saint-Simon, who had annotated the courtier Dangeau's historical journal of the reign of Louis XIV before realizing that he, not Dangeau, was the one to memorialize the age.

Céleste, however, never kept a diary. And Proust never did have the opportunity to jot down his commentary. That is a loss.

But the greater—incalculable—loss is the disappearance of Proust's *cahiers noirs* (black books), which Céleste describes as containing "the first drafts of the book, long fragments and even whole chapters written in the course of earlier years, even of his youth." Proust had ordered her to burn all thirty-two of them. She obeyed. Sometimes, because he had more than just a tendency to distrust everyone and must have suspected her slightly mischievous side, he began to fear that she might disobey him and spirit the notebooks away. But no, Céleste was faithful to a fault. She carried out the incineration, blindly, reducing all thirty-two notebooks to ashes. Max Brod proved himself a far more judicious friend when he broke his promise to a dying Kafka and decided not to burn the latter's manuscripts.

History, meanwhile, has not only forgiven Céleste Albaret her obedience; it has showered upon her recognition the likes of which very few servants have known. One is hard put to think of another servant who was made a commander of the French Order of Arts and Letters, or who has had a movie devoted entirely to her career in the service of a famous artist—as was the case with the charming German film *Céleste* (1982). No biographer writing about Proust today can afford to overlook Céleste's testimony.

By her own admission, Céleste Albaret never had any intention of entering Proust's permanent employ. Because her husband was Proust's personal chauffeur, she was asked to fill in for a few days and help run errands. Surely the starry-eyed, easily intimidated young girl from the country must have had something that pleased her employer, and over the course of weeks and months he not only decided to keep her on a full-time basis, but ultimately fired the woman for whom she was originally meant to substitute. But what she never could have dreamed is that she would wait on his every need for nine years. After his death she opened and ran a small hotel in Paris, keeping her silence and, for reasons known only to her, distancing herself both from those who wished to seek her out and from the ever-rising wave of Proust's fame. She disappeared as quietly as she had tiptoed into his life.

Then, in the very early Seventies, fifty years after Proust's death and after a half-century in which Céleste kept his memory to herself, the French publishing house Laffont approached her and persuaded her to tell all she knew of the private life of Marcel Proust. Céleste Albaret dictated seventy hours of taped material to Georges Belmont, a man known to French letters for his interviews with American movie stars and for his translations of Anthony Burgess, Graham Greene, Henry James, and Henry Miller.

The book did exceptionally well, not least because what emerged was a portrait of Proust that was not drastically different from the Marcel of the novel. Monsieur Proust may have been more retiring, more reticent, and far more intimidating as an employer than one would imagine the perennially dreamy, starstruck, awkward adolescent Marcel to be. But both are fussy, calculating, whimsical, ironic, and unremittingly penetrating in their perceptions. They see through people, through things, through life. And everyone around them knows it.

Céleste's Monsieur Proust and Marcel Proust share one further trait: both are locked in the past and are eager to find a pathway to the bygone universe of their childhood. They are loyal to anything that reminds them of it—old stores, old clothiers, old ways of doing and of cooking and of saying things.

And perhaps there is a reason why Céleste Albaret's Proust, unlike the Proust of so many recent biographers, is so similar to the narrator of *Remembrance of Things Past*. Either the two were indeed extraordinarily similar individuals, which suggests that Céleste's portrait is perhaps the more accurate of the lot; or, something else is afoot. Perhaps Proust's compulsive nostalgia may have belonged less to the man who paid Céleste's salary than to the man she came to read and reread and had heard everyone rave about for fifty years. Even if Céleste had never read *À la recherche* in its entirety but was able to piece together a good-enough likeness of it from what others had said, perhaps she simply transferred to the man she had known in the flesh the very same yearnings and personality he claimed were his in his prose. By echoing his own voice, by frequently repeating that Proust was obsessed with memory and lost time, Céleste Albaret reproduced the same character we encounter in his novel. In the end, she gave to his readers a Proust whom Proust had labored a lifetime to create, to perfect, to invent.

Which is another way of saying that she not only echoes his vision but fails to see through so many of his disguises. Her inability—or unwillingness—to accept that Proust had a homosexual side is a large-enough blind spot to alert the reader that hers is not only the voice of a loyal partisan who will continue to transmit to posterity Proust's elaborate fibs about his sexuality, but that, all told, she would rather be taken in by them than expose areas to which, without knowing, perhaps, she had already turned a blind eye during his lifetime.

And yet Céleste Albaret is by no means naive or so easily bilked. She understood that between Proust's self-sacrificing devotion to his magnum opus and his irrepressible capacity to see through everyone's most elusive foible there really was no room left for a human being to step into his life and do what would have been so normal to anyone else: share it. She understood, more-over, "that he must have let, or even made, a lot of people think he felt affection and friendship for them, whereas in fact—it was the thing that always struck [her]—he could do without all of them with the greatest of ease." She also understood that "by dint of analyzing himself and others . . . he'd left himself with nothing but motives and explanations."

There is a sort of trenchancy to these observations that is as much Proustian as it is Freudian. One is tempted to suggest that perhaps these insights are less those of the chambermaid Céleste than of Georges Belmont, the man to whom she dictated them. The taped conversations with Céleste, when and if they are made public in their entirety, could resolve the matter easily enough.

But what if—what if these insights into the man Proust are indeed those of a chambermaid who saw him as he really was, dirty linen and all? Then the answer stares at us with a starkness that is almost frightening: Marcel Proust had found in his cham-bermaid a sister-soul whose sensibility was not only supremely compatible with his own but who, within a short period of time, turned out to have the one quality he sought as desperately as he sought to avoid it: she had become indispensable. To have her and yet keep her at bay, Proust did something that readers of *À la recherche* will recognize—he made her his prisoner. And Céleste, as was her wont, was only too happy to oblige.

—ANDRÉ ACIMAN

INTRODUCTION

When Marcel Proust died in 1922, already famous throughout the world, there was a general rush to procure the memoirs of the woman who for Proust remained always "my dear Céleste." Many people knew that having lived close to him day in, day out, through the eight key years of his life, she alone was in possession of essential truths about the character, the friendships, the loves, the view of the world, the ideas and work of this great invalid genius. For hours every night—nights that were day for Proust, whose morning began at four in the afternoon—Céleste Albaret had had the extraordinary privilege of listening to Proust reminisce about the past and describe the evenings he had recently spent in society—mimicking, laughing like a child, reciting what would become this or that chapter in one of his books. In short, in her presence he lived and revealed himself as to no one else.

Céleste was a key witness, in the middle of everything; but for fifty years she refused to talk. Her life, she said, had ended with Proust. Just as he had shut himself up in his work, she wanted to retreat into the memory of him. There alone would he remain the splendid monarch of the mind, the monster of tyranny and goodness she had "loved, enjoyed, and put up with," as she now says. To try to describe all of this—and to do it poorly, she thought—would be to betray him.

If she has changed her mind at the age of eighty-two, it is because she has come to the conclusion that others less scrupulous have betrayed Proust grossly, either because they lacked her access to the truth, or through excessive imagination or the temptation to promote their "interesting" or self-interested little theories.

I hope the reader will forgive a personal word here. But I owe it to myself to say that I would not have agreed to become Mme. Albaret's echo if, after just a few weeks—our conversations lasted five months—I hadn't been convinced that her candor was absolutely genuine. For this book is bound to contradict many accepted ideas and cause some chagrin, and I wanted to be sure that for my part I wasn't contributing, as I said to Mme. Albaret, to another kind of betrayal: to make of Proust an idol.

Seventy hours of interviews by dint of tests and countertests finally gave me the proof. I would, for instance, return seven or eight times to some point or another, trying to surprise her with different approaches, but I never encountered any contradiction. Moreover, there are certain tones of voice which cannot deceive. If those who read this book could actually hear the story the way it was told to me and as I myself have heard it, I am sure they would recognize the most sincere of all voices —the voice of the heart.

My tasks have been to respect that voice in the transition from the spoken to the written word and to organize the material into subjects and chapters. And there is another thing I must say, for this was what convinced me most deeply of all. During the months that followed our interviews and in which the book took shape, not only did I live completely involved in Proust, thanks to the voice I had been listening to, but I also saw and heard him in a way that at times was almost hallucinatory. Not once did I doubt that this was the real Proust. Until then, no other book had ever given me this experience.

—GEORGES BELMONT, 1973

I should like to give special thanks to Odile Gevaudan (Mme. Albaret's daughter), Suzanne Kadar, and Hortense Chabrier for their invaluable help with the research and verification involved in this work.

MONSIEUR PROUST

For my daughter
Odile

1

A GRAND SEIGNEUR

It is sixty years now since I saw him for the first time, but it is as if it were yesterday. He often said to me: "When I'm dead you'll always think of little Marcel, for you'll never find another like him." And now I see he was right—as he always was. I've never been separated from him; I've never stopped thinking of him or taking him as a model. When I can't sleep at night, he seems to be talking to me. If I have a problem, I ask myself, "What would he tell me to do if he were here?" And I can hear his voice: "My dear Céleste, . . ." and I know what he'd say. All the happy things that come my way, I think it is he who sends them, because he wished only for my good. Whenever something pleasant happened to me when he was alive, or if anyone praised me to him, he was always pleased. When someone has been great in this world, as he was, he must still be so afterward, and I'm sure he still cares for me even in the other world.

Ten years is not such a long time. But those ten years I spent working for M. Proust, in his house, are for me a whole lifetime, and I thank heaven for them—I couldn't have dreamed of a more beautiful life. I didn't realize this at the time. I followed the daily routine, and I was happy to be in his household. When I said so to him, he'd give me his searching look, teasing and kind at the same time, and reply:

"Come now, my dear Céleste, surely it must be dull to live only at night, with an invalid."

And I would protest. He was joking, but he had realized, long before I did, what.that life meant to me. It is difficult to put this into words. It was his charm, his smile, the way he spoke, holding his delicate hand against his cheek. He set the tone of the song. When life stopped for him it stopped for me too, but the song is still there.

Meeting him must have been fate. How could I have guessed that my marriage itself would lead me to him?

It was 1913: I was not yet twenty-two, and I had never left my village of Auxillac in the Lozère. My maiden name was Gineste. I lived in a big house with my adored mother, father, sister and brothers, and as I grew up I had had no intention of either marrying or leaving home. Odilon Albaret, who later became my husband, used to spend the holidays with my family, at my cousins' house. He was a very nice young man, with an honest, round face and a full moustache, in the style of the time. He lived in Paris, where he drove a taxi. He was born in 1881, which means he was ten years older than I was. I knew he'd lost his mother when he was still a boy, and perhaps the affection I had for my mother, and the grief he still felt over having lost his, brought us close to each other.

He had a married sister, very dynamic and bossy, who had been a mother to her brothers and now ran a café in Paris, at the corner of rue Montmartre and rue Feydeau. Her name was Adèle—she had become Mme. Larivière—M. Proust mentions her in his book—in *Le Temps retrouvé*, I think. And one of my cousins told me that Adèle would like her brother to marry me. I knew Odilon well; I liked him; we used to write to each other. But we didn't meet very often, and the idea of marrying hadn't really entered my head. Besides, my family had some reservations about Odilon. It was only ten days before our wedding took place that another cousin of mine told my mother that Odilon wasn't right for me—probably because he lived in Paris and his work would keep him there so much. In those days families used to live close to one another; to marry didn't mean a couple left their community. On the other hand, I could no

2

longer see much of a future in Auxillac. Anyway, Odilon had proposed and I had finally accepted.

We were married on the twenty-seventh of March, 1913. And that day, just as we were setting out for the church with all the family, the postman brought Odilon a telegram. I could see he was very moved, and I asked, "What is it?"

He said, "Congratulations and good wishes from one of my clients in Paris." He found it hard to believe. "He's no ordinary client, I know that—a very special man—but I'd never have thought he'd take the trouble to send me a wire."

He was deeply touched. He showed me the telegram, which was indeed more than kind. I have kept it. It reads: "All my congratulations. I can't write at greater length because I have the grippe and am tired, but I send my best wishes for your and your family's happiness." It was signed "Marcel Proust."

It was the first time I heard of him. All the while Odilon and I had known each other, all the while we were engaged, Odilon hadn't said a word about him. Later that day he told me that M. Proust was a good client, and so, before leaving Paris for our wedding, Odilon had informed him that he would be away for two or three weeks and would not be able to chauffeur him as usual. He explained why.

"And where is the wedding taking place?" M. Proust had asked.

"In my home town," Odilon said.

"And where is that?"

Odilon told him, and M. Proust asked, "And on what date?"

From what I knew of him later, I am sure, just by the way he asked, that he already had thought of sending his congratulatory telegram.

After the wedding, which we had planned for Easter so that the whole family could attend, we all set off for Paris to spend the rest of the holiday together. There must have been nearly a coachful of us. I didn't sleep that night, and I remember being furious because my husband slept like all the rest and no one took any notice of me. In the morning, when we arrived at the Gare de Lyon and I saw all the smoke and all the people rushing after taxis, I felt completely lost. Odilon finally found a taxi. I remember, as we went past the Théâtre-Français, my husband pointed and said, "Look there—that's the Opéra."

I looked, saw a greenish roof, and, disappointed, replied: "Is that really it?"

We finally got home—a little flat in a new building at Levallois, which Odilon had found with great difficulty. The problem, as he later explained to me, was that he wanted it to be near a café that stayed open as late as possible at night, because M. Proust, who was then "his" M. Proust, would sometimes telephone, or leave a message, asking him to pick him up with the car, as late as ten or eleven, even midnight. Although until then Odilon's sister Adèle had taken the messages at her café, my husband preferred to live at Levallois because it was easier there to find a garage for his taxi. And nearby was a café which had a phone and stayed open late—just what he was looking for.

The apartment was brand new, tidy, and comfortable, but I don't know why—probably tiredness, overexcitement, the new surroundings—I started to cry as soon as I got inside. Then I fell fast asleep.

A fortnight went by. I had great difficulty sleeping and getting used to the new life. Fortunately I had my other sister-in-law, Julie Albaret, who was like a mother to me then. I didn't know how to do anything. At home in Auxillac my mother had spoiled my sister and me and always did all the housework. I couldn't even light a fire. My sister-in-law gave me advice and taught me the basic housekeeping tasks. More importantly, she took me shopping with her, teaching me how.

And my husband was so considerate in everything, so kind and patient. I remember one instance of his kindness in particular. In the country we never locked doors. And one day in Paris I pulled the door shut behind me, and there I was with the key inside and myself outside. I found the concierge and we went out into the street, thinking there might be a way in through the kitchen window. At that moment my husband arrived. He had a key, but as mine was still in the lock he had to climb through the window just the same. Afterward he simply said to me very gently, "This isn't the country, you know, my darling. You must try not to forget your key."

I took this as a reproach and began to cry. The slightest thing upset me. And yet my husband did everything he could think of to please me. He brought home flowers to cheer me up. And once, thanks to my sister-in-law Adèle, whose café was frequented by singers, we got seats for *Mignon* at the Opéra-Comique. In the middle of it Odilon asked me, "Do you like it? Isn't it beautiful?" But I was tired by all the singing, and replied, "Will it be over soon?"

He laughed over that for the rest of his life. I was so young. But he was never sharp with me; he just waited for me to adjust. During those first two weeks he said to me, "You'll get used to it, and when you do, I'll go back to work, but not before."

So, after about two weeks—that is, in April—he said, "If you would like to come with me for a walk, we'll go as far as boulevard Haussmann to Monsieur Proust's house, to tell him that from now on he can send for me if he needs me. I'm starting work again."

So off we strolled to 102 boulevard Haussmann. We went up the service stairs to the first floor. The kitchen door opened onto the landing. Nicolas Cottin, the valet, let us in. His wife, Céline, who also worked for M. Proust, was there too. They were charming, especially Nicolas, and seemed very pleased that my husband was back. I myself, because of my shyness, wasn't inclined to meet new faces. I was there because I had to be, for my husband's sake, but I wanted to leave as soon as possible. I remember noticing the big stove, the roaring fire, and the cleanliness of that shiny kitchen. My husband didn't want to disturb M. Proust; he just wanted Nicolas to tell him he had come back to work. But Nicolas insisted on announcing that Odilon was there.

M. Proust entered the kitchen. I can see him now. He was wearing only a jacket and trousers and a white shirt. But I was impressed. I can still see that great gentleman enter the room. He looked very young—slender but not thin, with beautiful skin and

5

extremely white teeth, and that naturally formed curl on his fore-head, which he always would have. And then his exquisite elegance and that peculiar manner, a kind of restraint, which I later noticed in many asthmatics, as though he were husbanding his strength and his breath. Because of his delicate features, some people thought of him as slight, but he was as tall as I, and I'm quite tall—about five feet nine.

My husband greeted him, and when M. Proust saw me, he held out his hand and said, "Madame, may I introduce Marcel Proust, in disarray, uncombed, and beardless."

I was so nervous I didn't dare look at him. He said a few more words to my husband, which I didn't hear, because as he spoke he was circling me and I sensed that he was studying me. I also sensed in him such a warmth and thoughtfulness toward me that I became still more nervous. And this time I heard him say:

"Well, Albaret, now that you're back, things will be the same as usual, if that's all right with you."

And he left the kitchen. We left, too, shortly after, and at the bottom of the stairs I asked Odilon:

"Why did he say 'beardless'?"

Odilon laughed. "Because he had a magnificent black beard. You couldn't have known, but he had it shaved off only last night. So he told you that as a bit of news."

My husband went back to work, and M. Proust began to send for him again. He would get someone to telephone. If Odilon was at home he would go down to the little café and take the call himself; otherwise someone at the café took the message.

My husband worked hard. He was entitled to use the car whenever he wished, and had no fixed hours; if he had a good client, he didn't want to disappoint him, for he was anxious to earn a decent living and add to our savings. He had had some savings when we married, and he planned to go into his own business as soon as I was used to living in Paris. Sometimes he came home for supper, some-times he didn't, but he usually managed to let me know. Gradually I adapted to our new life; I waited for him to come home, but it was difficult—after all, I was still a country girl. It wasn't that I felt lonely, really—rather, I felt isolated. There was always my sister-in-law, true, but I didn't care much for the café atmosphere. There was also my brother-in-law Jean, Odilon's youngest brother, who had moved to Paris too. He and his wife ran a café on the corner of rue de la Victoire and rue Laffitte. My husband and his brother adored each other, and Jean was very kind and full of life. Odilon suggested, "Why don't you go to Jean's? You'll learn something there about business, for later on." But there was a café atmosphere there too, and I preferred to wait. My husband worked nights and often went out very late, between ten and midnight, and of course came home extremely late, so I didn't get much sleep. Without realizing it I was practicing for my future life. But I could hardly imagine that in the following years we three—M. Proust, my husband, and I— would live completely upside-down lives.

The summer was over. M. Proust had gone to Cabourg on the Normandy coast, as he had done nearly every year until then, my husband told me. He came back in September and started sending for Odilon again.

One evening—it must have been toward the end of October—he asked Odilon how his young wife was getting along.

"Not very well. I don't know what's going to happen—she rarely leaves the house. I keep telling her to visit her family instead of just waiting for me to come home. She does go sometimes but not often. I'm working, and you know how it is—I'm not always home for meals and return at all hours. So she hardly eats or sleeps. I don't think it has only to do with leaving the country."

M. Proust listened, then said, "She misses her mother, Albaret. That's what it is."

Considering that he only had seen me once, I wondered then, how could he have understood that? But of course I didn't know him yet.

And that wasn't all. He went on:

"Since your family does not seem to be the answer, we must find some other way of getting her out of the house, and I think I've got an idea. Grasset has just published my book *Du côté de chez Swann*, and I'm now signing copies for friends. If your wife likes the idea, she could deliver the books for me. It might help her to pass the time."

My husband told me about this conversation, and added:

"If you like the idea, go; if not, don't. He said he suggested it for your sake, but it might please him, too."

Odilon gently urged me to accept, and finally I said, "All right, I'll go."

After that I remember him saying, "You'll see, Monsieur Proust is a very nice man. You must be careful not to displease him, because he notices everything. But you'll never meet anyone more charming."

That's how it all began. I would never forget, after I knew and understood him better, the way he had figured me out right away. I myself wasn't at all conscious of being unhappy, even when my husband was out and I was alone. And I wasn't really aware of missing my mother and family; I wrote to them, and they wrote to me. Odilon was very considerate; and he too was concerned, because he was a good man. But only M. Proust understood that even if I wasn't really unhappy then, I soon would be. And what he said about my mother was actually true. My husband spoiled me, but it wasn't the same thing. Our little flat at Levallois overlooked a courtyard, whereas the house at Auxillac was spacious and airy and set in the middle of the village, surrounded by meadows belonging to my family, alive with activity and cheerful voices echoing back from the nearby hills. And M. Proust had sensed it all.

Later, because of that and too many other things he noticed about me and other people, I called him a magician. I said to him, "Sir, you are not only a charmer but a magician as well."

He looked at me with his piercing glance, to see if I meant it.

"Do you really believe so, Céleste?"

But I think he was quite pleased.

2

A CLOUD OF SMOKE

I arrived, ready to deliver the books containing M. Proust's inscriptions. I took the bus from Levallois; it wasn't a tiring journey—we lived not far from Porte d'Asnières. I would climb up the little staircase and pick up the parcels waiting for me in the kitchen. During that time I never saw M. Proust, only Nicolas Cottin,
His wife, Céline, was away. M. Proust had thought she seemed a bit nervous and had persuaded her to go away for a rest.

At that time there was also a young couple who lived in the house on boulevard Haussmann: Alfred Agostinelli, about whom so much has been said in connection with M. Proust—I'll come back to him in due course—and his friend Anna. At that time all I knew was that Agostinelli had once been one of M. Proust's chauffeurs (Odilon told me) but then had gone back to the Côte d'Azur—he had come from Monaco. He returned to Paris not long ago with his friend, but this time as a secretary, to type M. Proust's manuscripts. Anyway, I didn't know them well—I only saw them once.

It was Nicolas who wrapped the books. The parcels were extremely neat—he was very meticulous. He used two kinds of wrapping paper, depending on whom the book was for—pink for the women, and blue for the men. Nicolas explained to me:

9

"Those are Monsieur Marcel's orders."

Then he would tell me what I had to do.

"Leave it with the concierge," or "Deliver this personally," or sometimes, "Deliver this letter with it."

From the first, he told me to take a cab—which suited me, as I still hardly knew Paris. There were many horse-drawn cabs in those days, four-wheelers and little coupés. I adored them—they were so pretty that I practically never took a taxi. The only time I remember taking one was while delivering *Du côté de chez Swann* with a letter to Countess Greffulhe. If I remember well, I was very ashamed and embarrassed afterward, because the Countess lived in rue d'Astorg, just across the boulevard Haussmann; but I hadn't known where it was, and the taxi driver didn't say anything. When I told Nicolas, he laughed and said it didn't matter; he just gave me the money as usual. Every time, when I had done my errands and come back to boulevard Haussmann, he would say, "How much were the fares?" I would tell him, and he would pay me without question. That was clearly the house rule.

Finally there were no more books to deliver. And this is where one can see how kind M. Proust was, how he thought of everything and never forgot anyone. Because he said to my husband:

"Your wife can still come if she likes, in case there's ever a letter to deliver." With his usual delicacy, he had asked Odilon beforehand: "Does your wife mind doing these errands? Do they bore her? Do they really help her to pass the time?"

And it was only when my husband thanked him for his thoughtfulness and said that the errands didn't bore me, on the contrary, that M. Proust made the following suggestion:

"All right then, from now on she can come every day. If there's a letter or something else, she can deliver it. If there isn't anything, she can go home—at least she will have taken a walk."

And from that time on I called at rue Haussmann every day.

We eventually moved to another apartment in the same building in Levallois. We overlooked the street now and there was more air. I could once again see the sun rise, and perhaps because of that I was now sleeping well. I would take a bus from Porte d'Asnières to Saint-Lazare, and from there I crossed rue de la Pépinière and rue d'Anjou to boulevard Haussmann—it wasn't far. If there were no letters I didn't necessarily go right home. Since I was already in town, I usually took the opportunity to visit one or the other of my sisters-in-law. In other words, M. Proust had had his way yet again: I still didn't see him, but it was as if he were directing me from within his apartment.

Life changed for me the day I met him and began to live near him, and those ten years from 1913 to when he died in 1922—the years when he actually wrote his books—feel either like just one year or a whole lifetime. Likewise, that early period, before I became part of the household, sometimes seems so long, as if unconsciously I had been impatient to be there, and sometimes very short, which in fact it was.

That is why I wouldn't be telling the truth if I claimed to remember the exact dates—to the day, the week, or even the month—of the period from the end of 1913 to the outbreak of war in 1914. But the sequence of events is perfectly clear in my mind, and that's all that matters. Knowing whether it was a Monday or a Tuesday when I first went into M. Proust's room would not change the way things happened nor add to or subtract from the truth.

For fifty years I refused to write the story of my life with M. Proust, because I'd promised myself I would not. The reason I finally changed my mind is that so many inaccurate and even completely false things have been written about him by people who knew him less well than I did or even not at all, except through books and gossip. The more they write, the more they distort his image, sometimes in good faith, because that's what they really think, though often simply to draw attention to themselves. But if an old woman like me, who at eighty-two makes up her mind to tell all she knows, why shouldn't she tell the truth? When M. Proust was alive I could never lie to him, and I'm not going to start lying about him, for I would be lying to him. All I want to do, before it is my turn to go, is to correct the picture people have of him, as best I can. That's all. It needed to be said.

To go back to that first period, for some time I was a "courier," as he called me in his books. The procedure was the same as it had been for the parcels: I got to the house, everything was ready, I went, came back, Nicolas paid me, and then I either went home or visited someone.

Then, around December 1913, a few things happened in the house on boulevard Haussmann. M. Proust's book was officially published; people were talking about it, though I didn't realize it at the time. Alfred Agostinelli and his friend Anna went back to the Côte d'Azur.

Most important of all, Céline Cottin, Nicolas' wife, fell ill and had to be hospitalized for an operation. For me that was the turning point. But before explaining why, I must tell you more about the Cottins. Because of M. Proust's character, his sensitivity to everything, and the peculiar life he led—the life of an invalid, already to a large extent the life of a recluse, calling for immense care, exactness, and attention to detail—and also his perceptiveness, the apartment on boulevard Haussmann was a confined little world in which the lives of the people surrounding Monsieur Proust, because he lived in such close contact with them, mattered a great deal to him.

Before the Cottins, there had been Félicie, the old family maid. She didn't actually see M. Proust and his brother Robert come into the world, but it was as if she had. I never knew her except through what M. Proust told me about her later. She apparently was a very good cook and spoiled everyone with her cuisine. He often told me about her *boeuf à la mode:* "The gelatine was so clear! It was delicious, Céleste . . . you can't imagine!" It was so marvelous, that *boeuf à la mode,* that he described it in his novel. Félicie was tall and thin and had great style. Sometimes she wore regional costumes. "You should have seen how magnificent she looked in them," he once said. After M. Proust's mother died, which was soon after his father's death, Félicie followed him first to the Hôtel des Réservoirs at Versailles, where he retired for a while, and then

12

helped him move into the house at boulevard Haussmann, where she stayed until Nicolas came.

Nicolas Cottin had also worked for the family before but had left to become a croupier at a fashionable club, the Cercle Anglais. Mme. Proust always told her son not to take him back.

"My dear Marcel," she said, "if Nicolas ever wishes to come back, don't take him. He was pleasant and charming, but working as a croupier has probably taught him to drink. He will never be the same man."

When Nicolas did ask M. Proust to take him back, as Mme. Proust cleverly had foreseen, Félicie repeated the warning and said that if he came she would go. And that's what she did. I'm sure M. Proust took Nicolas back out of loyalty to the days when his parents were alive; it was a time that was dear to him. Besides, Félicie was quite old by then, and Nicolas was the perfect valet—well trained, attentive, dignified, aware of his place. Nevertheless, M. Proust had found him terribly changed. Later on he told me:

"At first I thought he was very ill. I even thought he might infect me, and I called in Doctor Bize to examine him."

Dr. Bize was M. Proust's own doctor. He examined Nicolas and reassuringly reported that the valet was neither ill nor contagious; he just had a tired heart and must be careful. This was odd, because all the time I knew him he looked as fresh as a rose. Anyway, M. Proust rehired him, and since Félicie had gone and Nicolas had married in the meantime, his wife, Céline, came with him. They'd had a room in the boulevard Haussmann since 1907.

I remember having been surprised when I first heard Nicolas refer to M. Proust as "Monsieur Marcel." When I now asked the reason he told me:

"When I used to work for the family, Professor Adrien Proust was 'Monsieur,' and to distinguish between him and his sons, we used to call them 'Monsieur Marcel' and 'Monsieur Robert.' I've never got out of the habit."

Nicolas displayed a certain freedom of speech, which dated back to the servants' hall in the days of M. Proust's parents. I remember one day, when I was in the kitchen and he stormed in, furious, carrying a pair of trousers over his arm. Pointing to the trousers, which had one leg turned up, he said:

"I'd just pressed them nicely and the idiot has to wet them washing his feet. Now I'll have to do them all over again."

I found this sort of thing strange, surprising, and sometimes even rather shocking—I knew very little about human relationships in those days. And there were other things that surprised me. For example, as I was leaving, Nicolas would often ask:

"Would you mind dropping this off at La Beaujolaise?"

La Beaujolaise was a shop that sold wine by the bottle in rue de l'Arcade. The owner, a big man and not very polite, used to take the envelope Nicolas had given me and toss it into a sort of basket full of other envelopes. I didn't understand what it was all about, but as I was obliging someone with no inconvenience to myself, I didn't puzzle my head. I noticed that Nicolas used to become agitated toward the end of the afternoon—used to fiddle with his hair, while looking at the time. Then he'd say:

"I'm just going down to get the evening paper—I'll only be a minute. If he rings I'll be right back. . . ."

And in a few minutes he would rush back upstairs, always opening the paper at the same page.

It was only a long while afterward, when I told M. Proust about it, that he enlightened me. He had a good laugh about it first.

"Didn't you realize, Céleste? The messages you carried for him were bets, and the owner of La Beaujolaise was what they call a bookie."

Poor Nicolas had not only learned to drink the leavings when he was a croupier; he had also become a gambler.

This didn't interfere with his being devoted and charming, and I can understand why M. Proust was so fond of him. He never gave me any cause for complaint either.

When Nicolas' wife Céline had to go into the hospital, Professor Robert Proust, who as Professor Pozzi's assistant was already a well-known physician and surgeon, took her as his patient at his brother's request and performed the operation himself at the Hospital Broca. Of course M. Proust said to Nicolas right away, "We

14

must arrange for you to be able to go to see your wife every day. Why don't you ask Madame Albaret whether she minds staying here while you are at the hospital?''

I told Nicolas it would be a pleasure, and that's how one thing led to another.

It was agreed I would arrive at two in the afternoon, at which time M. Proust would let Nicolas leave, and then I would wait in the kitchen in case he needed me until Nicolas came back at about four or five. Then I could go home.

Nicolas explained everything to me very carefully. The arrangement was that when I arrived M. Proust would already have had the *café au lait* and croissants he sent for when he woke up, so I didn't have to worry. The only thing was that "M. Marcel" took his coffee in two stages: after the first cup, with which he ate a croissant, he had a second, and for this a second croissant was kept ready. If he hadn't sent for the second croissant before Nicolas left, I might have to take it in to him on a special saucer that matched the coffee cup that would be left ready. There were days when the extra croissant wasn't required. But in case it was, or in case "Monsieur Marcel" needed me for any other reason, Nicolas had shown me the long passageway leading from the kitchen, and the panel on the wall with a black disc for each room: I might hear the bell ring twice and one of the discs would turn white—always the same one, the one for the bedroom. If the croissant was still in the kitchen, I'd know what I had to do; otherwise I was to go and see. He explained in great detail:

"Answer as soon as he rings. Go into the passageway—you haven't been over the apartment, but it's very simple, you can't go wrong. Go along the passageway, across the hall, and through the big drawing room, and then there's another door—the fourth. When you get to this door, you mustn't knock but go straight in—he has sent for you, so he knows you're coming. If it's for the croissant, you'll see a big silver tray on the table by the bed, with a little silver coffeepot, the cup, the sugar bowl, and the milk pitcher. Put the saucer with the croissant down on the tray and go." Then: "Whatever you do, don't say anything unless he asks you a question."

15

So I went to boulevard Haussmann and waited in the kitchen. I couldn't help feeling rather nervous in that great, strange, silent apartment I wasn't supposed to go into, and knowing he was there, invisible and not even audible. The funny thing is that I don't ever remember being bored in all the hours I waited. I didn't do anything; I didn't even read. And at first never a bell ring. And never any visitors. Nothing. No one.

This went on for days, and I thought M. Proust never would send for me. When Nicolas came back he always asked, "He didn't ring?" and I said no. We chatted for a bit, and I went home.

And then one day, all of a sudden, two rings. The second croissant was still in the kitchen, so I put it on the saucer as Nicolas had told me, and off I went. I went across the hall and through the big drawing room. I reached the fourth door, opened it without knocking, pushed aside the heavy curtain on the other side as Nicolas had told me, and went in.

The smoke was so thick you could have cut it with a knife. Incredible. Nicolas had warned me that sometimes, when he woke up, M. Proust, who suffered terribly from asthma, burned fumigation powder—but I wasn't prepared for this dense cloud. It was a very big room, but the smoke absolutely filled it. The only light was from a bedside lamp, and that gave just a little glow, through a green shade. I saw a brass bedstead and a bit of white sheet with the green light falling on it. All I could see of M. Proust was a white shirt under a thick sweater, and the upper part of his body propped against two pillows. His face was hidden in the shadows and the smoke from the fumigation, completely invisible except for the eyes looking at me—and I felt rather than saw them. Fortunately there was the gleam of the silver tray and coffeepot on the table by the bed. I made for these without looking at anything else. When I left the room, I would have been incapable of describing any of the furniture that became so familiar to me afterward—everything was so confused in the half-light, and I was too intimidated by those eyes I couldn't see. I bowed toward the invisible face and put the saucer with the croissant down on the tray. He gave a wave of the hand, presumably to thank me, but didn't say a word. Then I left.

A Cloud of Smoke

I must admit I wasn't very bold in those days—in fact, I was shy, more like a child than a woman of twenty-two, especially since leaving the shelter of my mother's affection. And then there was the mystery of this apartment, of this man in bed, his silence and the clouds of smoke, and the room that seemed larger than it really was because everything in it was so lofty: the windows, the long blue curtains drawn to keep the light out in the middle of the afternoon, the ceiling that looked many yards high, and the chandelier hanging there unlit in the gloom.

It was only later, when I found myself back in the kitchen, that the most striking thing about the room I'd just left—the walls and ceiling—came back to me. It was as if I'd been inside an enormous cork; there were panels of cork nailed everywhere to keep out the noise. The effect on me was especially strong because it brought back a vivid childhood memory. When I was a little girl in the Lozère, I went to a school run by nuns who took us out on excursions every Sunday. One Sunday we went to see a new quarry, two or three miles from the village. I don't know whether I was more curious than the other girls, but I found my way alone into one of the stone corridors. It was quite silent—I no longer could hear my friends' voices. What struck me especially was the color of the earth in the dim light. It was honey brown, and I thought that it was exactly as if I were inside a cork. It had that magical feeling things have for children, and I was in awe. But as in the case of M. Proust's room, I kept these feelings to myself.

What I remember clearly is that from the very first time I went into the bedroom I was fascinated. I felt as if I'd been transported back into the quarry, amid the color of the sliced earth, with the noise all shut out behind me. I must have looked like an astonished child. I'm sure, in the shadows, the eyes in that invisible face were watching me. I'm certain too that that day he'd deliberately waited for Nicolas to leave for the hospital before sending for his croissant. To see what I was like. Even when I was still delivering the parcels, then the letters, he used to have the concierge sent up when there was no real reason: before, it had been the concierge and Céline who'd done that kind of job, but now I was the "courier." So if he

17

sent for the concierge it could only have been to ask questions, to find out how I behaved, whether I gossiped or was too familiar. Of course I had no more idea of this then than I had about the whole system in which I was about to become enmeshed.

Nevertheless, without realizing it, I'd taken the first step. It wasn't so much the fact of having gone into the bedroom and having the honor of serving the croissant. Nor was it a matter of curiosity, as it had been the time I wandered off into the quarry. No, it was something I was certainly not conscious of then, something that came from him. It's strange, when one thinks about it, that even during that first period, when I didn't know anything about him the idea never once entered my head that there was any mystery about M. Proust or the upside-down world he lived in. On the contrary, I was attracted. None of the other impressions he left me, in all the days that followed, could ever efface that first one of him lying there in the brass bed, with the face invisible, motionless except undoubtedly for his eyes and the slight gesture of appreciation more eloquent than any word. He was an extraordinary presence, and that was because of the natural distinction that made the man himself, and his feelings, no less great than his genius.

So, just as there was no reason for him to have any further concern for me, I myself would never have dreamed that I would soon work for him. I thought that when Céline was better, the situation would return to what it had been before. Céline would come back to work, or at least Nicolas would not need time off.

It wasn't even a question of handing her place back to Céline, because I hadn't taken it. Only if I had been told that I was no longer needed at boulevard Haussmann would I have realized how much I liked being there, how much it was already a part of my life.

3

AND THEN THE WAR

I think it must have been the beginning of 1914, January probably, when Céline Cottin came out of hospital, but she only dropped in at boulevard Haussmann, then went straight on to convalesce at a little house belonging to her mother, at Champigny-sur-Marne, not far from Paris.

All the time she was convalescent I carried on with my tasks at M. Proust's, at his request. But now that Nicolas didn't have to go to the hospital any more, I wasn't needed to take the coffee in, and I went back to being mainly the "courier." No more of those long sessions, waiting in the kitchen for the bell to ring. Or if I was left sitting there, with no letters to deliver or other errands for Nicolas, instead of going home as I had done at the beginning, it was agreed I should stay and do some sewing and mending. While Céline was away I was to look after the household linen—the least personal part of her job as chambermaid.

So again I didn't see M. Proust for a while; Nicolas was there to attend him directly. The only difference—you might say the only step forward, so to speak, though it was none of my doing—was that being there at the same time as Nicolas, I couldn't help noticing, while attending to my own little tasks, the way he did various things, especially prepare the coffee. As these preparations were always rather special and unlike anything I'd seen before, I was naturally curious and took in the whole routine. Without realizing it, I was learning.

I knew no more about M. Proust than what I'd learned from the two glimpses I'd had of him, except that Nicolas would occasionally make some remark in the kitchen about his duties (like the one about the trousers that had to be pressed twice). As for Odilon, he would no more gossip about M. Proust than about any of his other customers. At the most he might tell me he'd driven him to such-and-such a place—a restaurant or the house of people whose names meant nothing to me then—and that he'd waited so many hours to drive him home again. Very rarely, in the afternoon, they might have gone for a drive in the Bois de Boulogne or the outskirts of Paris because M. Proust wanted to see again certain parts of the countryside, but I don't think this happened more than once or twice at that time.

Anyway, although I liked going to boulevard Haussmann and would have missed it if it had to stop, deep down I thought it was only a temporary arrangement. But the strange thing was I was not concerned. I just let events take their course.

Then Céline came back from the country, and things started to move quickly. She was a strong character but a strange one too. M. Proust told me the details of what happened a few months later.

"She meddled in everything, you see," he said. "She wanted to control everything."

Perhaps her illness and the operation had made her worse, but probably my presence, too, especially as I was a woman, had its effect. Anyway, soon after she came back matters went wrong for the first time. M. Proust had suddenly had enough. He told me afterward:

"I said, 'My poor Céline, I'm afraid you'll have to change if you want to stay with me. I don't need your advice—it's not for you to tell me I spend too much money, or whatever. But I can't educate you either. I'm too busy, I haven't the time. So if you don't mind, why don't you take a couple of months' rest, three if necessary?

And when you're properly rested, I trust, I hope, things will be better. For I must tell you plainly, if you were to go on like this I couldn't keep you.' ''

So Céline went away again. When M. Proust made up his mind about something, he displayed a studied politeness, a way of saying "If you please" which was more compelling than a direct order.

So she went back to the Champigny, and since even when she was there, M. Proust had let me know through Nicolas that I was welcome, it didn't make any difference to me.

After a few weeks she came back, and it really seemed as if the rest had calmed her down and put some sense into her. She was better-tempered, quiet as a lamb. But it didn't last; her nature soon got the upper hand. Perhaps it was then that she really became jealous of me; perhaps it was then, as some people alleged, that she said things about me to M. Proust and even made scenes and said I was a "little schemer." M. Proust never talked to me about it, except just to say, "She was jealous of you."

What is certain is that soon M. Proust had had enough of it again. As he told me later:

"She became so impossible that I finally saw the truth, and I could not understand how I had put up with her so long. And this time I said to her: 'See here, Céline, I can see the rest hasn't had the effect I hoped. I've already explained I don't need your advice, and I need peace and quiet to work. I have done all I can, but unfortunately it is no good. As you cannot keep to your place, there's no point in going on. I can't endure it and you'll have to go.' ''

And to round it off he added: "If Nicolas wants to go too, he can go. If he wants to stay, he can stay. I've nothing against him, and I'm quite willing to keep him on. But not you. I've too much to do and I'm too tired."

It was an absolute bombshell for Céline. She left 102 boulevard Haussmann for good. But Nicolas stayed on. M. Proust asked him to manage with me. I was now to come in every day.

I think that quite apart from his affection for "M. Marcel," Nicolas saw the situation for what it was and was aware of the difficulties with his wife's character. He was very discreet, and there were no problems between him and M. Proust. Nor between him and me. Céline's departure didn't spoil our good relationship, but it was her influence that spoiled it later, when Nicolas too had to leave boulevard Haussmann.

During the weeks that Nicolas remained, when I came every day to help him, I continued to learn the rules of the house. What fascinated me most was watching him, in the afternoon, prepare the coffee for M. Proust's breakfast. Even at that time the meal consisted of practically nothing but coffee.

It was a ritual. First, only Corcellet coffee could be used, and it had to be bought at a shop in rue de Lévis in the seventeenth arrondissement where it was roasted, to make sure it was fresh and had lost none of its aroma. The filter, too, had to be Corcellet. Even the little tray was from Corcellet. The filter was packed tight with finely ground coffee, and to obtain a coffee as strong as M. Proust liked it, the water had to pass through very slowly, drop by drop. The whole process was carried out, of course, in a double boiler. There had to be just enough coffee for two cups, the amount the little silver coffeepot held, so that there would be some left over in case M. Proust wanted more after the first portion which was equal to one large cup.

And that wasn't all. Monsieur Proust usually decided the day before what time he would have his coffee, and we prepared it slightly before that, in case he rang earlier. But sometimes he rang later. He might have said that he wanted his coffee at about four o'clock—he never said "at," always "about"—and then he might not ring until six, either because he'd decided to rest a bit longer or because his asthma was especially bad that day and he had to prolong his fumigation when he woke up. If four o'clock went by and the bell still hadn't rung, the filtering had to be done all over again, taking care not to start too soon, for if the coffee had either been filtered too fast or left standing too long in the double boiler, M. Proust would be sure to say, as Nicolas told me: "This coffee is revolting—no flavor at all."

22

Lastly there was the milk. It was delivered every morning from a neighboring dairy. Like the coffee, it had to be fresh. It was left outside the kitchen door, on the landing of the little service stairs, so that M. Proust wouldn't be disturbed by the door bell—or by any other noise—while he was sleeping or resting. On the stroke of noon the woman who brought the milk came to see if the bottles had been taken in, and if not, she took them away and left fresh ones.

Three months or perhaps four went by like this, and then one evening Odilon came home to Levallois earlier than I had expected him. That morning he'd taken the taxi out of the garage and gone off to work, not knowing what had happened. War had been declared and general mobilization called. When he found out, the posters were already up. His mobilization papers said he had to report at once to the Ecole Militaire in Paris. "At once" meant the following morning at six o'clock. It also meant two lives turned upside down, like thousands of others.

But what was amazing in such circumstances was the concern and respect felt for M. Proust by everyone around him. My husband's first thought, even before coming home to tell me, his wife, had been to go to boulevard Haussmann, because he was afraid that if he didn't see M. Proust straight away he might not have time later. Both of us must have found this quite natural, because when he told me about it immediately after, it didn't even occur to me to complain.

So, as he'd done eighteen months before when he left his work to get married, he told M. Proust he would not be available for an indefinite period. It must have been quite late, because I was back in Levallois when Odilon told me the news. Still, certainly it was too early to have seen M. Proust, who often wasn't available until ten or eleven o'clock, or even midnight, unless he himself rang. As on the previous occasion, Odilon would not have disturbed him if Nicolas, with his usual kindness, had not insisted on breaking the rules. As soon as M. Proust was told, he sent for Odilon. And lying there in bed, he said, "My dear Albaret, what is this I hear? You've been called up? And you have to report tomorrow?"

And then, after some kind words about how sorry he was to hear it, he asked; "And what will your wife do? Go back to her mother, or stay in Paris?"

"I don't know," said Odilon.

And he explained he had only just heard about the mobilization and hadn't seen me yet for the simple reason that he had gone straight to boulevard Haussmann. M. Proust thanked him and said he was touched.

"I'm very sorry about this for both of you, Albaret. But don't forget—if by any chance your wife decides to stay in Paris, if there is any danger and there is anything I can do for her, I shall be here and she'll always know where to find me. Be sure to tell her. Meanwhile she can come here as long as she wishes."

My husband was not only moved but also reassured because, as he told me, he knew M. Proust well enough to be sure this wasn't just an empty promise. So I decided to stay where I was for the time being and see what happened.

It was a good thing I did, because for a time Odilon remained in Paris. As a young man he had had a passion for cars and had become one of the first taxi-drivers. So, during his last period of training as a reservist, he had been assigned to transport, and when he was called up he was sent from the Ecole Militaire to rue de Lourmel in the fifteenth arrondissement and assigned to supplying fresh meat to the front. The Paris buses had been requisitioned for this purpose and were being fitted up in rue de Lourmel. Every day it was announced that the convoys would leave the next morning, but the front shifted about so much that no one quite knew what to do. As it turned out, Odilon remained there for a whole month or even more. I was glad I'd stayed, because even if I couldn't see him—I only managed to do so two or three times—I felt close to him. And going regularly to boulevard Haussmann seemed like another link still between us.

But things soon changed. Years later, thinking about this early time, I came to the conclusion that M. Proust foresaw what would happen—that he knew the day would come when he would be left alone. He told me himself that, unlike most people, he had always

24

believed that the war would be a long one and that sooner or later it would take Nicolas away from him.

Nicolas was in the reserves and had thought he was safe. He hadn't been affected by the call-up, and he said to me:

"It won't last long. They won't call me for at least a fortnight, and by that time we'll have killed them all and be in Berlin. I shan't have to go, you'll see."

He said the same to M. Proust, who apparently said nothing but remained preoccupied.

Anyway, two weeks later, Nicolas was called.

When Odilon was called up, M. Proust wrote to me suggesting that I move to boulevard Haussmann and work for him full-time. I answered that I would continue to come every day but preferred to go home and sleep in our little place at Levallois. He wrote again, saying: "Do as you like. Stay in your own place. Come when you like. One can't do good for people against their will."

Almost immediately after that, Nicolas went, and M. Proust renewed his offer, this time in person.

"Madame," he said, "what was bound to happen has happened. You see, I am alone. You could have Nicolas' room. I shall not deny that I would be very pleased if you came here."

He asked with such dignity, such feeling, that I couldn't refuse. I said I would come. Then he added:

"Madame, I thank you profusely for agreeing to look after a sick man. You are doing me a great service, and I can't be too grateful. But you mustn't worry; you won't have to stay here long, for it's not proper for a man like me, who spends most of his time ill in bed, to be waited on by a woman, especially a young woman. So this will be just a temporary solution while I look for someone to replace Nicolas. But of course it is not easy to find someone like him at a time like this."

I still can see him looking at me as he went on:

"I will not surprise you, madame, when I say you don't know anything and can't do anything. But don't worry: I shan't ask anything of you; I'll look after myself. You'll just see to the coffee— that's the most important thing."

25

Then he added, still looking at me: "You can't even address people in the third person."

Then I answered. "No, I don't, monsieur," I said. "And I never shall."

There was a good reason for this: I didn't know what the third person was. He must have guessed, and I think it amused him.

"Madame," he said, "I'll never ask you to."

I've always been rather impulsive and quick to speak my mind. And although I was impressed by the grandeur of his manner, even though he lay in bed, I felt free to say what I thought because it wasn't by my own wish I was there. I remember I was bold enough to ask:

"Monsieur, why don't you call me 'Céleste'? It makes me self-conscious when you call me 'madame.'"

It was true. But he answered, "Because, madame, I cannot."

That was that. I didn't say any more.

4

THE LAST TRIP TO CABOURG

He went on calling me "madame," and I moved into Nicolas' room and started serving the coffee. I continued to learn the ways of the household and of M. Proust's life, and I became used to the smoke when I went into his room carrying the big silver tray with the little coffeepot, the bowl, the pitcher of milk, and sugar bowl, and the croissant.

Nicolas had told me that when M. Proust woke up in the morning he often had difficulty breathing, probably because of the congestion caused by his asthma while he was asleep, and the first thing he did was to burn his special medicinal powder in a saucer. But as the smell of a match might have brought on a coughing fit, he lit the powder with a little square of white paper, which itself was lit from a candle. One of the first things I learned was that always, night and day, there had to be a lighted candle kept handy on a little table in the hallway behind his room. There was another door to the bedroom from this hallway besides the regular entrance, which opened to the salon.

I'd come in and set down the tray, and usually he wouldn't say a word—just that graceful wave of thanks, to save himself the effort of speaking. Then I would leave. In those early days he used to wait for me to go before he drank his coffee. I never saw him even take a piece of sugar or start to sit up in bed. No, he just lay there with the upper part of his body slightly raised on the pillows, as if shut up in himself and only emerging with a slight wave of the hand and that keen look in his eyes.

There were other things I had learned from Nicolas, either because I'd seen him do them or because he'd explained them to me before he went. What I had learned was how to be silent while M. Proust was resting or working and how to wait for him to wake up in the afternoon or to come home if he had been out at night. That was when I began my night training; the all-night vigils had not yet begun, but even then I was never in bed before midnight or one o'clock.

All this remains in my mind as fresh as yesterday, the confusion one feels entering upon a life completely different from anything one has known before, with the fascination in an extraordinary person who becomes, with a gentleness more powerful than any force, the center of that new life and who sometimes seems very close because of his kindness and sensitivity and sometimes far away, deep in his thoughts.

Back in the kitchen or in my room, I used to think over what he'd said about it being improper for a woman to look after him, and I remembered how careful he was to lie still in bed when I was there, quite apart from any precautions his illness might require. I thought he must surely have to sit up to drink his coffee, perhaps even sit on the edge of the bed. But while I was there, nothing: he just lay with the sheets pulled up and his arms resting on them. Nothing but the keen look in his eyes.

Of course, because of his scrupulousness and because I was only supposed to be there temporarily, he did try to find a valet to replace Nicolas. Because he didn't want just anybody, he enlisted the aid of friends, so he could be certain of the references. Count Gautier-Vignal, who admired his work, asked his maid to look for someone, and after a while a young man turned up—very nice, I'll say that, very eager to please, but shy. I remember that when I opened the door he took me for the lady of the house. He told me afterward. He was ill at ease. He'd been before the medical board and been deferred, not because he was ill—M. Proust told me himself: "Count Gautier-Vignal guarantees he's healthy"—but because he was slight and delicate.

M. Proust engaged him but asked me to stay on a while and not change anything. I could see he didn't like new faces or changes.

"Madame," he said, "you've already got to know my ways, and I've got to know yours. And this young fellow hardly dares open his mouth. I have to tell him everything, and that tires me. So when I ring, I'd be glad if you kept answering, if you don't mind. We'll wait awhile to see how he works out."

But the poor man didn't have the chance; he was stopped before he even began. It was August 1914, and things were going badly at the front. The allies were retreating, and they had to draft anybody they could get. He was called up before the board again, and this time they passed him. So now he went too; it seemed he was with us one day and gone the next.

M. Proust resumed the search and took on a Swede this time, perhaps thinking that because the man was a neutral he would be able to stay longer. He was quite different from the first one, and as pleased with himself as if he were King of Sweden, if not God Almighty.

To cut a long story, M. Proust asked me to stay on a bit longer. And then suddenly, early in September, he decided in spite of the war, which still wasn't going at all well, to go to Cabourg on the Normandy coast, as he'd done nearly every summer up till then. He felt too lonely in Paris. The war had taken away nearly all his friends. He himself had just been rejected on grounds of general health, and he was in fact so sick that if he had volunteered they wouldn't have taken him even as a noncombatant. Many of the others—the women, and the men too old for the army—had left the capital, which was said to be directly threatened by the Germans.

Ah, the luggage for that trip! It was no small matter. I packed under M. Proust's strict instructions. Then Antoine, concierge of 102 boulevard Haussmann, arranged for the railway people to pick up our things. M. Proust kept for himself a large valise, old and battered but still very strong, made of cardboard hard as iron and covered with beige canvas. Just by looking at it one could tell it had made dozens of journeys. The manuscripts were packed in it. M. Proust told me he always took them with him wherever he went. They were his most precious possession. He never parted from them, and the valise always traveled with him.

Then there was a huge trunk on wheels that traveled in the luggage van. It was packed with outer clothes, underwear, jumpers. As he was always well wrapped up, even in summer, and never wore the same underwear twice, it was a sizable amount. There were two overcoats.

"I had those specially made for the seaside," he told me.

It was true—I never saw him wear them in Paris. They were both made of vicuna; one was light gray with a mauve lining, the other was brown. Each had a matching bowler.

His blankets also were packed into the trunk.

"The hotel closes in winter, you see, and no matter how much they air them their blankets smell of mothballs."

And then there was a whole pharmacy for treating his asthma.

Finally the three of us got on the train—I with M. Proust, and the Swede (his name was Ernest) in the next compartment. Traveling was a nightmare in those days, and the journey took much longer than we had anticipated, gauging the trip as we had on how long it had taken M. Proust before the war. He was very tired when we arrived, but happy, too, to be back in the Grand Hôtel, in the same room he had had every summer—number one hundred thirty-seven, if I remember correctly.

At the hotel they welcomed him with open arms. It was plain that he was respected, admired, and loved. Everyone was at his feet; they couldn't do enough for him. He was at home. They would have shifted all the guests around to find a room to his liking if he'd asked.

He explained to me that the hotel was the same as in other years except that there were more people, as many had given up their houses or country places because of the war.

I can still see the big terrace on the ground floor facing the sea. We went directly up to the top floor, where three rooms were reserved, all also overlooking the sea. Above, there was another terrace, but because of M. Proust, no one was allowed to use it throughout his stay.

"I don't like having people in the next room or walking about over my head," he said. "So you take this room next to mine, madame, as Nicolas used to do, and Ernest can have the one next to yours."

Each room had a door opening to its own bathroom, which isolated it from any noise in the corridor. M. Proust's room—the first on the left, followed by mine, then Ernest's—was very simple, much less grand than mine, even. It contained just an ordinary double bed, a few chairs, and some tables on which he arranged his books and notebooks. There was no fireplace—no need, as the hotel was open only in the summer. From the window you could not see the terrace below, but there was a view of the esplanade.

It was essential there should be no interruption of his routine. He told me he wanted me to see to his coffee.

We hadn't brought any equipment for that, but at the end of the corridor there was a pantry for the floor waiters and chambermaids, and there every day, with utensils provided by the hotel, I prepared his coffee as usual. The staff made sure I had everything I needed. He said to me:

"There isn't a bell from one room to another, so to call you I shall knock on the wall."

So life became organized much the same as in Paris. In the morning, silence: he was working. Then, when he needed me, he banged on the wall as he used to do with his grandmother when they both used to come to Cabourg in the old days, as he tells in *Sodome et Gomorrhe*. It wasn't difficult, as my bed was back to back with his on the other side of the wall. When he'd done his fumigation, I brought in the coffee. Then he rested a bit longer or worked on his notebooks. As in Paris, he spent a lot of time in bed. Sometimes in the evening he would go downstairs at dinnertime, but he didn't dine.

I myself had lunch in the hotel restaurant, in haste to return upstairs in case He should call. Some evenings he said to me:

"Don't go down to lunch tomorrow. I feel tired. Ask the head waiter to send something up to your room, in case I need you."

During all our stay he didn't have one engagement or invite anyone to dinner at the hotel. He didn't go out much in the evenings. Even the casino was closed. He told me he used to like to go there, "But not to gamble—it was just very interesting to watch." I don't remember that he saw many friends either, though several were not far away: the Comtesse Greffulhe at Deauville, Comte Robert de Montesquiou at Trouville, Madame de Clermont-Tonnerre at Bénerville, and Madame Straus, one of his oldest and greatest friends, at her nearby estate, the "Clos des Mûriers."

It was at Cabourg that I began to notice this trait in his character: he liked to be near people in case he should want or need to see them for his own purposes, but he wouldn't let himself be put under any unnecessary obligations. I remember that the Countess Greffulhe and Count de Montesquiou called one day at the Grand Hôtel and had themselves announced, but he wouldn't see them.

It was there, too, that the relationship between us strengthened and advanced.

At Cabourg he was less of a recluse. At boulevard Haussmann, the curtains of his room, let alone the windows, were never opened while he was there. But at the Grand Hôtel the curtains were drawn back in the afternoon, and he himself seemed to open up much more.

It was there too, that he finally gave up calling me "madame" and started to call me "Céleste." And it was at that time that he began to keep me with him, talking, now and again. Sometimes he would be on the hotel terrace, and if he saw me going by or sitting in the sun, he would beckon to me to join him, and we would talk as we strolled or sat watching the sea. But that didn't happen more than a couple of times, for when he left his room I always had plenty to do to tidy it up.

I could feel his confidence growing, and I myself was more at ease, less constrained in speech and attitude—though we kept to our respective places.

I think Ernest, with his pretentiousness, helped us to relax with each other. It was about all he was good for. I did everything, and he must have been bored to death just hanging about. M. Proust hardly ever made any demands on him.

"You know, Céleste," he said several times, "Ernest gets on my nerves."

Anyway, he became a great topic of conversation for us. I used to imitate his high and mighty ways, and so did M. Proust, and we both had many a good laugh.

When we joked together like this, the spontaneity natural to my temperament and my twenty-three years was set free. I could tell from his laugh that my replies amused him, and this encouraged me to go on. He must have felt my eagerness to please, and the pleasure I took in his company, and I think he liked it.

He tried to interest me in Cabourg and its environs. He often chided me for not being curious and not wanting to go out. One day he was singing the praises of a place that served delicious crêpes, a place he had visited in the past.

"Why don't you go one afternoon?" he said. "Order a car—I'll treat you to the ride."

"But I don't want to, monsieur," I said. "I'm quite happy here with you."

We were strolling up and down on the terrace, I remember. He was wearing his light-gray overcoat. He stopped and gave me a warm smile.

"Thank you, Céleste," he said.

It was at Cabourg, too, that he began to talk to me a bit about himself and the past; about when he used to go there as a child with his maternal grandmother; about later visits, when he came partly out of loyalty to those early memories, partly because his father and other doctors had said the change of air was good for his asthma, and partly because in the summer the region was full of friends of his from Paris. That was how I first heard names that were to become familiar to me: Horace Finaly, the banker; Mme. Straus, who had been the wife of Bizet, the composer of *Carmen;* and many others.

He spoke of it as a glorious time, when he used to drive about the country. He told me how it was there he had got to know my husband, because Jacques Bizet, who was the son of Mme. Straus and the composer and had been at school with M. Proust at the Lycée Condorcet, was director of one of the first car rental firms. In winter the cars were in Monte Carlo, and in the summer he sent them to Cabourg. M. Proust, who was always very careful, had asked who were the most reliable drivers to take him on his visits and excursions. Jacques Bizet gave him the names of three, two of whom became his favorites. They were Alfred Agostinelli and my husband.

I was young and listened in amazement. I was gradually falling under his spell.

One evening I was in his room. He was up that day, and said confidentially, "I want to show you something you've never seen before. But first just look and see there's no one in the corridor. I'm not dressed to go out."

As usual, when he stayed indoors but not in bed, he was wearing slippers, shirt and trousers, and a smoking jacket.

I looked. Not a soul.

"Come with me," he said.

He took me by the hand as if I were a little girl and led me to the end of the corridor, where there was a big bull's-eye window. Framed in it was the sunset, with the sea glittering below. And while I was looking, moved both by his gesture and by that beautiful sight, he said:

"Look at the reflection. My god, how beautiful! For me it is always a marvel." The ecstasy in his voice captivated the child that I still was. He took me to that window several times, but never again was I as moved as the first time.

I remember one other evening, toward the end of our stay. It was the equinox. He was up that evening too, looking out through the closed window. He called me over.

"Look at that, Céleste. They'll have to bring everything up onto the esplanade, or it'll all get smashed or carried away."

I had already seen from my window, and I was shaking with fright. He had told me what to expect, but I didn't know the sea and hadn't imagined anything like this—the raging flood and the noise, the waves that looked as if they would rise taller than the hotel, the spray dashing against the windowpanes. I said I didn't fancy the Last Judgment just yet. He laughed at me for being afraid and took me by the arm.

"Come, see how beautiful it is! There's nothing to be frightened of. What would you say if you saw Brittany!"

And he told me how he'd once made a special journey, with his great friend the composer Reynaldo Hahn, to see the equinoctial tides at the Pointe du Raz.

"It was magnificent, Céleste! I'd love to go again!"

And he said for the first time something that was often to occur in our conversations later:

"Perhaps, one day, if I'm better . . . And I'll take you. You absolutely must see it."

And again, in his voice, there was an almost childlike wistfulness for scenes he longed to see again.

It was marvelous at Cabourg, but it didn't last. The war produced complications. The first to affect us was the requisitioning of the hotel for the army and the wounded from the front. There was a shortage of accommodations for them, for this was the time of big battles such as the Battle of the Marne. M. Proust was very worried about his brother, Robert, who, like my husband, had been sent to the lines almost immediately after the mobilization. Robert had been sent to Verdun and was performing operations in military hospitals at the front.

Nearly all the guests had left the hotel. A few who wanted to stay on had moved into an annex. As a special favor, M. Proust was allowed to stay where he was: no wounded soldiers had arrived yet. As a matter of fact, we never saw one right up to the last day. I know that people said otherwise later—that M. Proust used to go to see the wounded, and even that he spent so much money buying them cigarettes and candies that he soon had none left and had to go home. All invention.

It's true that money was the second complication, but the reason was that the banks were in a state of confusion. Panic had overwhelmed the government, and thousands had fled to Bordeaux. Many of M. Proust's friends had gone too; some went as far as Biarritz. Bank transactions were more or less suspended or else made practically impossible by difficulties in communication. M. Proust had brought a supply of money with him from Paris, but when it was exhausted he couldn't get any more.

"My securities have gone to Bordeaux with the bank," he said. "And, my poor Céleste, I've spent all my money."

The money shortage was a hazard of his style of living, which, though simple, must have been very expensive, even if you take into account only our rooms and the big tips he gave. As a result we left Cabourg toward the end of September. The Germans had been halted; people were breathing more freely; civilian trains were running again.

I shall never forget that awful journey home.

We were on our way, everything was fine, when M. Proust suddenly had a terrible choking fit. We were near Mézidon, in Calvados, and between attacks he told me it was always there that he had an attack—always passing though Mézidon, and always on the way home from Cabourg. I remember quite clearly his telling me right in the middle of it all:

"It always comes on here. There must be something in the air that disagrees with me—perhaps because it's haymaking time. On the way to Cabourg, I know I'm nearly there when we pass through here, and it doesn't have time to affect me much. But coming back . . . the very thought of all the distance still to go. . . ."

I was almost out of my wits, because on top of everything I'd forgotten, not knowing any better, to put his medicines and some fumigation powder in the valise with his papers. Everything was in the trunk, in the luggage compartment.

At the next stop I leaped onto the platform and rushed to the back of the train. I explained the situation to the guard, who could see I was genuinely upset. He was very kind. We found the trunk, and I rushed back with the fumigation powder to our compartment, where M. Proust used it right away.

I don't remember how we finally got back to boulevard Haussmann. But there more trouble awaited us.

Every year, while he was away at Cabourg, M. Proust had the apartment thoroughly gone over with huge vacuum cleaners that sucked up all the dust from the parquet, the carpets, the furniture, and the walls—especially those in his room which were covered with cork. As ill luck would have it, we arrived just as the work was in progress.

I already thought I had a dying man on my hands—but when he saw that! He said, with the wave of the hand:

"They must go away, Céleste, they must go away. I must go to bed."

I sent them all packing; then I helped him to his room and asked what I should do.

"Prepare me some hot-water bottles right away," he said.

I brought the hot-water bottles and arranged the lighted candle within reach, with the squares of paper and the box of fumigation powder. Then I asked if there was anything else I could do.

"Just leave me here on my own; don't send for anyone. All I need is my bed. And whatever you do, don't come unless I ring."

I left him. I can still see him as I went out of the room: he was streaming with sweat and still choking as he bent over the fumigation powder. I was terrified. I waited in the kitchen, convinced I'd never see him alive again. But gradually the attack passed. During the evening he rang for me. He was lying back in bed.

"My dear Céleste," he said, "you've had a fright. I'm grateful, and I understand—you'd never seen that sort of thing before. But, you know, when I was young I had many more attacks than I have now."

Afterward he talked about our arrangements. He explained what he had in mind:

"I don't want to keep Ernest, and I don't fancy looking for

someone else—it's too tiring. I'd like us to stay as we are. Will you?"

"Why not, monsieur?" I said, as if it were the most natural thing in the world.

He looked pleased and went on with what he must have been turning over in his mind since the worst of the attack was over.

"My dear Céleste, there's something I must tell you. I've just been to Cabourg with you, but that's all over. I shan't ever go out again, to Cabourg or anywhere else. The soldiers do their duty, and since I can't fight as they do, my duty is to write my book, do my work. I haven't the time for anything else."

So it was that evening in September 1914 when he deliberately entered into his life as a partial recluse—the last eight years of his life and of his work. And it was then, although I didn't realize it, and although, as he said, it wasn't proper, that I entered into that life too—to remain to the end.

5

THE LIFE OF A RECLUSE

When we got back from Cabourg the luggage was unpacked, the books put away, the notebooks and manuscripts restored to their table in the cork-lined room, and the summer and traveling overcoats hung up in the wardrobe never to be brought out again. And gradually life settled into a pattern that was never to vary except for a few little incidents that would only help me to better understand M. Proust's goodness. I think these incidents throw light on an aspect of his attitude toward other people and his refusal to be burdened by them unless he so chose.

He was always kind and loyal to anyone who had ever worked for him, no matter what the reason for their leaving. For instance, not only did he never forget Félicie, the old cook, but every so often he would send her a banknote. And each time she would write back to thank him, calling him "Dear Monsieur Marcel," like Nicolas. Then, toward the end, she stopped answering and M. Proust worried about her, although his letters were not returned by the post office. Often, when he was tired, it was I who wrote the letter and enclosed the money, and one day he said:

"Céleste dear, are you sure you remembered to post that last letter? . . . Yes? Then I'm very much afraid our Félicie must be dead."

But she wasn't. He went on worrying, but unfortunately I discovered the facts too late to be able to set his mind at rest. Once she had returned to Gers, where she was born and had retired with her family, she'd gradually stopped bothering to write and to thank M. Proust. It was only when she learned of his death that she came to life again. She then wrote to the family to express her sorrow.

At first Céline, too, after she was dismissed, was the object of M. Proust's kindnesses, especially after Nicolas went into the army. M. Proust wouldn't have wanted her to be in difficulties for anything in the world. So he gave her some money and told me that he had given her permission to come for the key to the cellar to help herself to whatever she wanted. Among other things, in the cellar, there was coal, which was scarce and expensive because of the war. She came to me for the key, and I treated her as if nothing had happened, partly because I knew what it was like to have a husband in the army and was sorry for her, and partly because I was young and didn't bear malice and had no reason to suppose she did either.

But things started to go wrong. It began with the couple who were the concierges, especially Antoine, the husband. They had always been protégés of Mme. Proust's; she must have relied on Antoine to do various odd jobs. At one time she had found him employment at the Saint-Lazare train station, and when she inherited 102 boulevard Haussmann from her uncle Louis Weil, she set him and his wife up as concierges there.

Antoine would talk to me and try to make me talk too, probably to find out what I thought and perhaps also to frighten me by telling me that it was no life for me, confined with an invalid, alone for hours at night in that huge apartment. At first I didn't say anything. I ignored the gossip, knowing M. Proust would hate it. But one day Antoine went too far and I put him in his place. I mentioned it to M. Proust that evening, and he laughed.

"My poor Céleste," he said, "you'll set everyone against me. Now Antoine and his wife will hide when they see me coming, instead of rushing out of the house to give me a chair while I wait for a taxi."

And indeed, for some time, when they saw me go out to call a taxi, they just hid in their quarters instead of going to their window to greet M. Proust and make a fuss over him. It was M. Proust himself who took the initiative one day and went inside, and then, finally, they emerged from the kitchen to offer him a chair, and all was as before.

But M. Proust had told me the real explanation the evening I spoke to him about Antoine.

"My poor Céleste, it's Céline plotting against you. She hasn't given up; she still hopes she'll be able to come back. Every time she's been to see me since she left she's told me I rely too much on you, and she's made Antoine and his wife jealous of you too. They're all in league against you. The funny thing is that before I dismissed Céline they spent all their time telling tales about each other. Céline said Antoine opened her letters. They were at each other's throat—they cheerfully could have murdered one another!"

He laughed.

Then there was the incident of the letter. It was anonymous, written by a woman who mysteriously claimed to have helped someone who knew M. Proust intimately, and that she had made this person promise to visit him to tell him certain things that couldn't be trusted to paper.

M. Proust showed me the letter.

"Céline's behind this too, I am sure," he said. "She is insane. She still has not given up the idea of coming back, and this is an attempt to get round me. It is probably some woman who has swindled her with the promise she will succeed. I don't know what this person proposes to tell me, and I don't want to know. Get a pen and paper and I'll dictate a letter to Céline."

It was a letter of refusal, and I posted it.

Céline turned up the following day, and when I showed her in, she brandished the letter in front of M. Proust.

"I told you you didn't know what she was really like, that schemer!" she shouted. "See for yourself, monsieur! Look at the letter she's had the cheek to write me!"

41

The schemer was I, of course. But M. Proust said:

"That's enough, Céline. I dictated that letter myself. And don't think you can make me change my mind. You're mad if you think I intend to have anything to do with that woman."

She went away, furious.

One day she came back to the kitchen door, with another woman. It was in the evening, at a time when she knew she had a chance of being received. She asked if she could see M. Proust, I delivered the message and came back, and just as she was going off to M. Proust's room she turned to the other woman and said:

"Wait for me here."

Some time went by. Then, suddenly, M. Proust's bell rang. I went in, to find Céline in a fury and M. Proust very pale.

"Céleste," he said, "I understand there's a person, a woman, in the kitchen. Kindly ask her to leave immediately and to wait for Céline downstairs. Make sure you lock the door. Then come back here."

Céline had started yelling as soon as she saw me, but when I came back it was deafening: "Look at that schemer, that traitor . . ."

Then suddenly M. Proust—it was the only time I ever saw him this way and I never shall forget it—sat up in bed and began to shout back.

"Go away, Céline—do you hear? And this time for good. Don't ever come back, not even for the key to the cellar. I forbid you. Go by the front stairs—it's quicker! And let that be the end of it!"

Céline must have been taken aback to see him really angry for once, for she did as she was told. We heard the front door slam. But he wanted to be sure.

"See that she is really gone," he said.

And then, calm once more, he told me what had happened.

"Imagine, Céleste. She had got it into her head—and put it into the concierges' heads—that you were trying to convince me to dismiss them and to turn her away forever. She certainly succeeded, all by herself, on the last score: I never want to see her again. But that is not all. Do you know why she brought the other woman? To help her give you a beating! As soon as she entered the room she said, 'I warn you, monsieur, I've someone with me, and we're going to give your precious Céleste a good thrashing!' That was why I rang: I was afraid she might hurt you. But believe me, this won't happen again."

I could tell he was very upset. So was I. Thunderstruck. I'd always been careful to keep out of the way. I'd never said or done anything against anyone. I'd tried to be nice to them all, including Céline. I lay awake all that night thinking about it. I couldn't understand how Céline had come to feel such ill will toward me, and it pained me to think of the scene M. Proust had had to endure because of me. Next day I was still so upset I told him. Or rather— because it was my turn to be furious—I began by saying that the day before, taken by surprise, I probably wouldn't have stood up for myself, but if it happened again, if Céline should ring at the door and have another try, I'd chuck her down the stairs like a sack of dirty washing. It was revolting to think of anyone setting traps for me as she had. I'd become so worked up I then said:

"Anyway, I'd rather leave than have you subjected to such scheming and scenes because of me. I never asked to come here; I never meant to lead this kind of life. All my husband's family are in business, and he got married to do the same as soon as we could manage it. I'm comfortable here, I like it, and I'm happy to be of service to you, but I don't see how I can stay. You know I didn't take Nicolas' place as a permanent thing. Now all this has happened. Tell Céline to come back, and I'll go. I think that's for the best."

He let me say what I had to say; then, very gently, he reminded me he was alone and ill and repeated that the matter of Céline was settled. He didn't want to hear of her again.

And that to all intents and purposes was the end of the Cottins. We saw Nicolas only once more. Before that he wrote to M. Proust from the army, with a photograph of himself in uniform. I remember he said in his letter: "I'm very comfortable here. I'm cook to

43

General Joffre. All the officers are delighted with my cooking, and as you can see, I'm very well." But M. Proust said as he read the letter:

"He's a lost man, Céleste! He obviously drinks the Madeira and the port instead of putting it in his sauces. Look how fat he's got."

Then came the day when Nicolas arrived back on leave. This time he was as thin as a rake and as sallow as a lemon—I hardly recognized him. He was quite changed toward me too, because of the stories Céline must have told him. He didn't even say hello, just asked timidly if he could see "Monsieur Marcel." M. Proust was awake and saw him at once. He told me afterward that Nicolas said he was very ill and begged him to help him get treatment. M. Proust sent him to Dr. Netter, a famous heart specialist, with a warm recommendation. After he had examined the patient Dr. Netter wrote to M. Proust saying that unfortunately it wasn't certain Nicolas' life could be saved. M. Proust said to me that day:

"What can you expect? He was all right here because he needed a quiet life, and like me he can't bear strain. But as I said to you before, you can't do good to people against their will. Take Céline. . . ."

Céline, too. We saw her just once more—when Nicolas was in the hospital. She came one day and cried; she said her husband was cold and asked if M. Proust could give him a blanket. He told me to give them one—a red satin quilt he'd never used in all the years he'd had it. It was a present from a little maid named Marie who had worked for his parents. She was very pretty and had been one of his sweethearts when he was still a young man. She had made the quilt and sent it to him.

With Céline and Nicolas gone for good from boulevard Haussmann and Ernest gone almost as soon as we got back from Cabourg, M. Proust began a life of partial seclusion in which he shut himself up for the sake of his work—and I with him—and which nothing disturbed for the eight years until the end.

44

It's been said he thought several times of going to live some-where else—Nice or Venice or I don't know where. It's even been suggested that when the air raids were very bad over Paris I tried to persuade him to go to Cabourg or the Côte d'Azur, to stay with Mme. Catusse, an old friend of his mother's. But it isn't true. He did sometimes feel a wish or even a need for a holiday, or a desire to see again a certain town, a landscape, a painting, a church—like Cabourg, when he'd talked about showing me the high tides in Brittany. But it was always:

"We'll go when I've finished my book, dear Céleste. Then you'll see how marvelous it is."

To finish his book—that was all that mattered now. And from autumn 1914 onward, his whole life was organized around that compulsion more than ever before.

He severed most communications. Before the end of the year he decided to give up his telephone. He may have told people it was because he was in financial straits, as has been alleged. But that was only an excuse; he indulged in whatever other expense he fancied. In fact, he didn't want to be disturbed against his will any more. He made himself sole master of himself and any visitors and all his connections with other people.

His only concern now was peace and quiet in which to write. For that he needed solitude. He shaped and molded me with this in mind. He taught me step by step what he needed in the same way one teaches infants to walk.

What still astonishes me is the ease with which I submitted and adapted myself to a way of life for which I was absolutely unpre-pared. All my childhood had been spent in the freedom of the country and the affection of my mother. We went to bed with the hens and rose with the roosters, or nearly. And here I was, taking quite naturally to living at night as he did, as if I'd never done anything else. And I not only lived in the same rhythm as he did, but twenty-four hours a day and seven days a week I lived entirely for him. I have nothing to do with the book he called *La Prisonnière*, but it would have been a good name for me.

45

I recall one little episode at the beginning, which other people have embroidered, saying it was the first Sunday of our life of seclusion and that I had dressed up to go to Mass, which is ridiculous since I was dressed up all day and every day at boulevard Haussmann. It was just an ordinary day, and I don't remember exactly how the subject came up. With M. Proust it could only have been in the evening, especially in those days, and therefore not the time for church, and he may have been talking to me about myself, my family, and my childhood. At any rate I said:

"You see how it is, monsieur. Here I am, I don't budge; I never go anywhere except to do something you want done and don't want to write about. And yet my mother brought me up to go to Mass every Sunday. But not only do I not go—I hardly even think of it."

I said this without any resentment, just eagerly, like a little girl. He looked at me from the bed, with magnificent serenity.

"Céleste," he said, very gently, "do you know you are doing something much greater and nobler than going to Mass? You are giving up your time to look after a sick man. That is infinitely more beautiful."

It was true. And I think that was the only time I ever made him think I was complaining, even though I didn't mean to.

When I recall the beginning, when I was first left on my own with him, it seems to me the chief difference between someone like Nicolas and myself was that Nicolas did his duties automatically, because he had to do them. Whereas I—I did everything. When it wasn't one thing it was another. I made the coffee, did the cleaning, went out to telephone or to buy something, delivered a letter, warmed up the linen, prepared or changed the hot-water bottles, tidied up the newspapers and manuscripts M. Proust left in heaps on his bed—if I hadn't tidied them away, there wouldn't have been any room left for him, there were so many of them—lit the log fire in his room, heated the water for his foot bath. I did all this as if I were singing, in a sort of joy, like a bird flitting from branch to branch. There were times when I was dead with fatigue, but I didn't feel it, didn't think of it any more than I thought of going to Mass, because not for one second was I ever bored. In one sense it was a life that was as regular as clockwork, and at the same time there was always the unexpected, the charm of a gesture or conversation, his pleasure at having worked well, mine at having done something satisfactorily. Also, I probably felt so lighthearted, because I never looked on it as a real job. Not once in those remaining eight years was there any question, either for him or for me, of my staying on indefinitely. When Odilon came back from the war he said; "Well, who'd have thought I'd find you still here!" It was like a lease renewed automatically.

I've said I fell into the rhythm very quickly. The rhythm of his life was unique. Though I don't think anybody else ever did live that way. Time contained no hours—just a certain number of definite things to be done every day. Everything else depended on his work; on some concern or need connected with his writing; or on a whim, the satisfaction or the disappointment over an evening out, a meeting, or a visit; and on the fatigue, beneficial or harmful, of going out, or of writing, with all the inevitable consequences to his sensibility and his illness.

At first I continued to get up fairly early, partly out of habit and partly because M. Proust didn't keep me up very late. In those days he used to tell me to go to sleep at about midnight or one o'clock in the morning. Before I left him I did all the things I had learned from Nicolas: I took the silver tray away from his bedside and put a lacquer one there for the night, with lime blossoms, a bottle of Evian water, and his little cup and sugar bowl, in case he felt like making himself some lime-blossom tea with his electric kettle during the night. He never did. In those eight years I never took back a single bottle of Evian from which he had drunk a single drop.

But that kettle was the cause of plenty of accidents. He turned it on and off with a pear switch. He had three of these within easy reach; the other two were for the bell and for the bedside lamp. Several times, absentmindedly, probably because he was so absorbed in his work, he pressed the switch for the kettle, thinking it was for the bell, and then forgot. Suddenly he would be struck by the awful smell of the burning empty kettle. And he couldn't bear smells! He panicked. I rushed in, and every time—though I could never do it today—I managed to mend a plug or change a burned-out fuse. Later I'd take the kettle to be checked or repaired at a special shop—Morse's, at the head of rue de la Bienfaisance.

But as a general rule, if all was well, I went away after checking everything for the night. But even then, after having said goodnight, sometimes two minutes or an hour later he'd ring. Sometimes I would be already undressed and in bed. I would put on my dressing gown and go to his room, my hair hanging loose.

"My poor Céleste, were you in bed? I'm so sorry."

He knew very well I was in bed, but he sugared the pill so sweetly that I would say: "It doesn't matter, monsieur. I'm always glad to come to see what you want."

I meant it, too. I remembered Nicolas, when he was there, grousing at the sound of the bell: "I've only just left him. What does he want me for now?" I didn't go at all unwillingly. And probably one of the things that made him trust me and brought us together most was that I was always smiling when I went into his room.

Sometimes he called me back for just a trifle—to make sure no arrangement about the night had been forgotten.

"Céleste dear, in spite of what I said before, I think I might go out tomorrow. There is someone I would like to see again if I feel up to it." He would say who it was and why. "We shall talk about it tomorrow. I may ask you to telephone that person to make sure he is available." Then he would send me off.

Or he might ask me to phone before he awakened. Sometimes he called me back because he had changed his mind about when he wanted his coffee.

"My dear Céleste, I may ask you for my coffee a little earlier tomorrow."

It was nearly always "maybe." And in the course of the night, or when he woke up next day, it was quite possible he would decide I wasn't to telephone, that he wouldn't go out, that he wouldn't ring for his coffee till six or eight in the evening. But I'd be up and dressed and waiting, and I'd make fresh coffee if necessary.

To give myself something to do while I waited, I sewed on lace borders and trimmings. One day he asked how I occupied my time when I hadn't anything to do. I told him.

"But Céleste, you ought to read!" he cried.

I even remember his suggesting *The Three Musketeers*. I read it and found it fascinating. We talked about it on several occasions in the evening. I was very simple and naïve and would say things like:

"I wonder how that woman Milady always manages to take everybody in."

He looked surprised and pleased. "Very true, Céleste," he said, laughing.

He suggested I go on to Balzac. "His novels are beautiful, you'll see. We will talk about them."

But I was just a girl and preferred sewing. How I have regretted it since, when I think of all he would have said and taught me in those evenings.

For we soon fell more and more into the habit of talking. And then I had no more regular hours at all. The time I got up depended on the time I'd gone to bed; the only item that had to be taken into account was his coffee when he woke up. So usually I didn't get up until one or two in the afternoon, and when he eventually woke up and we were talking about his plans, I got into the habit of saying quite naturally:

"Well, yesterday evening you said . . ."

"Yesterday evening" had sometimes been eight or nine o'clock that same morning.

It was a completely upside-down life, even in the simplest things. For example, I couldn't clean the house or do his room unless he was out, and since when he did go out it was rarely before ten in the evening, I never did housework except at night, never opened the windows of the flat except onto darkness.

In the kitchen and in my own room, I could still see what daylight was, when I got up. But in all the rest of the flat the curtains were kept hermetically sealed and daylight never entered. The cork-lined room itself was guarded by closed shutters, and the big thick blue curtains were always drawn. Between the curtains and the shutters there was a double window to keep out the noise. You couldn't even hear the sound of the trams down in the street. We lived by electric light or perpetual darkness.

Now I realize M. Proust's whole object, his whole great sacrifice for his work, was to set himself outside time in order to rediscover it. When there is no more time, there is silence. He needed that silence in order to hear only the voices he wanted to hear, the voices that are in his books. I didn't think about that at the time. But now when I'm alone at night and can't sleep, I seem to see him as he surely must have been in his room after I had left him—alone too, but in his own night, working at his notebooks when, outside, the sun had long been up. And I think how I was there, not suspecting up till the end, or almost, that he had chosen that solitude and silence, though he knew it was killing him. But then I remember what Professor Robert Proust said to me later:

"My brother could have lived longer if he'd been willing to live the same way as everyone else. But he chose what he did, and he chose it for the sake of his work. All we can do is bow our heads."

And above all I hear the voice of M. Proust himself:

"I am very tired, dear Céleste. But it has to be like this. It has to be. . . ."

1 The picture taken at my second meeting with Odilon Albaret, at his in-laws in La Canourgue in the Lozère. I'm sitting in the middle, with Odilon to the left. Behind him is his sister Adèle Larivière, the matchmaker. Seated at the right, M. Larivière.

2 Odilon and me, married in 1915, on his first leave from the war.

3 Above: Odilon and his car, a Unic, before I knew him. He already worked, from time to time, as a driver for Monsieur Proust at Cabourg on the Normand coast.

4 Right: Depending on the season, he also worked in Monaco and in Paris. This is how you started the car with a hand crank. Odilon bought a red Renault, in which he regularly drove Monsieur Proust in Paris.

5 Opposite: I had this picture taken during the 1914 war, though I was already living at Monsieur Proust's on the Boulevard Haussmann. It was intended for Odilon, who had gone to the war, and for my sister Marie.

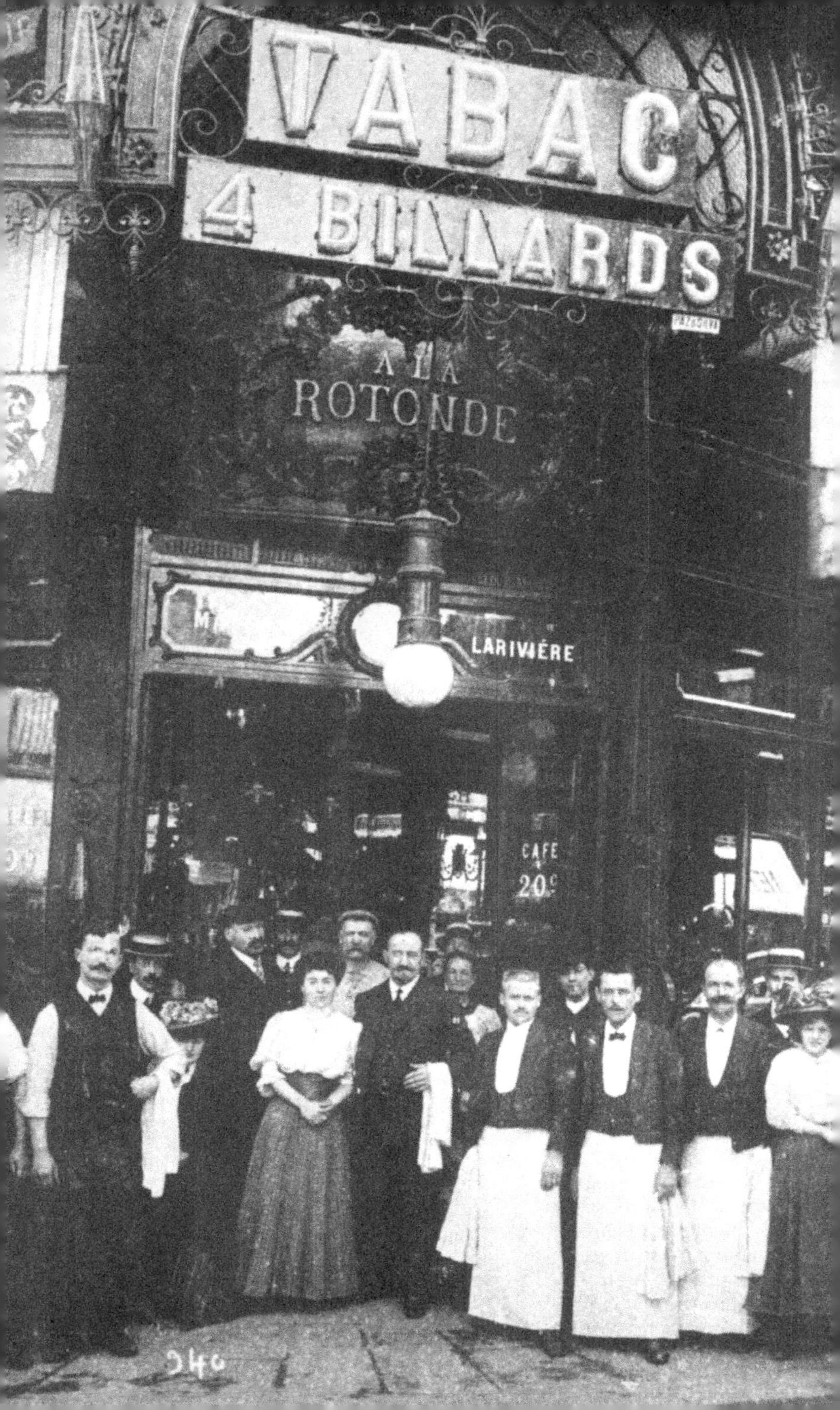
TABAC
4 BILLARDS
A LA
ROTONDE
LARIVIÈRE
CAFE

6 Opposite: The café Larivière, at the corner of the rue Feydeau and the rue Montmartre, where Monsieur Proust called in a message when he wanted to retain Odilon's services. My sister-in-law Adèle and her husband are at center, surrounded by their staff.

7 Right: My sister-in-law Adèle. She didn't take kindly to contradiction, but was always charming and good to me.

8 Below left: My sister Marie, who joined me at Monsieur Proust's in 1918, after our mother died. Picture taken at Auxillac, when she was still in mourning.

9 Below right: My niece Yvonne, who stayed for a month at Monsieur Proust's, on the rue Hamelin, typing the manuscript of *The Prisoner*.

10 This is a reconstruction of Monsieur Proust's bedroom on the rue Hamelin. I stood just the way you see, when he spoke to me from his bed. Photograph by André Dunoyer de Ségonzac.

11 Top: When Monsieur Proust summoned me after I'd already gone to bed, I'd arrive looking like this, with my hair down and in a bathrobe too. He'd say, "It's the Mona Lisa."

12 Left: He inscribed this photograph to me, one evening in 1915 or 1916. He thought he was "old" by comparison to me.

6

RETREAT INTO ILLNESS

Even now, I believe, there are still many people who think or say that M. Proust was, if not actually a madman, then at least slightly mad, and that he deliberately exaggerated his illness. They say his asthma was not nearly so bad as he made out; that he was not only to some extent a *malade imaginaire* but also made a display of his illness in order to gain sympathy. Some have even said this condition has its basis in the great but possessive love he had for his mother as a child and ever afterward—a love made even more jealous by the birth of his younger brother, Robert. It has been hinted that he invented his asthma, as a child, to monopolize her attention, and then continued at it to draw the attention of other people.

All this is ridiculous. Those who have said such things have done so for their own ends. Anyone who could have seen M. Proust during that attack when we got back from Cabourg—pale as death, crouching over the fumes, choking for breath—wouldn't need any more proof that it was not play-acting.

True, I never saw him have another attack as bad as that one. But that may have been because we never left Paris again. Most likely if we'd gone back to Cabourg he'd have had the same choking fits as before if we'd passed through Mézidon at haymaking time.

It's probably because of the resemblance to hay fever that people have said his illness was worst at the change of season. This may have been so before I knew him, but all the time I was with him I never saw this to be so, and he never said anything to me that suggested it. I remember his saying several times: "The rising of the sap is bad for me." But I don't remember that he had any especially bad attacks in the spring, for example. What I recall particularly is a letter—I think it was to his friend Jean-Louis Vaudoyer, the writer—in which he said: "Nothing announces the onset of my attacks, nothing their end."

That was more like the way it really was.

What is certain is that after September 1914, when he shut himself up at boulevard Haussmann and never left Paris again, only going out to see friends or to meet someone for some specific purpose, I never knew him to have any of the deathly attacks he must have had before. Once he said:

"Céleste, it is a fact that since I have lived the life of a recluse I have had fewer attacks."

And when I asked him what could have been the cause of his illness, he said, "No one has ever been able to say, not even my father, and he was a famous doctor. One thing is certain: I had my first attack when I was still a child, one day when I was playing in the gardens in the Champs-Elysées, and already then there was nothing anyone could do."

Speaking about that time, he went on:

"I'm quite well now in comparison to what I was then. You cannot imagine! My parents were distraught whenever I had an attack. Sometimes both of them would sit up all night by my bed, thinking I was going to die, as you did when we came back from Cabourg.

"One of those nights, Father had to fetch the big medical dictionaries from his office to put behind my pillows and prop me up to help me breathe. But I didn't get any better, so he sent for one of his colleagues. His solution was to give me a morphine injection, but that only made me worse."

Here he started laughing.

"My dear Céleste, how glad I am it did! I never got rid of my asthma, and if the injection had helped me I certainly would have had the weakness of giving myself one every time I had an attack, and perhaps—who knows?—I might have become a morphine addict. It makes me shudder to think of it. I might have ended up a complete ruin, like a friend of mine."

He didn't say at the time whom he meant, but I realized later he was referring to Jacques Bizet, his old schoolmate, who shot himself.

The full significance of his words emerges especially when one knows that even if he was no longer ill as before, he was still an invalid, with the threat of an attack always hanging over him. For even if I no longer saw him have acute attacks, I saw him suffer all the time.

The way he resigned himself was wonderful. I never heard a word of complaint from him. And not only did he not complain, but he wouldn't be pitied either. At such times all he wanted was that everyone leave him alone with his suffering. If he sent for me, it was just to say with the usual, inimitable gentleness:

"Céleste, I am not well, I can't talk, and I need to be left quiet. Just put the candle and the powder where I can reach them, and leave me, please."

That was all.

If the attack was lengthy and severe, he perspired a lot, and the resulting exhaustion would bring on a kind of chill. Then he'd ask me to change the hot-water bottles, and he'd put an old fur coat, kept specially for the purpose, over his legs. He had another beautiful coat with a sealskin collar and lined with mink, which he wore going out when it was cold. But the old coat always had to be hanging over the foot of the brass bed, together with a magnificent black overcoat with a black and white check lining—very smart and not at all old—which his mother had ordered for him but which he used as a dressing gown. He didn't have an ordinary dressing gown; when he was alone and wanted to walk about the room, or when the barber came, he would just wear Turkish slippers, and the overcoat over the clothes he wore in bed.

Perhaps I should say something about his room, because for all those years, it was his stage, and in a way it was mine. Even later when we moved, he did everything to keep the setting unchanged. He arranged to be surrounded by all the furniture and other things he was used to—to part from them would have been heartbreaking.

As I've already said, the room was very big and lofty, with a ceiling twelve feet high, and two large double windows always sealed while he was there, as were the shutters and the blue satin curtains lined with felt. The soundproofing was completed by big sheets of cork over the walls and ceiling.

The most striking thing in the room, apart from the cork, was the color blue—the blue of the curtains, to be precise, which reflected the big chandelier that hung from the ceiling—a sort of bowl ending in a point, with lots of lights and several switches, which was never lighted except for visitors, or when I tidied the room in M. Proust's absence. There was a thick white marble mantelpiece, with two blue-globe candelabra and a matching bronze clock in between. The candelabra were never used either. The only light came from the small long-stemmed bedside lamp—like a desk lamp—which lighted up his papers while leaving his face in shadow. It had a green gathered shade lined with white silk. It turned on and off with a key switch.

The room needed to be large in order to accommodate all the furniture, which was M. Proust's share of his parents' furniture, divided up after their death between him and his brother (Mme. Proust had, as I said earlier, inherited from her uncle Weil). Although M. Proust had generously let his brother have most of it, the flat was still crammed with furniture. The dining room, which was never used, was full to bursting, and since 1906 three big roomfuls had been stored in the Bailly furniture warehouse. Only the main and small salons were properly set out.

Occupying the whole space between the two windows was an imposing rosewood mirror-wardrobe with bronze trimmings and a bracket lamp. In front of the wardrobe was a grand piano that belonged to M. Proust's mother. He played it sometimes but not often; sometimes his friend Reynaldo Hahn, the composer, would play. The piano was jammed so close to the wardrobe that the latter was never opened.

To the left of the piano facing the windows was a massive oak desk piled with books. The wall to the left, still facing the windows, was the one with the mantelpiece, the candelabra, and the clock. In the right hand wall were two tall double doors, one at each end, opening into the main salon. The one nearer the window was the usual entrance to the bedroom; it was covered by a curtain, and one half of the folding door was always kept shut. The other door was never used at all, in any case, it was blocked by two revolving bookcases, laden with volumes as was the oak table. Against the wall, to the left of the door that was used, there was a pretty little Chinese cabinet with photos on it of him and his brother as children. M. Proust kept his money and bank papers in the drawers of this cabinet; when he went out he usually asked me to get from it whatever money he needed. Next to the little cabinet was a large rosewood chest matching the wardrobe. It had a white marble top, on which there were two white bowls with scalloped edges, on either side of a white statuette of the Infant Jesus crowned with bunches of grapes. Above it was a big mirror reaching to the ceiling. Also on the chest were the thirty-two black imitation-leather notebooks containing the first draft of his book, which he always kept there. In the drawers were all sorts of photographs and souvenirs amassed in the course of the years.

Finally, in front of the two revolving bookcases, there was a worktable, a copy of a Boulle, with his mother's initials, "J.P.," Jeanne Proust.

Then came "his" wall. Beside the huge folding door that was always kept shut was a small door opening into a passageway, through which he reached his dressing room (a large bedroom which had been converted) and the lavatory. This door was supposed to be used only by him, but gradually I came to use it too. But I never once did so of my own accord; as always, it was he who decided.

"Come through the little door, Céleste," he would say.

That meant entering the room between his mother's worktable and the foot of his bed.

So his wall was the one facing the windows. And the bed was against it, lengthwise.

There was a striking contrast between the large pieces of furniture, with their gilt and bronze fittings, and the others—those that made up his corner, between his wall and the wall with the mantelpiece. Apart from an exquisite five-paneled Chinese screen behind the bed, everything was very plain. The bed was of brass, with bars, the metal tarnished from the fumes of the Legras powder. Then there were his three tables, arranged within arm's reach. One was of carved bamboo, with a lower shelf that held a pile of books, a pile of handkerchiefs, and the hot-water bottles. There was also an old rosewood bedside table with doors, which held his work things: manuscripts, notebooks, a schoolboy inkwell, penholder, a watch, a bedside lamp, and, later on, several pairs of spectacles. A third table, of walnut, was for his coffee tray, and for the lime and Evian water at night. And all this was very simple, like a little island in that vast room amid all that massive furniture.

The only places to sit were the piano stool and, near the bed, for visitors, a velvet armchair that had come from his father's study.

The floor was bare oak parquet except for an oriental carpet that made a rather large bedside rug. He had inherited a number of very good rugs from his parents, but they were all in the other rooms—in the main salon and the dining room, and one in the hall, on top of the red moquette. Since the time we got back from Cabourg to find the vacuum-cleaning in progress, that operation had never been repeated. When M. Proust was out I took the opportunity to go around with the carpet sweeper—that was all. I was even forbidden to polish the parquet; he had warned me early that the smell would disagree with him. Anyway, I didn't know how; at home we used to wash the floors and sweep them with a broom.

His acute sensibility, which was connected with his illness, showed itself in all sorts of ways.

Princess Marthe Bibesco says in a book she wrote about him that one day he told me he couldn't see her because she used too much scent. I don't know where she got the idea: it isn't true, at least as far as she was concerned. What is true is that M. Proust couldn't stand perfumes, either natural or artificial: they brought on his asthma. He couldn't bear flowers, even if they had very little smell or none at all. A few times, while I was with him, he asked my husband to drive him to the Chevreuse Valley to see the apple trees or the hawthorns. According to Odilon, M. Proust would sit for a long time in the car admiring the flowering trees or bushes; then he'd ask Odilon to go and cut off a branch for him. He'd look at it through the window of the car, sometimes for quite a long while, and then generally tell Odilon to put it in the trunk to take back to boulevard Haussmann. There, in case he should want to look at it again, it was to be left out on the landing of the service stairs.

I also remember a conversation we had about hawthorns, after one of his excursions. He told me he was very fond of it, and I said politely, and rather vaguely:

"Yes, monsieur, it is a very pretty flower."

"But do you really know it well, Céleste?"

I replied in the same tone; "I think so, monsieur. There was a field at home that had a hawthorn hedge. So I always saw them when they were in flower."

"But I am so fond of them I have written an article about them, the white ones and the pink. I am sure you have never looked at them closely. There are some on the service stairs that Odilon brought back for me. Go have a look. Look very closely at those tiny roses, and see how perfect they are in their tininess. I don't know of anything prettier."

And he insisted on my going. But he didn't go himself.

He had a great admiration for all flowers; I often think he must have been sorry not to be able to have them in the apartment, let alone in his room. His friends knew there mustn't be any flowers around when he went to see them. But he was always giving flowers to other people. I was forever going to order them at "his" florist's, Lemaître's on boulevard Haussmann, never the other shops.

"And remember, Céleste," he might say, "they must be beautiful." Or: "Céleste, I want you to order some orchids for Madame so-and-so. I know they are expensive, but it can't be helped; I want them to be beautiful."

It was as if by giving flowers to other people he was trying to make up for not being able to live with their beauty himself.

On the question of smells, I remember another example. One evening when he was going out in full evening dress, I had prepared some white gloves, very elegant and spotless. I had just had them cleaned—it was at the beginning, and I didn't know. I helped him on with his fur coat. He was in a very good humor, laughing at something I'd said that amused him, probably. Then suddenly, when he went to pick up the gloves that were waiting as usual on a little silver salver, he stopped laughing and looked at me searchingly.

"These gloves have been cleaned, Céleste."

I guessed I'd done something wrong and tried to look innocent.

"I don't think so, monsieur."

"Come now, Céleste, you know whether you've had them cleaned or not. Anyway, I tell you they have. They smell of benzine."

Having got to know him a little, I'd sniffed them all over to make sure they didn't smell. So I tried again.

"Monsieur, I assure you they're immaculate."

"And I tell you they smell of benzine. Get me some others."

I hung my head and said; "Very good, monsieur." And I was never guilty of that sin again.

But it wasn't only smells. Like all asthmatics, when he had an attack he sneezed and had to keep blowing his nose. So, just in case, there always had to be piles of handkerchiefs ready on the little table by his bed. When he had wiped his nose once with one of them—he never blew it—he threw it down. And so on. When I first went to boulevard Haussmann and was exclaiming at the fineness of the cloth, he explained that it had to be like that because the membranes of his nose were extremely sensitive. One day—it was just after the 1914 war, when at M. Proust's suggestion my sister Marie had come to help me look after him a bit—one day he asked me to buy him some handkerchiefs. I said to my sister:

"Go to the Bon Marché and get some very good ones, the finest they've got."

Marie came back with some very good ones, finely woven and with a handsome embroidered initial, but I could see at once they were a bit too coarse. I showed them to M. Proust. He gave them one look and said:

"It's no use, Céleste. I shall never use them. Do as you like with them."

"But monsieur, you just see—once they've been properly washed and ironed, they'll lose their stiffness."

He didn't say anything. I washed them, ironed them very carefully, and mixed them up one day among the others. When he came to them he sent for me.

"Céleste," he said, "I told you I couldn't use these handkerchiefs. Please understand it's not just a caprice or a whim. They're just not fine enough. They irritate the inside of my nose and make me sneeze, and that's very bad for my asthma. So don't give them to me again, please."

I wanted to have another try. I washed and rewashed them, ironed them again, and again mixed them up with the others. At first he didn't react. He waited for me to come in about something else. When I did, he was holding a handkerchief in one hand and in the other the small pair of scissors he used to cut his nails. He looked at me, and said with his inflexible gentleness:

"My dear Céleste, I see you haven't understood at all. So I'll show you."

And he started to cut up the handkerchief, not stopping until it was in shreds. Then he said:

"Now do you see? Get it into your head once and for all, Céleste. Handkerchiefs are like shoes: None but the finest are pleasant until they've been broken in. From now on, let's be satisfied with the old ones."

If he'd been the *malade imaginaire* some people say he was, or the real invalid trying to attract attention, he would have had a bevy of doctors and a whole pharmacy by his bed. But during the eight years I knew him he never called in anyone but Dr. Bize, the doctor he was accustomed to and in whom he had confidence.

"He is very good," he used to say. "He may overprescribe a little, but I don't need to be told whether to take a medicine or not."

It shouldn't be forgotten that M. Proust had come from a medical family and had the example of his father. There was a story that he liked very much and told me several times.

"One day when my father was just finishing lunch, he was told that a gentleman urgently insisted on seeing him. Father refused at first and sent a message to say that he meant to have his lunch in peace and that afterward he was engaged, so the patient must make an appointment. The gentleman implored. Father flung down his napkin and had him shown into the drawing room. There he examined him and asked him questions. Suddenly he broke off in the middle of a sentence, leaped up, and cried: 'Fire! Fire! Quick, monsieur, run!' And the patient ran like a hare. My father had seen at one glance that his problem was emotional."

Then, with his subtle smile:

"It was like that all the time. At meals the telephone was always ringing for my father. They sent for him in the evening, and when he came back he would say: 'I have seen so-and-so, he has this or that the matter with him, and I prescribed such-and-such a treatment'— and he would explain it to us. When you are a doctor's son, you see, you end up being a doctor yourself. You learn your lessons. So I know very well what is good for me and what is not."

That is probably why he preferred Dr. Bize to any other doctor. He was a little man going gray, very calm, serious, pleasant, and polite. He called M. Proust "Mâitre." It was M. Proust's brother, Robert, a famous professor like their father, who had recommended Dr. Bize to M. Proust as a very good general practitioner—they had been students together. But M. Proust never consulted his brother about his health, except at the very end—and then it was Dr. Bize and I who took it upon ourselves to call him in.

Actually, M. Proust did not usually do as Dr. Bize told him and took a mischievous pleasure in gently teasing him. Once he told me: "I said to him, 'My dear doctor, today you want me to take such-and-such a medicine, and the other day you said it might poison me. How do you account for that?'" The story amused him so much he put it in *La Prisonnière*.

He only took what he wanted from among the prescriptions. Contrary to what anyone might think and to what some have said, he wasn't at all keen on drugs. It is true he always had to have his tablets on the table within reach. But there were only two kinds— Veronal and caffeine—and it is quite untrue to say, as some have, that he took them regularly. The only regular aspect was that they had to be there in case he needed them. But one followed the other. I mean, if his heart was tired in the evening, as may happen to any asthmatic after an attack, or if he wanted to work particularly hard, he would take a caffeine tablet; then, to restore the balance, when he wanted to rest or when he stopped working, in the morning, he would take his Veronal. But always in very small and carefully measured doses, and never in any excess. And those were the only tablets he took. Adrenalin has been mentioned, but that too is untrue.

He did frequently call in Dr. Bize, though it was often I who had to insist.

"I'll see, I'll see," he would say. Then, a few days later: "All right then! Send for Dr. Bize!"

It was always he who made the decision.

When he did send for Dr. Bize—who always hurried up—it was usually for something so trifling that for a long time I wondered what the explanation could be. They would stay closeted together much longer than was needed for an consultation. M. Proust never talked to me about it, but from what I knew of him I came to the conclusion that he sent for the doctor mainly to talk about details he was putting into his book: with Dr. Bize providing the information, he could be sure it would be sound. When I saw him after these sessions he usually looked pleased, wearing the mocking smile he always wore when he had been enjoying himself. Yes, I've seen him at it too often not to be sure he sent for Dr. Bize mainly to bombard him with all sorts of questions, leaving him outmaneuvered and backed into a corner.

His chief remedy against asthma, and the only one he used regularly, were the fumigations. Between ourselves we used to call it "smoking"—I think he got the expression from me.

I remember once he said, his face still pale and drawn after he had crouched over the fumes for a long time:

"This is the only thing that has ever given me any relief. I once tried the cigarettes made with this same Legras powder, but I am sure the paper they use, though thin and carefully prepared, disagrees with me. I prefer just the fumes."

It was a dark-gray powder that had to be ignited; he never used any other kind. We ordered several cartons at a time, each containing ten packets, and always from the same place—the Leclerc pharmacy in rue Vignon, at the corner of rue de Sèze. Everything was organized. As I've said, behind the wall where the bed was, there was a corridor with a door opening into the bedroom. In this corridor, on the other side of which was the dressing room, was a little table with two candlesticks, one always lighted and the other kept in reserve. I used to buy the candles in rue Saint-Lazare, in ten-pound boxes—you can imagine how many we must have used up. And they were big candles too. They were lighted in the kitchen, for there mustn't be the least smell of sulphur near the bedroom; and when he had finished with a candle, I had to take it away.

Every morning—*his* morning, in other words, every afternoon—after he awoke and before he had his coffee, he "smoked." If I was there I would bring him the candlestick. But he always measured out the powder himself. I handed him the little box; he opened it and poured the powder into the saucer, then lit it with a little square of white paper lit, in turn, from the candle. It was ordinary writing paper, which we bought (fifteen or twenty boxes at a time) at Printemps. I used to keep a box of it by the bed, carefully shut to keep out the dust. He was always afraid of dust, because of the sneezing.

Sometimes he lit only a few pinches of powder, which lasted just long enough to produce some wisps of smoke. Sometimes he needed more—half an hour, an hour, several hours. Then he would add more and more powder; sometimes he even asked me to hand him a second box. Then the room would be thick with smoke, as it had been the first time I entered it. Sometimes he would ring for me after having got everything ready, and then say, pointing to the open box:

"Take it away, Céleste. I decided to try not to smoke."

The box was rarely empty when he had finished. He never shut it himself; I always cleared it away. For him, once opened, it was ready to be thrown away. When Nicolas was still there, he used to keep the partly used boxes in the kitchen for someone he knew who suffered from asthma and used to collect them. Nicolas knew that once they had been opened, M. Proust could never be persuaded to use them again.

But after the coffee and the fumigation were over, M. Proust wouldn't "smoke" any more for the rest of the day. Not even on those nights he went out and sometimes came home very tired.

Of course all those Legras fumes presented a problem, as there could be no question of opening the windows while he was there. Fortunately the apartment had deep chimneys with a good strong draught. So we lit a fire every day after the fumigation, even in the middle of summer—a wood fire, of course, because he wouldn't have been able to stand the smell of coal—and the Legras fumes would disappear quite quickly. He used to signal me to light the fire. Not a word, just a wave of the hand—he never spoke after the fumigation. Or he might take one of the little squares of paper and start to write, "Would you light . . .," but before he'd finished I'd have understood, and he'd thank me with a little gesture and a smile. When it was very hot outside we just made one short blaze, enough to draw out the fumes. If it was cold, I made up the fire with logs. At night, if he was working and felt the fire dying down, he'd ring for me and ask me if I would mind putting on more logs.

Apart from my oven purring away in the kitchen, these fires were all the heating there was in the apartment. There was an excellent central heating system, very well insulated, but this too, he said, disagreed with him because it dried up the air, which in turn dried up the membranes of the nose and bronchial tubes.

The best of it was, the chimney was never swept in his room for as long as we were at boulevard Haussmann. I never thought of it at the time. Now I realize how lucky it was the soot never caught fire. But he wouldn't have stood for having the chimney swept any more than for polishing the floors. Think of the dust!

And as his wish was my command, I had no complaints about the winters in the apartment.

Yet heaven knows he felt the cold himself—partly because of his illness and partly because of his refusal to eat properly and his lying still most of the time in bed.

There weren't many bedclothes—just a woolen blanket and a rustic quilt with a pattern of yellow apple blossoms on a red ground, which had belonged to the Cottins. He'd seen it and asked Céline to sell it to him, because he found the apple blossoms so pretty. It reminded him of the summers of his childhood, at Illiers. Above all, he told me once, it resembled one that used to be on his aunt's bed, the aunt he made into Tante Léonie in his writing—he had been very fond of her. There was also an eiderdown, put away in a cupboard, that had been specially made for him at great expense at Liberty's, on boulevard des Capucines. But he soon gave up using it because the feathers were bad for his asthma.

He relied for warmth mainly on his hot-water bottles and woolies.

Imagine him lying in bed, his head only just raised although he was propped up by two pillows. He wore white pajamas—but only the top: instead of the trousers he always wore a pair of long woolen underpants. I never saw him in these, but I could tell from the washing. Under the pajama top he wore a soft wool jumper. There were heaps of these indoor jumpers, very thick, with buttons, and edged with silk. There was always a pile of them on the armchair (I whipped them away into the dressing room if there was a visitor). It would be typical for him to ring for me and say:

"I am sorry to bother you, dear Céleste, but I feel a bit chilly. Would you mind handing me a jumper to put over my shoulders?" Then he would simply throw it over his shoulders like a cloak, without actually putting it on.

"Won't you let me just tuck it in for you, Monsieur?"

"No, no, please! Don't touch—I might catch cold."

The jumpers used to slip down behind him, so that finally he might have four or five behind him like that, almost forming a sort of seat.

It was the same with his hot-water bottles. He always had two to start with. When he was out I used to put his pajamas, underpants, and jumper round them, so that they would be warm for him when he went to bed. He'd have one hot-water bottle at his feet and the other by his side. But he'd often ring.

"Dear Céleste, I am afraid my hot-water bottle has got rather cold."

So I'd go and prepare one or two more. I'd give them to him, and he arranged them by himself after I'd left the room. No question of my taking away the ones that had cooled. He kept them all.

When I think of the number of hot-water bottles I fixed for him in eight years, and of all those I made for my husband, poor fellow, who had albumin trouble and was always cold, I think I must have been born to prepare hot-water bottles.

The miracle with M. Proust was his will power. And his will power was all directed toward his work. His body was already exhausted by continued asthma.

"If you knew, Céleste," he once said. "My bronchial tubes are like worn-out elastic."

The continual effort to breathe put a strain on his heart. Yet apart from the choking fits, which it was impossible to hide, he rarely let me see the state of his health.

He used to tell me he was tired, yes. I can still hear his voice saying "Oh Céleste, I do feel tired." He might just mention his health, as when he compared his bronchial tubes to old elastic. But that was all. Sometimes I'd see him lying motionless in bed, his eyes closed, signing to me not to speak. And two or three hours later he would dress and go out for six or seven hours, return at four or five in the morning, and then talk to me for another three or four hours as if he were a young man of twenty!

I've often wondered how he was able to do it—to go from his silence, his rest and solitary labor, the glow of his little lamp, to the glare and noise of lights and people, and the air, which, in his view, was full of germs. Whenever I asked him about this, the answer was always the same: "I have to, Céleste. . . ." He had to for the sake of his work—that's what he meant. To find material for his book he would have done anything. That was what kept him going.

I know there are lots of stories about various illnesses he was supposed to have complained of in conversations or even in his letters. He is said to have suffered from dizzy spells and to have fainted sometimes in his room. I don't think this ever happened to him outside—he would have told me if it had—and as for fainting in the apartment, I'd either have seen him or been the first to know about it—he certainly would have rung for me. He was *afraid* of dizzy spells in the last few months of his life—he told me as much. But he never actually fell.

The same with the otitis he was supposed to have had suffered after using Quies ear-plugs, which supposedly was cured by Dr. Wicart, the famous ear, nose and throat specialist. The whole thing is an invention. I know all about the Quies earplugs. A great friend of his, the Duchess de Guiche, had recommended them to him. He told me about it, laughing:

"Do you know what, Céleste? The Duke goes out reveling with friends. The Duchess stays at home with her earplugs. That way she never knows what time her husband comes home, and all is for the best."

He did use the earplugs for a while; then, though he still kept them by the bed, he gave them up simply because they irritated him.

But he never had otitis, then or afterward. And the only time he ever mentioned Dr. Wicart to me was to say once, in passing, that he had met him once but had never seen him professionally.

I know it's also been said that at one time he had uremia, and that at another he was afraid he had a brain tumor, and that he complained of speech difficulties and symptoms of facial paralysis. I can vouch that I never saw him unsteady on his legs; on the contrary, you should have seen him cover ground in the apartment when he had a mind to! He flitted about like a butterfly—so the uremia, the tumor, and the facial paralysis are all untrue. And I never heard him stammer or even trip over a word. It was always that same even, gentle voice, at once warm and virile. And every word clear as a bell!

On the other hand, it wouldn't surprise me at all if he had written to Dr. Babinski, a famous specialist who attended his mother, to find out about the symptoms and death of someone with a tumor of the brain, because one of the characters in his book dies this way. And to make sure his inquiries were taken seriously, he might well have pretended he was talking about himself. He was quite capable of this, just as he was capable of harassing Dr. Bize with questions hour after hour if he needed to do so for the sake of his work.

I think the truth is that he used even his illness as a further means of shutting himself up in his work and cutting himself off from the world outside. He wasn't afraid of illness. The only thing he feared was dying before he had finished his work. So he did all he could to erect as many walls as possible around himself.

I am sure that if, with other people, he acted or talked as if he were more ill than he actually was, this was merely another way of ensuring peace and quiet whenever he wanted it, of ensuring that he need see only those he wanted to see and go out only when he wanted to—always to verify some fact or idea or to see again one of the models for one of his characters. He was very fond of Jean-Louis Vaudoyer; yet he wrote to him: "Every day I have fumigations lasting seven or eight hours on end. How can I see anyone?"

And I'm afraid this was done only to put off a visit or an evening out, because he didn't want to interrupt his work or because Jean-Louis Vaudoyer didn't fit with the work at that moment.

With me too, and even with visitors, he would suddenly withdraw completely and say:

"Forgive me if I close my eyes and don't say anything. I need to rest."

I knew very well what that meant. It wasn't a lie—such a word would never have come into my head. He might talk of rest, but I knew very well that as he lay there motionless in bed, he was journeying forward in his book and in his time regained.

7

AN APPETITE FOR MEMORIES

The most extraordinary thing of all was that he could survive and work, ill as he was, without taking any but the most meager nourishment. Or rather, by living on the shadows of foods he'd known and loved in the past.

I remember one day I had an attack of sinusitis, and he insisted on sending for Dr. Bize. After he'd examined me, the doctor went in to see M. Proust and took the opportunity to say in front of him:

"And you must take proper nourishment, Céleste. You don't eat enough. Don't be like M. Proust!" And turning to him he added: "It's true, maître—you work like a plowman, and you don't take any food!"

After he'd gone, M. Proust said, "Did you hear, Céleste? 'Like a plowman.'" And then, with a broad smile and a gleam of amusement in his eye: "I'm honored."

But Dr. Bize was right.

I still wonder where M. Proust found the will power to live as he lived, without any respite. I never knew how many hours he slept, or even if he slept at all. It was all between him and the four walls of his room. Sometimes he shut his eyes and was silent, and then he blanked out. He was frighteningly still when he did that. He scarcely breathed; seeing the green light, the white of the pajamas and the sheet, the pinched nostrils and motionless arms, anyone coming in to his room might have taken him for dead. He would repose like that even in the presence of a stranger, and no one would have dared to disturb him, he was so much the picture of a prince.

But when you think of the energy he expended, in his work, in his going out, and in the hours and hours he kept talking, he couldn't have made up for it all by staying in bed for half a day. He may not have been actually using the physical mechanism of his body during that time; but where did he get all the energy?

It isn't an exaggeration to say he ate virtually nothing. I've never heard of anyone else living off two bowls of *café au lait* and two croissants a day. And sometimes only one croissant!

Not only that, but even the one meal, if you can call it that, gradually grew smaller and smaller. During the 1914 war he stopped eating the croissants and never took one again. I tried to steer him on to *sablés* instead, as they were fluffy and light. I'd been told about a cook in a big house who made very good *sablés* and at my request he made some delicious ones for us. I took them in on the tray. M. Proust tasted them, asked where they came from, and said:

"Please thank the man for his trouble, just as I thank you for having thought of it, dear Céleste."

But he wouldn't eat them, and I gave up the *sablés* as I did the rest.

Why had coffee survived as his only food? I never asked him. I didn't like to ask questions. But he was very particular about the taste. Once you knew the exact strength, there was no problem, and not much danger of not doing it right. But sometimes, just the same, he would sigh:

"What have you done with the coffee, Céleste? It's awful. Is it perhaps a bit stale? Are you sure it's the right blend?"

"I don't know, monsieur. It's the same as usual."

I didn't dare suggest that, perhaps, he couldn't taste it properly that day.

As he had to have everything at once when he asked for it, there was no question of my suggesting making some fresh coffee. So he'd

70

drink it, his eyes apologizing over the rim of the bowl for what he had said. I never saw him with a wry face.

I'm sure he drank coffee mainly because it was a stimulant. It had to be made very strong, even if he did put lots of milk in it.

In fact, the *café au lait* was meant as a meal. His real nourishment was milk—he sometimes used as much as a liter a day. If he had only wanted a stimulant he would have drunk just black coffee, but in all the time I was there he never drank a single cup of black coffee.

I can see it all before me now: the silver coffeepot with his initials; the lidded porcelain jug to keep the boiled milk hot; the big gold-rimmed bowl with the family monogram; the croissant, in its own saucer, from a baker in rue de la Pépinière, opposite rue d'Anjou.

He poured out the coffee himself, but he waited until he was alone. He would make a gesture with his hand, and I would go. But it was easy to work out the proportions of coffee and milk. The coffeepot held the equivalent of two cups, and he poured the equivalent of one and a half cups into his first cup, adding milk to bring it up to about half a litre in all. The milk had to be boiling hot. If he had a second cup, it was usually soon after the first. He poured out the rest of the coffee, which had cooled meanwhile, but there had to be fresh milk. There was no question of warming up the other. I boiled more and brought it in with the second croissant if he asked for it.

All this was carefully organized and measured. I never saw him exceed the two cups held by the little coffeepot. After a certain point he didn't even drink the last half-cup. Sometimes, but very rarely, he might want some coffee before he went out in the evening or at night, either to fortify himself a bit or because he just felt like it. Then he wouldn't ask for fresh coffee but just have what was left. I'd give him this, cold, but with boiled milk.

Many people imagine he drank vast quantities of coffee. But no, if anything was excessive with him it was the meagerness of the nourishment he took and the all-importance of work. But the real stimulant for the latter was in his mind.

Of course I'm speaking about the period after which I went to live with him. And it's certain that the return from Cabourg, and the war, were a great turning-point in his life and mode of existence, including the question of food.

At the very beginning, before the war, he did eat a little from time to time. He would ask Nicolas to cook him a sole or to order a dish or a delicacy from a restaurant. In fact, with very rare exceptions, all Nicolas and Céline's own food came in from outside so that there could be no smell of cooking. There was a good plain restaurant, the Louis XVI, nearby on boulevard Haussman; the Cottins' food came from there. M. Proust's came from Larue's, which no longer exists but was once a famous and fashionable restaurant at the corner of rue Royale and place de la Madeleine, where M. Proust had often dined and had supper with friends. Finally, at the beginning of the war, he used to go to the restaurant of the Ritz.

Anything he wanted Nicolas to bring him he usually asked for if he had had his coffee at about two or three o'clock in the afternoon. Nicolas would serve the sole or the dish from the restaurant at five or six o'clock. But when I joined the household this was already a rare occurrence—once or twice a month at the most, when the fancy took him, or sometimes deliberately, to strengthen himself before going out, for example.

But it was mostly whim. After I took over from Nicolas this went on, but less and less frequently. In those days he never asked me to cook anything. Even in Nicolas' time, cooking in the flat had been reduced to a minimum, but when Nicolas left, there was a further reason: As M. Proust had immediately realized and as he told me, quite accurately, I didn't know how to do anything. I could just light the stove once my sister-in-law had shown me how, and I had done a little cooking for my husband.

But there came a time when there was no more Louis XVI restaurant. As far as I remember, it had been closed and pulled down together with the rest of the block to make room for the Bank of Indo-China. So M. Proust said I could cook for myself, and when the occasion arose, for him or for a guest. I didn't have too much difficulty: I'm curious and observant, and I'd had a lot of time to watch Nicolas. Anyway M. Proust's demands were not complicated. He was simple in his taste for food as in everything—but it had to be prepared exactly to his liking. He was a connoisseur, or rather, he had been one. I could see that his fancies were really sudden memories. For he had learned in a good school, with his mother and Félicie, his parents' cook. I've already described his memory of Félicie's *boeuf à la mode*.

"Oh Céleste!" he'd say. "Cold! It was cold I like it best, with the jelly and little carrots . . . ."

And his eyes would gleam with sudden craving and delight. Sometimes he might go on:

"I could eat some right now."

He'd laugh, and I'd say:

"If you like I'll go and get some, monsieur."

But he would shake his head. This was as far as it went. If I pressed the matter he would answer:

"No, no, Céleste, better not."

And I think it wasn't so much that he wasn't hungry as that he feared, in fact, he knew, he would be disappointed. He preferred to savor in his memory.

Then there was a dish called *la petite marmite*. The first time he mentioned it I didn't know what it was. And although he knew what it tasted like, he was just as ignorant as I was about the recipe.

"I don't really know how to describe it," he said. "I think you have to mix special bits of beef with chicken gizzards and many other little things. And it has to simmer for a very long time on a low flame. But it's delicious."

I ordered it sometimes from Larue's. I would bring it in, and he ate it out of the pot, never off a plate. He picked at it rather than ate, really—two or three mouthfuls and that was that. When he saw the lid taken off, he didn't even say "There is too much—take some away," or "Keep some for yourself if you like." No, he just had two or three nibbles and then the pot had to be taken away immediately. At the beginning I dared to press him.

"Just a little bit more, monsieur. What am I going to do with all the rest?"

"Just throw it away, Céleste."

Anyway, he wasn't really keen on any kind of meat. At the most—and that rarely—a bit of chicken.

But sole, yes, sometimes he would again fancy a sole.

"My dear Céleste, I think I could eat a fried sole. How long do you think it would take, if it is not too much bother?"

"But you can have it right away, monsieur."

"You are so kind, Céleste!"

There was an excellent fish store nearby, at Félix Potin's on place Saint-Augustin. I'd hurry there, rush back with the sole, fry it, and take it in to him as fast as I could on a large china plate, the fillet resting on a folded clean damask napkin to absorb the fat, with half a lemon at each corner. Just as I'd seen Nicolas do it.

Sole was about the only thing he ever finished. Usually, by the time a dish was put in front of him, he no longer wanted it—he had thought about something else in the meanwhile. Either he picked at it absentmindedly, or he rang and I took it away untouched.

Apart from *la petite marmite,* chicken, and sole, the only solid foods I saw him touch in eight years was, once, mullet, twice whitebait or eggs, and a few times, Russian salad or fried potatoes. But I never saw him eat even a mouthful of bread, for example.

I never would have dared to make the Russian salad myself. It would have been impossible—all the vegetables and the mayonnaise—for I wouldn't have had the time as he wanted it straight away. So I bought it from Larue's.

I prepared the other things myself.

The mullet had to be small and from Marseilles, and I had to buy them at Prunier's near la Madeleine, because, according to him, nowhere else in Paris was it so fresh and succulent and of the right size. He remembered them because his father had taken the family there sometimes; Prunier's was also a very good restaurant.

I remember the first time he asked me for whitebait, teasing and kind at the same time.

"I would like some fried whitebait, Céleste. But I don't think you know how to cook it, do you?"

I was piqued and said of course I knew. And off I went to the fishmonger's. When I saw the things, like little snakes, I wondered what you do with them. Did you have to gut them? As soon as I got home I didn't hesitate; I called at our neighbors' on the ground floor—Dr. and Mme. Gage's—whose cook was a friend of mine. She was a very kind woman, an excellent cook and extremely obliging. She was the only other person in the building I got to know. I asked her what to do. Eventually I served the whitebait, and M. Proust complimented me on them.

He had them again, and then when he asked for them a third time he said:

"If by any chance there aren't any, you could get gudgeon. As long as it is fresh."

With that sort of magical power he had, it was as if he'd guessed that there wouldn't be any whitebait. So I got the gudgeon and cooked them. But when they were ready he didn't want them—they were too big. He must have thought they'd be the same size as the whitebait.

Eggs were a story in themselves.

"Céleste, do you know how to make scrambled eggs?"

"Yes, monsieur, I should think so."

"Well then, I think I could eat two scrambled eggs."

"Very good, monsieur. Right away."

I hurried back to the kitchen, very sure of myself, and cooked two fried eggs, which looked marvelous to me, and took them in on the tray, not only confident but proud. First he looked at the eggs, then he looked at me.

"Are those scrambled eggs, dear Céleste?"

"Yes, of course, monsieur," I said innocently but already a bit put out.

"Are you sure?"

Then I wasn't sure of anything. "I thought that was what you meant, monsieur," I said.

"No doubt," he answered, amused. "But that is what I call 'fried eggs.' Next time I shall explain myself better."

Probably because he saw I was humilated, he kept them and toyed with them. But I was so furious I rushed to my friend the cook downstairs and begged her to show me how to scramble eggs. She had a good laugh and then showed me. Afterward I told M. Proust that I now knew. He didn't say anything, but I remember very well that another day, probably long afterward, he again fancied scrambled eggs, and this time he found them satisfactory.

As for fried potatoes, I think I could count on the fingers of my two hands the number of times he asked me for them. It was usually late at night, when he wasn't going out or, two or three times, when he had a visitor. I would serve them on a folded napkin, well drained, like the sole and the whitebait. He was fond of them.

I think now that those sudden fancies occurred at moments when he was seeking times he'd lost—lost in the sense that a paradise is lost. And every fancy always corresponded to a particular shop or caterer, dating from his youth or at least the time when he was still living with his parents. And all this was of course connected with his mother, who took great trouble over her table and her housekeeping.

Sometimes he would feel like something sweet. If it was *petits fours,* they could only be from Rebattet's, because his mother had decided that theirs were the best in Paris.

"One day when my friend Reynaldo Hahn, the composer, had called to see me," he said, "and we were having tea with Mother, Reynaldo began teasing her about her *petits fours* and said, 'I bet that if I were to bring you some from Potin's instead of from Rebattet's you wouldn't know the difference!' You should have heard Mother! 'All right, my boy. Just try, and then you'll see.'"

One evening M. Proust suddenly said:

"I think I could eat a brioche from Bourbonneux's. But Céleste, it must be from Bourbonneux's."

It was in rue de Rome. I went. I put it on a little plate on the tray. He ate a bit of it, and I took away the rest.

Or else: "Céleste, I think I would like something with choco-late."

"What kind of thing, monsieur?"

"You choose."

Sometimes these sudden longings would occur at ten or eleven at night. I would rush off to Latinville's in rue la Boétie, which fortunately stayed open late. I'd bring back some sort of confection—it didn't have to be pastry. He would eat a couple of spoonfuls and that was all.

Or else it would be a Bourdaloue pear I ordered from Larue's. The same thing would happen again. Or all of a sudden it would be an ice.

I would get the fruit at Auger's on boulevard Haussmann. I could be sure of getting excellent fruit there summer or winter, and they always had whatever he happened to want, which was usually a pear or a bunch of grapes. Just to nibble at, of course. But as the years went by his sudden fancies for fresh fruit disappeared. Sometimes he would ask for some kind of compote, with very little sugar, which I had to cook for exactly the number of minutes he told me. But I usually found it left untouched on the tray, and he might say, I think to disguise his own disappointment:

"My dear Céleste, I don't know what you did with it, but it was unedible."

When he fancied an ice it was almost always very late in the evening. When the war was over and Odilon was back, it was his job to get one—always raspberry or strawberry, never any other flavor—at the Ritz. Sometimes this would be in the middle of the night, when M. Proust returned from one of his outings.

Once or twice, no more, he asked for preserves or syrup.

"Get them at Tanrade's, rue de Sèze, behind la Madeleine. That's where Mother used to go."

It was red-currant syrup he asked for, I remember. When I went back into his room later he'd hardly touched the glass.

"Was it all right, monsieur?" I asked.

He looked up at me and sighed.

"Not really, Céleste. It's strange. I remembered it as much nicer than that."

He smiled as he said it, but in his eyes there was a wistful dream of childhood.

He hardly ever drank. Every day I took away the previous night's bottle of Evian water just as I'd left it. But since it had been opened it couldn't be used again. Apart from his coffee he didn't drink anything—especially not wine, never a drop—except beer, for which he might suddenly have a fancy. It was the writer Ramon Fernandez, then a young man, who gave him the idea by telling him how nice and cold the beer was at the Brasserie Lipp on boulevard Saint-Germain. In the beginning—during the war—we fetched it from there, filling a bottle from the tap. After my sister came to join me at boulevard Haussmann I used to send her, in a taxi. Then when Odilon was back we got it from the Ritz restaurant. He used to take the car and bring back a little carafe, well chilled. As it was almost always in the middle of the night, Odilon had an agreement with Olivier Dabescat, the manager of the Ritz. The kitchens were usually shut at that hour, but the chefs had shown Odilon where the beer and ice were kept, and as it was for M. Proust, who was a good customer, Odilon was allowed to go in and help himself when everyone else had gone home.

There is one ridiculous story, told by I don't know whom and repeated in some book which says that at a supper at the Ritz, M. Proust drank champagne and "devoured a leg of mutton." Nonsense.

Of course I wasn't there when he dined or had supper out. But I'm sure he wouldn't have touched food or drink any more than he did at home, whether he was the guest or the host. When he got home he used to tell me the menus, but not greedily, just for amusement and because of his constant and unique concern for facts. Sometimes he hadn't eaten anything. And I don't see why he should have eaten any more when he went out than when, for example, he had a guest at home.

He didn't invite people often and never more than one at a time. This suited me. I wasn't keen on cooking. In fact, it rather bored me.

When he had a guest, he stayed in bed, wearing fresh pajamas. I cleared the little table where the tray was usually left, and laid a cloth and set a single place for the visitor. M. Proust used to decide on the menu, which was always much the same—I think he adapted it to my ability. Usually it was fillets of sole, chicken, and an ice from Poire-Blanche's. Sometimes there was just chicken and ice, or fruit. I remember one dinner with his friend Henri Gans, the banker: I carved the chicken very carefully so as to serve it without any bones, and M. Gans asked for the "parson's nose."

The only more or less full meal I remember was the one M. Proust gave toward the end to his brother Robert, to celebrate his Legion of Honour. He asked me to get melon, chicken, cakes, and fruit.

I have said he sometimes asked me to fry potatoes in the middle of the night, to have with some cider for a guest he'd brought back with him. It happened two or three times, just about as often as he fancied them for himself. But cider wasn't served very often.

For the dinners he gave I had to buy good wines, red or white according to whether there was meat or fish, or both. Apart from the dinners it was champagne—only Veuve Clicquot—or port, with *petits fours* from Rebattet's.

For me it was important that M. Proust should be pleased, even more than the guest. You should have seen him when someone praised my chicken to him. He would tell me he was proud on my behalf.

When I look back on all these things now and see them clearer than I did at the time, I realize that two things emanated from him as a man and from his life: his taste for quality, for perfection in everything—a perfection that belonged to the past, and which showed his loyalty to shops and restaurants. This attachment to the past in his everyday life is all the more strange when you realize how far, in his books, he saw into the future—when you think of all he wrote about the dissolution of a certain kind of world and society.

The other thing that recurs again and again was his devotion to the work to which he'd completely sacrificed his health. Often, when I saw him looking tired, I'd be overcome with grief and anxiety. Seeing the untouched tray, I'd say:

"Why don't you eat, monsieur? How can you expect to be able to go on if you don't?"

"Think now, Céleste. When someone has had a good meal he feels torpid, his mind is not alert. And I need to have my mind completely alert."

I remember telling him one day:

"When my mother was at school there was a lay sister who was always afraid of giving the children too much to eat. She would say: 'Children, don't eat too much, and your minds will always be alert and you'll always be healthy.' You're just like the lay sister, monsieur!"

He laughed.

"Tell me about the lay sister again," he often used to say.

Perhaps the two things—the urgency of his work and the love of the past—were connected. Perhaps, if he struggled so against time in order to finish as soon as possible, it was because he sensed the approaching end of many of the things he'd loved, which were already no more than shadowy memories. And because he himself was being pressed by death.

8

AN EXTREME MODESTY

He sought perfection in what he wore, too. There was the same fastidiousness in that as in all his tastes, and here, too, he showed attachment to the past. I know that in his last years there were some people, especially those who only knew him when he was famous, who said he seemed to belong to another age. That was because although fashion had changed considerably with the war, he kept to the old tailoring and to his high stiff collars. But nobody in his right mind could have thought him ridiculous or failed to sense the extraordinary natural elegance he maintained. I'm sure that for most of those he knew, or who met him, he was always the *grand seigneur* he was for me that first time, and forever. He had the supreme elegance of being quite simply himself.

First of all there was his bearing. I've already said he was quite tall. At the same time he was slender and held himself with his chest thrown out slightly and his head held high, an aristocratic stance which made him look taller. There was no affectation in this. It's well known that asthmatics often carry themselves like this, as if to ease the difficulty of breathing.

He didn't look stiff at all. It was surprising that someone who spent more than half his life in bed and who might have well been expected to become completely rigid should be so supple and graceful in his smallest gestures and movements. Even while he was in bed his charm would immediately captivate any newcomer, as M. Proust looked at him with his unruly lock falling over his forehead, his head bent slightly to one side, and his delicate hand gracefully supporting his cheek. For me seeing him this way was a pleasure that never faded.

I remember that when after the war, in 1919, at last he agreed to see Mr. and Mrs. Sydney Schiff, two great English admirers of his work who very much wanted to meet him, he reserved a little private salon at the Ritz for this first encounter. And he told me that when Mrs. Schiff saw him come in wearing a dinner jacket she stifled an exclamation.

"And do you know what she said, Céleste? 'I expected someone elderly, with white hair, and I find a young man!'"

He was forty-eight at the time.

Another surprising thing about such an invalid was his complexion. Sometimes, yes, as he lay in bed, he did look like a corpse. But whenever he was animated, or about to go out, or had just come in, even though he might be tired, he had a magnificent complexion, made even more vivid by his black hair and moustache and shining eyes and beautiful white teeth. That alone is extraordinary enough: although he was ill and ate nothing, his teeth were perfect. I never knew him to have toothache or anything else the matter with even a single tooth. The funny thing was that an excellent dentist, Dr. Williams, an American, had his office right above us on the second floor. Mme. Straus, one of M. Proust's great friends, used to go to him. Two or three times, on her way out, she called in to see her "dear Marcel," and when he returned the visit, he told me, laughing, that she was always trying to persuade him to go upstairs and have his teeth examined. "Take advantage of it, Marcel, even though there isn't anything the matter with your teeth. Promise! He's the best dentist in Paris!" And he would promise, but with his tongue in his cheek. He never went.

Many silly stories have been told about his vanity, including that he dyed his hair and even made up his face and eyes. It's the stories that were made up, not he. The dark rings around his eyes were from work, illness, and lack of sleep, and he didn't do anything to his skin. It was very delicate, with a naturally high color exactly as in the portrait Jacques-Emile Blanche painted of him. The portrait is much more like him than many photographs, precisely because the color makes the skin come alive. As for his hair and moustache, they never needed any dye to remain black.

He changed the shape of his moustache once, just as he had had his beard shaved off just before I first met him. After that he wore his moustache rather long and curled with a curling iron. Then one day after the war—it was his sole concession to fashion, if it really were a concession—he decided (was it on the advice of his barber or of his friends at the Ritz?) to have a sort of Charlie Chaplin moustache, though not without considering the question and talking about it to me.

"Would you believe it, Céleste! They say I should have a Chaplin moustache! 'You look so young,' they tell me."

Once it was done he wasn't altogether sure about the result.

"Dear Céleste, do you think I look foolish with this little toothbrush under my nose?"

"No, on the contrary, monsieur. It really does make you look younger."

He was delighted. And I wasn't telling a lie either: he really did look younger than ever.

You can't really say he was vain about clothes. His wardrobe was very simple, very correct, that's all. He didn't need to fuss about his wardrobe; since he was always in bed, his clothes never wore out. In addition to the Cabourg overcoats made of vicuna, which he never wore again, there was the one that hung over the end of the bed for indoors, a new one with a sealskin collar and a mink lining, and a black one I've already mentioned. As for suits, he had two or three made during my time, that's all.

He'd always got his clothes at the Carnaval de Venise, on the boulevards not far from the Opéra. The fittings took place at home. He was very fond of the elderly English cutter who always attended him, a very kind man. I remember him well, because several times he came and rang at the door and I had to tell him M. Proust couldn't see him—because he was too tired or working or had asthma. The tailor was used to it. He greeted me nicely, said politely in his English accent, "Whenever Monsieur Proust wishes," and went away. Of course, after all that time he knew he would receive a good tip and M. Proust's practiced but genuine affability.

As well as tails and dinner jacket, he had several jackets which he wore with striped trousers, and to these he added a black jacket with piping. Everything was of course made to measure.

He had a collection of waistcoats, handsome but plain. I remember he had one made because he particularly liked the material. It was red silk with a white silk lining. He tried it on and showed me. I can see him now turning this way and that in front of the mirror, then saying:

"Definitely not. It would be all right for a dandy like Boni de Castellane, but I don't want to look ridiculous."

And he never wore it. I put it away in the cupboard.

It was exactly the same with his ties. There were black bowties to go with his dinner jacket and white ones to go with his tails, but all the rest were very sober too. He only had one that was brightly colored—the shade was called "opéra," a little brighter than wine color. He wore it very seldom. At one time he'd worn loosely tied bows bought at Liberty's, but he'd given those up; I only saw them lying put away in a box.

And shoes—I never saw him in anything but the same kind of button boots, except for one pair—in ten years—which he sent me to buy for him.

He'd asked me to get the same black patent leather boots he was used to, from Old England, the shop on the corner of rue Scribe and boulevard des Capucines. I got the address wrong and went to a little shoemaker's, very smart, as a matter of fact, also on boulevard des Capucines but between Old England and the famous Café de la Paix. There I bought a pair of patent leather boots with beige canvas uppers. I took them "on approval," because they weren't entirely black, but when M. Proust saw them he thought they were very nice.

"We'll see," he said. "I shall try them on."

He liked them. In fact, he thought them so smart he always wore them, except of course when he wore black.

He didn't wear his shoes out any more than his clothes. He always traveled about in taxis and never walked except on carpets and parquets. And then he was a person of habit; he hated any kind of change. He felt especially comfortable in things he'd worn for a long time. What's more, choosing, buying, trying things on, were tiring and took up time. Also, we mustn't forget, he only went out at times when the shops were shut. He never bought anything himself—he ordered it.

Washing and dressing were themselves no small tasks and made him very tired, especially as he could not stand any assistance but that of the barbers.

I often saw him trimming his nails in bed with a pair of small scissors, very neatly and fast, as he did everything, but with such meticulousness! But he never shaved himself. If he wasn't going out and hadn't to see anyone, he didn't shave. If he was going out, I got the barber to come as fast as he could. His name was M. François, and he lived within easy reach in boulevard Malesherbes. I believe he was the barber of M. Proust's father and to M. Proust himself when he lived with his parents. He would come right away. It was always in the evening; there weren't fixed hours. He kept a whole set of his equipment—brushes, scissors, shaving brushes, razors—at boulevard Haussmann. When M. Proust needed a haircut, M. François did that, too, on the spot. But all the rest of M. Proust's toilet was a secret. Everything was prepared, but beyond that it was forbidden ground, just as there was no question of putting in a hot-water bottle while he was in bed or even of helping him to arrange his woolies over his shoulders. He was extremely modest about this sort of thing. And I don't think my being a woman made the slightest difference; I had been observant enough to see that it was just the same during Nicolas' time.

Never, never, did anyone ever go into his dressing room while he was in there.

There is one thing that always makes me laugh, and that is when people take as fact, referring to M. Proust himself, everything he attributes to the "Narrator" of this book. Because he talks of Françoise, the maid, going into the Narrator's bedroom without warning and surprising him in an intimate embrace with Albertine, or even seeing her naked beside him; and because it's well known that he used Félicie, Céline, and me for the character of the maid, some people deduce that I must have gone into M. Proust's room unannounced and seen things. All I can say is that obviously these people never knew M. Proust. It was strictly forbidden for anyone to go into his rooms without being sent for! As for surprising him, there is another long story which I'll come to in due course. But to think M. Proust's books are a factual account of his life is to give little credit to his imagination.

When I first began to live at boulevard Haussmann, before M. Proust had given up the telephone, in other words before the end of 1914, the telephone used to be in his room. And as I often had to make calls for him before he went out and he liked to listen to see whether I was getting the messages right, the doors of the bedroom and dressing room were left open onto the corridor, and so I glimpsed a few details of his toilet.

But it never went beyond my discovering that he brushed his teeth over and over and that he never washed with soap. He just dabbed his face with damp towels. This was because his skin was very delicate, he told me later, and couldn't stand being rubbed, especially with all the soda in the soap. But when I saw him dabbing his face, it meant he was almost finished. He had put on his trousers, his shirt, and the woolie he wore underneath it. The face was the last stage.

I know some people will think what others haven't hesitated to say: How could he really be clean by this method? In the same way it's been claimed he was slovenly, because by chance someone saw a bit of the cotton-wool he sometimes put round his chest sticking up out of the collar of his shirt.

The truth is he was meticulously clean. It mustn't be forgotten that his father was not only a famous doctor but also a specialist in hygiene. This had left M. Proust with a fear of germs which itself would have been enough to give him almost an obsession with cleanliness.

After all, he wasn't the only one never to use soap. I've been told that the famous English writer Bernard Shaw thought it was unnatural and bad for the skin and always washed in pure cold water.

M. Proust didn't carry it that far. He had to have hot water—very hot water, in fact. And although he never used any toiletries—eau de Cologne, cream, or anything else—for general purposes he used one well-known disinfectant. He used it not only as a mouthwash, but for everything. At the slightest sign of a sore throat he used it as a gargle.

And I remember one very rare occasion when he had a pimple on his nose. Without saying anything, he put on some of this disinfectant, undiluted. It became inflamed and turned so nasty it was one of the very few times I saw him worry about a minor detail of health.

"It's getting bigger. It looks as if it's spreading," he said to me finally. "I think you'd better call Dr. Bize."

When he saw him, and M. Proust told him what had happened, the doctor exclaimed:

"You were very rash! You could have contracted a serious infection, what's called a 'phenic complication.' There have even been cases where it's reached the brain."

M. Proust told me all this. Once the danger was over, he laughed as he imitated the doctor's concern.

At any rate, it wouldn't surprise me if he put this disinfectant even in the water he used to wash his hands.

The whole toilet, of course, was a meticulous ritual, like everything else. First there was the footbath, then two jars of hot water—all from the big boiler in the kitchen. Running water was still rare in those days; at boulevard Haussmann we only had it in the kitchen.

He had a very handsome white enamel footbath with a wide gold stripe. That and a big set of ebony brushes with silver initials were the only luxury objects in the dressing room.

In the early days I was alarmed at how hot he wanted the water: it had to be about fifty degrees centigrade. Then I realized that this too had been carefully worked out. He knew himself very well and could tell that by the time he'd finished doing this and that, most of the heat would have dissipated and the water would be just the temperature he wanted.

It was the same with his underwear. He always changed completely when he went out. Next to his skin he wore a vest and long underpants, both woolen and made by Rasurel. I bought him some others once which to me looked just as good. But they weren't Rasurel. He never wore them.

Vest, pants, and shirt all had to be warmed to the right temperature, like the water. The big boiler in the kitchen blazed away day and night, the brick oven always ready. I used to put the underwear in the oven to warm wrapped up in towels, and it would stay in there cooking until he asked for it.

So when he wanted to wash and dress, everything had to be ready—water, clothes, underwear, towels—all properly set out where needed, on the dressing table and on chairs within reach. I would then withdraw, and he would get up, in his pajama top, woolies, and long pants, and if he was cold, his black overcoat with the black and white check lining. He replaced the little socks he wore in bed with a pair of Turkish slippers or a pair made of coarse cloth with buckles, which he wore indoors when he was up.

Try to imagine the ceremony of the towels. They were of very fine cotton, and I always arranged a pile of twenty or twenty-five of them on the dressing table. There were hooks for towels on the sides of the dressing table, but he didn't use them. He dabbed himself with each towel once, either to wash or to dry himself, and then threw it aside. There was an enormous stock of them, and they were all sent to be laundered at Lavigne's (it used to be the Maison Bleue, I remember, and his mother had been a customer there too), while the woolen clothes used to go to the cleaner Garobi's, on the boulevard Haussmann. Few things were washed at home.

Sometimes, looking at all this mess (later, after his death, I managed a hotel on rue des Canettes in Paris; it had about fifty rooms, and I sent out no more laundry there than I did at M. Proust's), I couldn't help saying:

"It hurts me, monsieur, to think of all the money you're wasting."

"What do you mean, Céleste—wasting?"

"All this linen hardly touched that you just throw aside!"

"My dear Céleste, you don't realize that if I use a towel twice it gets too damp and chaps my skin."

The way he used to clean his teeth was unusual too. He only used powder, always the same kind, very white and fine, specially made from an old prescription of his father's, in big round jars, which I bought at the Leclerc pharmacy. He put a lot on the brush and scrubbed and scrubbed about fifty times. Everything was be-spattered afterward—the mirror, the dressing table, even himself.

That was how I found out that quite often he must have left his face and teeth till last, when he was already dressed, because when I saw him afterward, all ready to go out, I might say:

"Oh monsieur, you've made your shirt collar wet. It's bad for your throat, and the collar will get all rumpled."

Or: "Monsieur, there's white all over your tie."

"But I put a towel over it."

And if I tried to brush it off:

"No no, leave it, Céleste dear. It's all right as it is. Do you think people want to see me for my ties?"

But finally he would let me brush it off.

But that was about all. It's been said I tied his ties for him. Never! He never would have allowed it. And I wouldn't have known how. But you should have seen how quickly he tied his knots and bows—as if he did nothing but that all day! The only thing he asked me to help him with sometimes was his shirt front, if the buttons were very stiff.

Just once, toward the end, one evening when he was very tired but had decided to go out just the same, he was sitting slumped in the armchair fully dressed—I can see him now. As I happened to be there because he'd sent for me for something else, he said:

"Would you be so kind and hand me my boots, Céleste?"

I gave them to him and he put them on, but before he had time to finish, there was I down on my knees like a girl, buttoning them up, click, click, click, without asking his permission.

He practically jumped back and said in a voice full of pain:

"Oh, no, please don't, Céleste!"

"But monsieur," I said gaily, "it only took a moment. Why should I mind?"

When I got up he almost had tears in his eyes. I'll always hear him say with that deep gentleness of his:

"Céleste, I love you!"

What was so marvelous was that with him there were moments when I felt I was his mother, and others when I felt I was his child.

9

THE DARK NIGHTS OF PARIS

The war certainly helped to bring M. Proust and me close together, and probably, by scattering most of his friends, it also contributed to transforming his life into that of a recluse. Although he would still have been obsessed by his work, if it hadn't been for the war I think he would have been tempted to continue to see the people he knew. But the parties, the receptions, the dinners, were over. The hostesses' châteaux were closed up or sometimes converted into army hospitals, and in Paris it wouldn't have been seemly to continue holding salons, not to mention the servant problem. Even if they didn't actually give up their houses, many of these ladies and their daughters devoted themselves to good works for the wounded and became nurses. As for the men who in peacetime gravitated around the cream of society, they were nearly all in the army. Life had lost its glitter, and what was left was anxiety and mourning.

M. Proust's brother Robert was a surgeon at Verdun, where he helped institute the first surgical unit at the front. M. Proust was worried to death about him. One day shells burst into the very place where the doctor was operating; subsequently he was made a captain for his bravery. M. Proust was very proud, but that didn't stop him from trembling for his brother.

All those with whom he had shared youth and a carefree life

were now risking death. The composer Reynaldo Hahn, the one he'd loved the most and longest, who through connections could have stayed safely in the rear, had asked to be sent to the front. He wrote M. Proust that he had composed a song for his infantry regiment, after hearing the whine of the bullets, and that all the men were singing it. M. Proust worried all the time about the danger he and the others were in.

"Look, Céleste," he once said, showing me their letters, "they are being shot at and I am here."

In the second summer of the war he lost one of his cousins. Before that, two friends he had been extremely fond of and who were, in a sense, the models for the Chevalier de Saint-Loup, one of the characters in his book, had both died. The first to go was Comte Bertrand de Fénelon, at the end of 1914. M. Proust hoped at first he'd only been taken prisoner, and anxiously followed all the inquiries. It wasn't until months later, in March 1915, if I remember rightly, that papers and photographs were found showing that he was dead. M. Proust saw it in the newspaper, and it was a great shock for him.

The second who had been very dear to him was Gaston de Caillavet, who died in January 1915. He wasn't killed by a bullet but by a serious illness to which he succumbed after an unhappy love affair. With mourning cards pouring in from everywhere, it was as if death had chosen this moment to strike at the world M. Proust had loved and to condemn him to a life in memory.

But still, though it wasn't a time for elegance and great receptions, there were enough people he knew in Paris for M. Proust to go out and see friends if he wanted to. If private houses no longer entertained in style, there were still the fashionable restaurants. And as people kept talking more and more about the recently published book, new acquaintances increased both in number and in importance. And when M. Proust did feel like going out, it was the same as with Bourdaloue pear and many other things: neither the hour nor the circumstances mattered—nothing could have changed his mind.

I know what people will think if I say this sometimes took a certain amount of courage. They'll say it was nothing in comparison with the real dangers faced by the soldiers at the front, or that it showed a kind of insensibility on his part. But I remember a particular example, after the Germans had started bombing Paris and the city was plunged into almost total darkness at night.

One night he wanted to pay a visit to the poet Francis Jammes, one of the first to have written favorably about *Du côté de chez Swann.* He lived quite a long way off, near the place des Invalides. With my husband away at war, M. Proust didn't have a regular taxi, so I had to go and look for one. They weren't always so eager to go out in the dark those nights, and it didn't make my search any easier to know he must be growing impatient waiting. But at last he got off. And then, before he would come home again, the antiaircraft guns would start—I can't remember whether they were shooting at a zeppelin or at planes, the Gothas. I was not myself, what with the noise and the bombs, wondering what he could be doing, where he was, and whether he'd be able to get back.

Once—the second and last time—I went down into the cellar during an attack. Then suddenly I heard the main doorbell ring.

"Imagine!" said the concierge. "What's he doing out? I'll have to go up and let him in."

I ran up to the apartment by the service stairs so as to be there by the time he was. I can still see him getting out of the lift, tranquil and smiling and obviously very pleased about something.

"Were you waiting for me, Céleste?" he said. "But I told you to go down to the cellar. Go back right away, please."

I protested that I didn't want to, knowing he wouldn't go down because of the dust and smell. But he insisted that I go and finally I did. But when I saw Antoine, the concierge, and his wife shaking with fright, I thought: "If a bomb drops we'll be suffocated whether we're in the cellar or anywhere else. I'd sooner die a bit farther up the heap than underneath everything." So up I went again. He laughed when I told him why. Then I began to put away the things he'd taken off when he came in—coat, gloves. . . . When I got to the hat I couldn't help exclaiming. The brim was full of bits of shrapnel.

"Monsieur, look at all this metal!" I said. "Did you walk home, then? Weren't you afraid?"

"No, Céleste," he said. "Why should I be? It was such a beautiful sight."

And he described the searchlights and the shellbursts in the sky and the reflections in the river. Then he said he'd had a very pleasant evening at Francis Jammes's—Tristan Bernard was there and was very amusing—and as M. Proust didn't think there would be a taxi on a night like this, he'd set out to walk.

It was so unlike him, who never set foot in the street, to have trudged so far, that I in all innocence asked him:

"But how did you find the way?"

He laughed and said, "Your celestial protection must have sent me a guardian angel, in place de la Concorde."

The square was deserted, he told me, and when he entered it a man came up to him in the darkness.

"He might have been following me already and seen me hesitate or stumble in the dark, because I only had the light of the bursting shells to go by. He said, 'You don't look as if you know your way very well. Would you like me to come with you? Where are you going?' I told him, boulevard Haussmann, and we walked along, chatting, side by side. He asked me what I was doing out in the dark like that. I told him I was going home after visiting a friend, and he said it wasn't a very suitable hour for walking the streets. We took rue Boissy-d'Anglas at the side of the Crillon Hôtel, which brought us to boulevard Malesherbes, and he didn't leave me until he'd seen me across the street."

He stopped and gave me an amused little look.

"And do you know, Céleste, to tell you the truth, he was a bad lot. I guessed it right away, but I didn't show it until we parted. I thanked him and said, 'It was very kind of you to see me home. Will you allow me to ask you, though—why didn't you attack me?' And you'll never guess what he said. 'Oh, not someone like you, monsieur.'"

He was very proud of that.

His attitude toward me at that time was strangely contradictory. On the one hand he was very solicitous and insisted I shelter in the cellar when there was an air-raid alert. He would try to persuade me:

"I want you to go because if anything happened it would be on my conscience, because I promised your husband I would look after you. Have you ever thought that if one of their bombs set this place on fire we would go up like torches in the middle of all the cork in my room?"

And when I protested that I didn't like going down into that hole and preferred to be burned to bits with him, he answered gently:

"But it wouldn't matter about me. In the first place, I am an invalid, and in the second, all the work I am trying to do would be destroyed with me. But you are young."

At the same time he was so oblivious of danger he saw nothing amiss in sending me out into the dark streets at night when he had to have something done, and it never seemed to occur to him that my being a woman made any difference.

But actually it didn't really surprise me either, and it was he who asked me to go. I was so blissfully happy with him, it must have made me a bit oblivious too. What did I know about life, anyway? After leaving my native village, I'd hardly gone out at all, and now I spent practically all my days shut up at boulevard Haussmann. Even there my experience was only just beginning; it was M. Proust who was teaching me to understand life. Then, I was still full of the naïveté that delighted him so much. For instance, when he sent me out at night I nearly always passed a big Negress walking to and fro on rue Tronchet, behind la Madeleine, with her handbag over her arm. One day I asked him:

"What can she be doing, monsieur, walking up and down for hours like that in the dark? She doesn't even have a little dog—"

"Come now, Céleste," he said, "you must know. She is one of the women who earn their living walking up and down."

I've rarely seen him laugh so much. And he had such a way of not making you feel ridiculous that I joined in.

The fact remained that I ran hither and thither as if it were noon instead of midnight. I'd got so used to turning day into night it seemed as natural to me as it did to him, and the only time I ever remember being frightened was once after I'd gone past the Terminus Hôtel at Saint-Lazare and a man followed me all the way along rue Pépinière. There wasn't another soul about, and I ran up rue d'Anjou like a hare. When I told M. Proust about it afterward, my heart still pounding, he said:

"Oh, you're quite strong enough to defend yourself."

I went out mostly to mail letters or packages, to make sure they would be delivered by the following morning. Depending on what time it was, I posted them on boulevard Malesherbes or at the main post office at the Bourse. The latter was a long way off, and I would go by taxi.

Sometimes a package would be a book that he had asked me to find in the various piles in his room but I couldn't locate because the light from his little lamp left much of the room in the dark and even though I could have switched on others, I didn't, out of habit and respect. Then he would become impatient in his mild way and finally say:

"I give up. It would be better if you went to buy a copy."

And I'd go. There was a local bookshop in rue de Laborde, between Saint-Augustin and boulevard Haussmann. The owner, an old man with a little skullcap and white overalls, was called M. Fontaine. He loved his job so much he couldn't bear to leave his books, and during the war he kept the shop open till one or two in the morning. I would go in and tell him what M. Proust wanted, and usually M. Fontaine would tell me that he had such-and-such and such-and-such but unfortunately not the book M. Proust had asked for. "But I think this one would do. If not, bring it back."

Sometimes I went home with several. I offered them to M. Proust, explaining what M. Fontaine had said, but often it was the same with books as with his other whims: between the time of my going and coming back, he'd gone on to a new matter of interest and he'd say:

"Leave them there, Céleste. They'll only make me waste more time."

And he didn't even look at them. But I didn't take them back to the shop. We kept them all.

Sometimes I delivered a letter personally in the middle of the night. I've woken more than one person like that. I remember once—I've never forgotten it, because it was another of the times I made M. Proust laugh—he'd been struck by a quartet of young musicians he'd heard at the Théâtre de L'Odéon, with the composer Gabriel Fauré at the piano. It was the Poulet quartet, and he'd been particularly impressed by the violinist, who was called Massis. When he came home he said:

"I had a marvelous evening. I met Gabriel Fauré again, and he gave a wonderful performance of one of his works. And there were four young musicians so remarkable I asked him to introduce me to them after the concert."

Shortly afterward he wrote to Massis to tell him again how much he admired his playing and that he'd like to know him better, if he'd be good enough to come to boulevard Haussmann one evening. Naturally, Massis had to have the letter right away without waiting for the post. So off I went.

Massis lived a long way distant on the other side of the river, in a street behind the Panthéon. I took a taxi, but when the driver finally left me off I hadn't the faintest idea where I was; and I had no light, not even a match. It was some time between midnight and two in the morning, and I was stumbling around in the dark when suddenly, fortunately, I came upon a policeman.

"Please, officer," I said, "I need your help. I want to go to"— and I gave him the number and street—"but I think I am lost. Could you kindly tell me how to get there, and perhaps, if you'd be so kind, show me the way?"

The policeman very politely took me to the door, and I, not quite sure how to thank him, gave him a five-franc piece. Then I woke up the concierge to find out what floor I wanted and started to climb. My legs still remember those rickety stairs. I rang at the door and woke the unfortunate musician to give him the message. But I wasn't at all embarrassed, since that was what M. Proust wanted. And as a matter of fact, young Massis didn't seem all that surprised at the late hour.

When I got home I told M. Proust all about it, saying how lucky I'd been to meet that policeman and how I'd been so grateful I'd tipped him. He started to laugh so much he couldn't stop. I don't know how often after that, through the years, he said to me when I set out as his "courier":

"Don't forget to give the policeman five francs!"

The way he imposed his own rhythm on the life about him, I 'wouldn't have noticed there was a war if it hadn't been for my anxiety about my husband.

Odilon didn't come home on leave more than four or five times in all those five years. It seemed a long time; there was rarely any news of him. His first leave was in 1915, nearly a year after he went away. Just before, I had received a postcard he had sent from a sector near Amiens—it was a photo of him with a beard. I wasn't very keen on that. And a few weeks later, there he was at the service door with the beard itself! Poor fellow! I can see him now. He wore big army boots, and when I let him through the door into the kitchen, he looked down at the clean tiles and didn't dare walk on them. Or perhaps he'd forgotten how to walk like a civilized person. I was mesmerized by the beard. I rushed to M. Proust's room. I was overjoyed, of course, but all I could say was:

"Monsieur, you should see Odilon! He's just arrived with a beard, and he looks frightful!"

M. Proust laughed. But he was glad, too, for the good news.

"Tell him to come in and say hello right away."

Odilon went in and they had a long chat. M. Proust inquired after his health and about the war. Then, looking up from among the pillows, he asked the reason for his beard. Odilon explained it had been so cold that when he shaved his skin got all chapped.

"Still," said M. Proust, "I am afraid Céleste is right. I don't think it really suits you."

So my husband shaved off his shaggy beard.

There are two other leaves of his I remember best. The first must have been in April 1917. I recall it because he had albumin trouble, which he never got rid of for the rest of his life. I remember that other leave because it was the last, on October 17, 1918, ten days long, and he mentioned rumors of peace in the trenches, saying: "If only it were true!"

It was when he was demobilized that I really saw how fond he was of M. Proust. He was ill when he came home, with a serious case of albumin, and had to remain in the military hospital at Le Vésinet for three months. Even after he resumed driving his taxi at the end of 1919, he had terrible dizzy spells. He was also very much affected by the death of his brother Jean, his favorite and the youngest of the family, who by sheer hard work had acquired his own business at the corner of rue de la Victoire and rue Laffitte. When he was reported missing, M. Proust asked Reynaldo Hahn to make inquiries, but alas, the only result was the confirmation of Jean's death. The two brothers loved each other like twins. When war was declared, Jean said to Odilon, weeping: "Come in the infantry with me and we won't be separated." But Odilon had been posted to supplies, and the war parted them. And now Jean had been killed on the ill-fated Chemin des Dames in the Argonne, and Odilon hadn't got over it.

M. Proust knew, and spoke to him with the greatest kindness. He literally took him in hand when he was demoralized. He asked his brother Robert to examine him and recommend him to other doctors and not content with that, called in Dr. Bize. I remember what he told me afterward.

"The doctor says he must go on a very strict diet. He discussed it with me. Odilon must drink lots of milk and eat plenty of purées and green vegetables, without any salt. But the doctor said, 'The only thing is he won't keep to it. That sort of person will never take any notice of doctors or diets.' So I said, 'We'll see. I'll make myself responsible; I know Odilon will do as I say.'"

He asked me to send for my husband.

"My dear Odilon, Dr. Bize claims that you won't be sensible

even if you know you're very ill—which you are. I don't agree with him. You've got plenty of will power, and I'm sure you'll look after yourself if I ask you to. Promise me you will."

Odilon promised, and he kept his word. From that day on he kept to a draconian diet. M. Proust supervised it and insisted on knowing every detail. When Odilon started working again, at night of course, M. Proust asked if he could always get sieved food at those hours, and he confessed he couldn't.

"I'm glad you told me," said M. Proust. "It shows you are taking it seriously. But don't worry. I shall ask Céleste to keep some purée always ready for me in the kitchen, and when you come in we will be sure that there is some for you and you won't have to break your diet."

In fact, in his own way, he was as fond of Odilon as Odilon of him. As time went by he had come to trust and rely on Odilon. And that was saying something, for before M. Proust placed his confidence in anyone, you can be sure he'd screened him thoroughly. And then he came to love him too, because of his devotion. He could send for Odilon at any hour of the day or night, just as he could me, and Odilon would bring the taxi around without a murmur. When we were still at Levallois I'd seen Odilon, who was sleeping like a log after a tiring day, get up in the middle of the night because M. Proust had telephoned. On one of these occasions he came back very late and told me he was so tired he'd just driven like a sleepwalker till he got to the gates of Paris—there was still a tollhouse there in those days—and only woke up properly when the man came out and asked if he had anything to declare.

He had a host of other good qualities which won M. Proust's heart just as they had mine. First, as I've said, he was extremely tactful and discreet. Although we were husband and wife, he never commented to me on what he did for M. Proust, even when both of us were living at boulevard Haussmann after the war and elsewhere after M. Proust had died. He would tell me where he'd driven M. Proust and how long he'd waited for him and what the weather had been like. That was all. When you think how M. Proust himself used to talk to me about his evenings out, it couldn't have been that he had ordered Odilon not to tell me anything.

Odilon was very honest and open, too. Once I was cross with him because he wanted me to visit his relatives. I was very fond of them, of course, but I was fonder of my own habits, which made me not want to go out. I was so piqued that I mentioned it to M. Proust.

"Come, come, Céleste, what does it matter? In fact, it does Odilon credit. Remember one thing, anyway. He is a good man and a good husband. And he has one virtue I value above all others: He never told me a lie, and I am sure he never told you one either."

Another time when I was complaining, he said:

"You don't know how lucky you are, my little Céleste. You have the nicest husband in the world."

"Do you think so, monsieur?"

He laughed. "I certainly do. In fact, I sometimes wonder how he puts up with you."

I was vexed. "I must say, monsieur, you are very kind to me! What does he have to put up with? I do everything he wants."

"If that is the case, you must be very fond of him. What are you complaining of, then?"

He told me how much it was to Odilon's credit that he'd made his way in life all alone. It was true. His parents were dead and he left home when he was fourteen and worked as a scullion in a restaurant in Paris, until he found out they were giving him the customers' leftovers to eat. He went off in disgust to become a coach driver, like one of his brothers who'd come to Paris before him. But he was bright enough to see that motorcars were the coming thing, and he soon passed his driving test with flying colors and started with taxis. Then he was engaged by Taximetres Unic to drive in Monaco, Cabourg, and Paris, according to the time of the year. It was a company formed by the Rothschilds and run by Jacques Bizet, who'd been at school with M. Proust at the Lycée Condorcet. M. Bizet's mother had married Mr. M. Straus after her first husband died, and Mr. M. Straus had connections with the Rothschilds. That was how Odilon met M. Proust, at Cabourg.

M. Proust told me Jacques Bizet recommended three or four drivers to him. But with his usual prescience, he soon came to prefer Odilon. At Cabourg he used to prefer Agostinelli's service, but one day he asked Odilon what he did when he wasn't in the south of France or in Normandy.

"I drive a taxi in Paris," said Odilon.

"Would you drive me if I needed you?"

"With pleasure."

"But how would we get in touch?"

So Odilon gave him his sister's telephone number at the corner of rue Feydeau and rue Montmartre. And that's how it all began. Soon complete confidence reigned between them, only interrupted by the war, and when Odilon was called up, M. Proust took on his elder brother Edmond as driver. Edmond was a little hard of hearing, and M. Proust employed him as long as his deferment lasted.

Of the things about Odilon that touched M. Proust most—I know because he told me—were the circumstances of his mother's death when he was still a schoolboy at La Canourgue, in Lozère. One evening when he and his mother returned home from an outing, he discovered that a button had come off his waistcoat. She said, "Leave it on the chair in the kitchen and I'll sew it on for you. But first I'll lie down for a bit—I've a pain in my chest." Next morning he got up and found his waistcoat on the chair with the button sewn on and the house all silent. He thought his mother must be so tired she was still sleeping, and he prepared for school as quietly as he could. But just as he was going out of the door, he thought his mother would be worried if he went off without a word. So he went back, found his mother, cold, in bed. M. Proust was always very moved when he talked of it. Anything to do with a mother's death reminded him of his own mother and moved him very much.

But he was so discerning about other people that when he spoke to me about his affection for my husband, he added:

"Yes, I love him very much. But you know, dear Céleste, it's not the same thing. What he does for me is quite different from what you do for me."

I'd have been very stupid if I'd taken offense on Odilon's

behalf. M. Proust was only telling me the truth. Odilon wasn't devoted to him exclusively, as I was.

Nevertheless, M. Proust knew quite well that one thing my husband and I had in common was that nothing could ever make us leave him. For when the war was over and Odilon had got over his surprise at seeing me settled at boulevard Haussman and sacrificing my independence for this strange mode of existence, he came to live there too without protesting. We never even discussed whether we should stay or go, and he never mentioned his ambition for us to go into a business of our own. His only ambition then was to get a new taxi, and that was as much in honor of M. Proust as to satisfy his own pride.

In the beginning, taxi drivers sat outside like coachmen, in the rain, heat, and cold. But as cars became more luxurious, my husband grew rather ashamed of his old Renault. Finally he spoke to M. Proust about it, though good taste forbade him to mention other customers' disparaging remarks. He said he was thinking of ordering a new car, more suitable to be seen waiting outside the Ritz, for example, or fashionable private houses.

"Oh no, Odilon," said M. Proust. "I don't want you to get a new car. I am very fond of your taxi, it is perfectly comfortable, and I am used to it. I don't want people to notice me as I go by."

My husband didn't insist. He was too fond of M. Proust to displease him. It was only in the very end, when the Renault became so decrepit it *would* make people notice M. Proust, that Odilon decided to buy a new car without telling him, and to give him a surprise, which he was sure would turn out to be a pleasant one. Even I knew nothing about it. But M. Proust died before he ever saw it. The remarkable thing is that my husband never used his beautiful new car; it was as if his ambition had died with M. Proust. We hadn't yet moved out of M. Proust's apartment when he sold it at a loss. He'd bought it for twenty-two or twenty-four thousand francs and sold it for eighteen. Odilon and I were both of the same mind. Neither of us hesitated when he said to me:

"Now he's gone, that's the end. It was only because of him I put up with the other customers."

10

YOUR MOTHER IS DEAD

Yes, it was those nights during the war, from 1914 to 1918, that encouraged the growing confidentiality of our evenings—if you can call them evenings, for unless he went out, they always lasted well after midnight.

At first it was I who did the talking, probably because I felt I was still on probation, so to speak. But another factor must have been his constant need to observe people and get to know them inside out.

It was then he started to ask me questions. He wanted to know all about me and my family and especially my childhood.

"That's where everything starts," he'd say. "Both heaven and hell."

I remember once stopping in the middle of what I was saying to exclaim:

"But what am I telling you all this for, monsieur? I must bore you to death, going on about my childhood and my home town."

"Not in the least, Céleste," he said. "I may even tell you a secret: I would like to write a book about you. But you must not become too haughty about it."

"Why should I, monsieur? You're pulling my leg!"

"Not at all. And don't be offended, because if I did write such a book it would be very instructive. People would see that what is in you doesn't belong just to you. That is one of the most fascinating things about human beings—to find out from where we inherit what we are. You have a beautiful soul, but where did you get it from? Your father, your mother, your grandmother, or further back still? That is what I would like to know."

The way he listened fascinated me—his cheek resting gracefully on his hand, and his eyes now gentle, now laughing, but behind it all always concentrating, as if he were already converting what you said into writing. So I chattered away.

He wanted to find out all the details about your life as well as about your character. I had to tell him my childhood pranks: how I climbed trees (what trees, he wanted to know); how in the winter, instead of having our lunch, we used to risk broken bones sliding on the ice in our wooden clogs; how I wore out three pinafores for each one of my sister's because I was always getting caught on things (what were our pinafores like?).

"Céleste," he would say, delighted, "you ought to have been a boy!"

I had to tell him about the seasons, the flowers and fruit, and how the bedrooms in our big house, which was a mill, were so cold in midwinter that mother used to heat the beds with a warming pan before we went to sleep. And how, because the schoolroom had no heating, she would give us each a foot warmer full of hot coals to take with us every morning.

He was much interested in my four brothers, all very bright and each gifted in various ways. The eldest had gone to the Jesuit school at Rodez, where he won the top prize every year. He was very handy and could make anything. When he was a young boy he put up the frame of a shed all by himself, and the roofer said he'd never seen such an expert job. But he hated the land and went away, which was a disaster for my father, for after he was grown up he only came back to help on holidays. He died when he was twenty-seven after a bicycle accident.

My second brother was just the opposite: Nothing would have

106

induced him to live in the city. When I married Odilon he said, "That's right, go to Paris and eat rotten meat and smelly chickens! Here at least, things are healthy." He even ground his own flour and built an oven to bake his own bread, because the flour in store-bought bread was not pure, he said, and gave him heartburn. It's true that an attack of scarlet fever had left him delicate. But what he lacked in health he made up for in inventiveness. I remember how, instead of using oxen, as was the custom, he built a threshing machine that worked by hydraulic pressure. He was very proud of it. "Other farmers have to have people help them, and then they have to feed them, and that costs money. But I don't need anyone." I remember that he had difficulty sleeping and used to toss and turn thinking of how to improve farming methods.

Without knowing him, M. Proust was fond of him. Before I myself married, this brother had married the niece of Monseigneur Nègre, the archbishop of Tours, and one day when M. Proust and I were talking about my family and I told him that, I think he was as pleased and proud as if he had heard that one day his great-niece would marry the son of François Mauriac. I don't remember if it was the next day or a little while afterward that he showed me a little poem he'd written about it. He read it to me with a mocking air:

> Grande, fine, belle, un peu maigre,
> Tantôt lasse, tantôt allègre,
> Charmant les princes comme la
>   pègre,
> Lançant à Marcel un mot aigre,
> Lui rendant pour le miel le vinaigre,
> Spirituelle, agile, intègre,
> Telle est la nièce de Nègre.

> (Tall, slender, beautiful, rather thin,
> Now tired, now gay,
> Charming both princes and riff-riff,
> Throwing Marcel a harsh word,
> Returning him vinegar for honey,
> Witty, nimble, upright,
> Such is the niece of Nègre.)

He was so pleased he laughed like a little boy as he read it. When he finished he asked:

"What do you think of it, Céleste? Good, eh? I like it. I make you a present of it."

I laughed too, it was so amusing to see him laughing.

"A nice picture you paint of me, monsieur! Vinegar indeed!"

"Yes, but 'beautiful' and 'charming princes' and 'witty, nimble, upright'! We will put it in my book."

He was almost clapping his hands. And he kept his promise: it is in the book.

He liked to hear about my youngest brother, too, perhaps because he felt a certain similarity. I think it was in this connection he first mentioned his own childhood. My little brother was very delicate and sensitive and gentle, and we were extremely fond of each other. If I did something silly he'd say to my mother, "Don't grumble at Céleste, you'll make me cry." He died when he was nine, of acute rheumatoid arthritis. He was my father's favorite, and my father never got over his death. Nor did my mother, especially as she'd already lost her seventh child as the result of a fire that destroyed the farm. While she was pregnant a barn full of straw caught fire, and there was a very strong wind fanning it on. She climbed up to throw water and fell, but she picked herself up and went to throw another bucket of water on the flames, which singed her skirt as she stood there. A week later the baby was born, but he cried all the time, and after a little while he died. My father, too, nearly died in the fire. The house itself was alight, and he went in to save some papers and things. But he didn't come out again, the place was full of smoke, and my elder brother just had time to get through a window and drag him out, half-asphyxiated.

In spite of this tragedy, I caused M. Proust much amusement telling him that my father, who'd lost everything, had to borrow a neighbor's hat to go to mass on Sunday, and the hat was too small.

But it was my mother he asked about most. He once said:

"It is plain your father was a good man. But goodness even in the best of men can never be what it is in a woman. There is always a layer of roughness. A man cannot be goodness itself, as your mother seems to have been.''

It was true. Mother had endless good judgment, wisdom, and endurance. She was deeply religious and bore her trials with wonderful patience and resignation. There had been four children in her own family, three girls and a boy, and all were dead except her. Her mother said to her, ''God preserve you from ever seeing your children go before you do.'' But now my two brothers had gone, not to mention the baby that hadn't survived. But this only increased her magnanimity and sympathy for others. We survived our sorrows; we weren't to be pitied. But at school there were children who said to my sister Marie and me: ''You at the mill have everything we haven't got.'' There were families with four or five children who starved in huts without light or heating. My mother would often give me a basket with a cheese and a loaf of bread to take to one or another of them. ''If anyone asks you where you're going,'' she instructed me, ''don't answer. Just go, give it, and come back home.'' And she always sent me in the evening, during the Angelus, so as not to humiliate people by letting them be seen receiving gifts. It was the same when she sold a chicken, to give one example. We always kept about a hundred fowl. Once my father was present when she sold one, and afterward he exclaimed: ''I can't understand! You sell a bird for eighteen sous, and everywhere else they ask two francs fifty or three francs.'' And I'm sure she actually gave some chickens away without telling us.

We also had a lot of fruit, and Mother fed the women who picked them for her. We were sometimes twelve or fifteen at supper. And in the evening the women went away with their baskets full.

She was incapable of doing anything dishonest, incapable of lying. She used to say to us: ''When anyone who's done something wrong or made a mistake admits it, he must be considered forgiven.''

From photographs I had, M. Proust thought I was very like her physically.

"Morally, too," he added. "There is an innocence about you that you certainly must have inherited from her. With me, and with your husband too, I feel you would not know how to deceive."

"That's because I see my mother again in you, monsieur," I said.

By that I meant the same care, the same warmth, the same kindness toward me.

I'd finished growing by the time I was eleven. I was as tall as I am now, but I'd become very anemic, and in the next few years my mother was afraid I might develop tuberculosis.

"How worried she must have been about you, Céleste," M. Proust said. "Just like Mother about me."

And when I told him that when I was fourteen or fifteen I stopped being a tomboy; that I didn't want to go out any more but stayed at home working and sewing while my elder sister Marie was out enjoying herself; that even after I was married and living in Paris, the thing I still liked best was pottering about at home, he looked at me with his warm, captivating smile and said:

"And you have stayed like that, fortunately. Without realizing it, you were made for devotion, like your mother. Otherwise you wouldn't be here."

To mention the last of my mother's misfortunes, my father died in the autumn of 1913, in September. He had been paralyzed for four years, after a stroke. He couldn't walk without help, but if anyone else took his arm he used to say, "I want your mother." They were very close and affectionate couple. I was already married when Father died, but I came straight back from Paris. My mother looked very tired.

"When you feel better," I said to her, "why don't you come to Paris for a few days, for a change?"

"No," she said. "Half of me died with your father, and the other half must stay here. I shan't ever go to Paris. Shall we ever see each other again?"

M. Proust's eyes filled with tears when I told him how I'd left her. The path leading to the road ran around the wall of our property and passed by the house again. My brother drove me the three miles to the station in a horse-drawn carriage, and my mother watched me for as long as she could see me.

And then one day in April 1915 there was a knock at the back door at boulevard Haussmann. When I went to open it, there was one of my sisters-in-law looking grave.

"Céleste," she said, "I received a telegram from your brother. Your mother's ill and they want you to go home."

"How can that be?" I said. "I had a letter from Marie written two days ago, and she said Mother was very well."

But she insisted, so since M. Proust was awake I went to his room and told him.

"How did she find out?" he asked immediately.

"By telegram."

"Did you see the telegram?"

"No."

"Bring it here quickly."

I went for it but did not dare to look at it. I shall never forget him, holding the blue telegram in his hand against the white of the sheet, his face pale.

"My poor Céleste," he said. "Your dear mother is dead. The telegram says, 'Be careful how you tell Céleste. Letter follows.'"

And he started to weep silently, like me. Then he wanted me to leave right away.

"I understand your pain, dear Céleste: I have been through the same thing myself. But you must see your mother once again, even though she is dead. It would be too awful if you didn't."

"But I can't leave you all alone, monsieur."

"I shall manage very well, don't you worry about me. Just go."

And he kissed me.

Finally we arranged for one of my sisters-in-law to look after him while I was away.

It was wartime, and the journey was even more difficult than in normal times. I had to stop overnight at Saint-Flour to make a connection. I had left in haste, without stopping to change my clothes. My pumps sank right into the snow, and I was wearing stockings with white spots. A peasant said in dialect, thinking I wouldn't understand: "I bet she's nice and warm in her net stockings!" At Auxillac my brother and sister weren't expecting me, and when I arrived my mother was already buried (she'd had a stroke and died within a few hours). So I didn't even see her again, as M. Proust had hoped.

I left again almost at once and wasn't away from Paris for more than three days. M. Proust wept again when I told him what had happened. He took my hand gently, and said:

"My thoughts were with you all the time."

It was true. This was about the same time that Jean, Odilon's brother, was reported missing, and M. Proust had asked his friend Reynaldo Hahn to try to get information about Robert through connections at the army headquarters. Before I left Auxillac he said:

"Don't worry about your brother-in-law, Céleste. If I get any news I shall send you a wire."

And he did send me a wire, though only to say there was still no news.

My sister-in-law Louise did the best she could during the short time I was away, but I soon realized it hadn't been enough. M. Proust said it seemed I'd been away ages, and told me that Louise, though she didn't gossip, hadn't been able to help getting into conversation with the other people in the house and reporting it all back to him—a thing he couldn't bear. He was too used to me now, as I to him, to be content with anyone else.

I'm almost sure he practically never got up while I was away. He said, as a joke rather than a reproach:

"Your sister-in-law was lost here; she wouldn't have known how to make my bed."

Of course, all this raised the question of what would happen if I were temporarily indisposed. But I didn't really trouble about that—I was too young and too happy in what I was doing. And during all those years I was ill only once. It must have been in 1917, during the epidemic of Spanish influenza that killed so many people. I remember I had a temperature and was streaming with perspiration as I dragged myself about. His eye and his sense of smell never missed the slightest thing. When I went into his room he said:

"What is the matter, Céleste? Are you tired? There is a just a faint smell of something."

"Oh no, monsieur," I said. "I'm perfectly all right."

But that evening Mme. Chevalier, the cook downstairs, who was my only friend, told me to watch out. She knew what she was talking about—she'd had the flu already. That evening M. Proust was going out, and I got everything ready as if nothing were wrong. Then, after spending part of the night tidying up the newspapers and scraps of paper in his room, as soon as he returned I went to bed with plenty of aspirin and a spare nightdress on a chair within reach. When I woke up a few hours later I was sopping wet and freezing cold and unable even to lift my arms. But I made an effort and forced myself to throw off one nightdress and grab the other. I changed and went back to sleep and got up about noon as usual to go on duty. At four o'clock I served the coffee. I felt weak in my legs, but the worst was over. I could do what I had to do, without having to say anything to M. Proust. He didn't say anything either, even if he guessed. That in itself was a sign of affection; how many times did he say to me:

"Céleste, you ought not to see so-and-so. I am afraid he or she is carrying a germ, and it would be a bad thing for us if you caught it."

But the real problem was fatigue. While he was sleeping or resting, I went about my routine, but as soon as he woke up, I was never still. So in the end my sister Marie came to help me.

She is three years older than I am, and we now live together. We're extremely fond of each other, perhaps because we're so different. I'm very active and energetic, even though I may collapse afterward. She retreats before difficulties and just lies down. After Mother died she went to bed and intended to stay there. When I got to Auxillac I found her in bed, yellow as a lemon and saying over and over, "I can't go on living without Mother." When I went back to Paris I was, because of her, twice as upset as I would otherwise have been. We wrote to each other all the time, and I constantly tried to persuade her to pull herself together and come to Paris for a change, instead of languishing away in the country, grieving for Mother. She did come once but didn't stay.

In the end I spoke to M. Proust about her, explaining that I couldn't be two places at once and assuring him my sister would be as devoted in his service as I was. He said yes, and Marie came to Paris again, this time for good. As M. Proust hadn't suggested she could occupy the maid's room, upstairs, I was too proud to suggest it myself, and I arranged for Marie to stay with my sister-in-law in rue Laffitte. She didn't come in the morning but arrived in time for lunch, which we had in the kitchen, and left again in the evening.

At first—Marie started at the beginning of October 1918, a little while before the armistice—M. Proust was rather mistrustful of her. I must admit she was as self-conscious with him as I was at ease. Once, in the early days, he said to me:

"I have to do whatever you want, you see? You wanted your sister to come, and here she is."

I bristled and said:

"Why do you say that, monsieur? If you really mean it, it must be because you don't like having her here."

He gave me a marvelous smile.

"No no, Céleste, I was only joking."

I got the message, just the same! His first feeling about my sister was a kind of jealousy. It belonged to the possessive side of him; the fonder I was of my sister, the less affection there was for him.

But later he realized Marie had very fine feelings and was as attached to him as I was myself. I remember how one day, when I wasn't there, he talked to her about his father, Professor Adrien Proust, and when I returned he was radiant.

"I was talking to your sister about my father," he said. "And do you know what she said? 'Lives like that of your father, monsieur, are lives offered up.' That is beautiful, and I shall put it in my book."

And he did.

But in fact he never made much use of Marie. If I was out he'd send for her and say:

"Is Céleste back yet? Well, send her to me as soon as she comes in."

Her chief job was running errands and doing the shopping, and she was a great help to me with the housework when he was out. His only real contact with her was when I was there.

In his book there is the famous scene where he describes us both with him while he's having his coffee. He sets this in Cabourg, and we are his "couriers." The scene is partly true and partly imaginary, a sort of compendium of many others that took place on days when he woke up as cheerful as a bird, either because he had worked well during the night or because his asthma wasn't too troublesome.

In this scene he makes me say: "Oh little black demon with jet hair, oh subtle mischief! What could your mother have been thinking of when she created you—you're just like a bird. Look, Marie, look at the graceful way he turns his head—doesn't he look as if he's preening his feathers? . . ." I did sometimes say things like that, comparing him to a bird ruffling its feathers, because of his rumpled hair when he woke up and his sharp little eyes. And he used delightful gestures; he would eat his croissant with an elegant air that seemed to be for our benefit.

In the same passage he also has me call him "Poor Ploumissou!" I'd called him that once, and he'd asked me what it meant. I told him:

"When I was small my mother used to say, 'Come here, my little ploumissou, and let me tidy your hair.' And your hair's just like a little bird's feathers, monsieur."

He was very taken with that.

"We will do what Reynaldo Hahn and I used to do when we were young. He called me 'Buncht' and I called him 'Bunibuls.' So now you will be 'Plouplou' and I shall be 'Missou.'"

And sometimes, after that, when I went into his room, he'd say: "How are you today, Plouplou?"

But I never called him "Missou"—it wouldn't have seemed right. I don't remember, either, if I ever said, "I've never seen anyone so awkward and clumsy," like the Céleste in the book. I might have, jokingly, just as I might have called him a "spend-thrift"! I often remarked to him:

"You're very lucky to have been born rich, monsieur. I don't know how you'd have survived if you'd been poor."

Then he'd say, like a scolded child:

"But I am not rich, Céleste."

"Rich enough, monsieur, to do as you like."

Once he answered:

"No, I am not, Céleste. Fortunately for me, because anyone who is rich . . ."

He didn't finish, but from his look I guess he was thinking of the duties it would have entailed, for he was a man who took his duties seriously.

To go back to the part of M. Proust's book that I was speaking about, it shows, I think, that he must have found in my sister and me a sort of natural freshness in comparison with other people he knew. And this was truer of me than of Marie, who was shocked some-times at the liberties I took. I think M. Proust teased me just to scandalize her—he enjoyed that immensely. In the book, he called my outbursts "whirlpools."

Yes, I'm sure he felt at ease with us. And when Odilon came back after the war and joined me in my room at boulevard Hauss-mann and started driving his taxi again, then I think M. Proust was quite happy, because his little circle was complete.

11

HIS EVENINGS OUT

In a way we were both orphans—he with his parents dead and his friends scattered, and I with my parents dead, my family far away, and my husband in the army. So we created our own sort of intimacy, though for him it was chiefly an atmosphere within which to work, while I forgot about my own tasks and could see nothing but that magic circle.

We even had what might be called our vigils, except that because we had turned night into day they usually began at about two or three in the morning, when he came in after spending the evening out; if he'd stayed in, they began when he stopped working. As time went on, these vigils grew longer and longer. In the beginning he used to let me go at about five or six in the morning, perhaps seven. Then he got into the habit of calling me back, and it got to be eight o'clock, nine, sometimes half-past nine. It was all one to me. As soon as the bell rang I was there, my hair down my back as I've said, always smiling, always ready to listen even if the bell had awakened me out of my first sleep.

"Here comes la Gioconda!" he'd say. "Dear Céleste, you haven't had any sleep, but as you are kind enough to have come, there is something I want you to do."

"Something" would be a telephone call he wanted me to make at once to someone he'd been thinking about. He'd say whom he wanted to see or to accompany him somewhere, and usually he'd add:

"What do you think? You know I can only do what my health allows. Do you think it would be sensible for me to go out tonight?"

"You know best about that, monsieur."

He'd give me a searching look, then either stick to his decision and I'd get dressed and go down to telephone, or he'd put off the question until later. But nearly always these impulses provided an opportunity for keeping me to his room, and we'd talk for a while longer, sometimes for another hour.

It wasn't just that he wanted company. He needed to recapitulate; to sort out what he'd been thinking or seeing. I'm sure he tried ideas out on me so as to see more clearly what he was going to write, and also because in talking he warmed up to different ideas. I struck sparks out of him just as he struck sparks out of me—he liked that.

He was as methodical about going out as he was in everything else, at least in the years I knew him. He never went out two evenings or two nights running. But each time he would bring back material for at least two of our all-night sessions, and sometimes he would still return to a subject days afterward, if something had happened to enable him to round out a picture or if on reflection he'd perceived some different angle. In either case he'd be radiant.

"Céleste, do you remember what I told you the other day about Madame so-and-so? That it was she who was Monsieur X's mistress? Well, today I have the proof."

And he'd tell me what it was. Or again:

"I have been thinking, Céleste. And I have changed my mind. I think that probably . . ."

And he would go on to see my reaction. At the time I didn't even realize that he was prompting me; I just fell in with his mood. It was only after his death that I understood. I wouldn't go so far as to suggest such a thing myself, except that Jacques de Lacretelle, the writer, who knew him well, said to me several times afterward: "Do you remember, Céleste, how he always had to have your opinion?"

118

And others said the same. I've had plenty of time to think about it since, and I've come to the conclusion that it wasn't so much my opinion he wanted but, as I've said, my emotional reaction. I have an ironic bent, and I told him sincerely what I thought and what I felt. The latter was what he wanted.

I remember once he read me some lines from some poetry he'd either bought or been given—I can't remember whether it was by Paul Valéry or Saint-John Perse. When he'd finished I said:

"That's not poetry, monsieur. They're riddles."

He laughed heartily. He told me he repeated it to everyone afterward.

When he dressed to go out, I prepared his gloves and handkerchiefs on a stand in the hall, on a little silver tray, which I also used to bring him his letters on when he woke up. Also ready were his overcoat, stick, and whatever hat was appropriate—opera hat, felt, or bowler. I would help him with his coat and give him his hat. You ought to have seen the elegant way he put on his hat and took his stick and gloves. It was fascinating and delighted me every time. Then I'd open the door for him and summon the lift. He always turned round on the landing to look at me and smile.

"Goodbye, Céleste," he would say. "Thank you. I am very tired, but let us hope it will pass. I don't know what time I'll be back. You will, of course, make the phone calls and tidy up my bits of paper."

As soon as he was gone I set to work on his room. As he never put anything away or picked anything up, the bed was always covered with papers and newspapers; pens and handkerchiefs lay around where they'd fallen or been thrown aside. I tidied the room and aired it and put some woolies on the chair in case he was cold or wanted to change when he came in. The time passed quickly.

When all the work was done, I waited for him to return. Even if he came home early it was late, too late for anybody else in the building to be coming in, so the house was quite silent as I waited. As soon as I heard the lift I'd be out on the landing, my hand on the knob ready to open the door for him. I had to be there, anyway: he never carried a key, and I don't think he ever bothered to ask if there was any, or where it was.

He always arrived with thanks and a warm smile. I held the door open, and he walked in and took off his hat with his usual elegance and charm—that was always the first thing he did. But as soon as I caught a glimpse of him in the lift he'd unconsciously told me whether he was pleased or disappointed with his evening. I could tell from his hat. If he was pleased, it was on straight, tilted back slightly from his forehead, and his eyes underneath would be shining. Otherwise it was pulled down over his eyes, and his smile, though warm, would be weary. In either case he knew I'd seen. We had a little ritual. He'd say, on the landing:

"Well?"

And I'd answer, "Well, here you are, monsieur."

In the hall, when he'd taken his hat off and I'd helped him out of his coat, if it had been an unsatisfactory evening he'd wait for me to ask:

"Didn't it go well, monsieur?"

"My dear Céleste, if you knew how sorry I am I went! I was so bored—I have so little time. I should have stayed home and worked."

But the amazing thing was that however annoying the evening had been, he was always even-tempered with me and kept his displeasure to himself. If it had been a good evening, well, then it was magnificent, a display of fireworks. His face would light up from inside.

"Is my room done, Céleste?"

"Yes, monsieur, everything's ready."

"Come in quickly then—I have much to tell you."

I followed him into his room; he sat in a corner at the foot of the bed, I stood facing him, and it began.

When I think now of the hours and hours I must have spent like that, standing in front of him like a policeman on duty! And it never even occurred to me to feel tired! We were too absorbed. If he never invited me to sit down, I'm sure it was because it never occurred to

him. And I was so engrossed that I never even saw the visitors'
armchair just a few feet away. He forgot his own tiredness too.
Perched on the end of his bed, he looked like a young prince just
back from the ball of life. It was all the more extraordinary when you
remembered him in the afternoon, emerging from the fumes, pale,
ill, and motionless, husbanding his strength, silent and signaling for
silence.

Now he was a fountain of youth, pouring out everything—the
wit or folly he'd met with, how this man was ridiculous or that
woman had been in splendid form all evening—and what she was
wearing. When he described a gown I could see every detail as
clearly as if I were looking at a fashion picture.

One day, a while after his death, Mme. Lanvin's daughter, by
then Princess du Polignac, came to see me. I told her I already knew
her through the description M. Proust had given me of one of her
gowns, which had dazzled him. At that time she had still been
married to Clemenceau's grandson, M. Proust told me, and then he
went on:

"The lapels of her dress made me think of Venice—they were
the color of a pigeon's breast."

From the things I was able to tell her about it, the Princess
could remember the dress very well.

Whenever he started to describe an evening, I'd say something like:

"Well, monsieur, I see there's going to be an analysis today!"

He'd laugh and say, "Perhaps, Céleste, perhaps."

Some people have said he was malicious about others, but I
think he was first and foremost a moralist. What he sought for in
everything, whether virtue or vice or pretense, was the honest truth.

I remember him telling me about another dress on which he'd
complimented a lady because the material and the style both seemed
to him really lovely—it was made of silver brocade or lamé—and he
was still indignant at the lady's reply.

"You will never guess what she answered, Céleste. She said,
looking down her nose, 'It's the last silver in France!' And do you

know who she was? The wife of the Minister of Finance! I came to the conclusion that on such an ugly soul, the prettiest dress could only be in the same bad taste as her remark.''

For his concern was to see into people, and if what he saw there was dark, he tore off the mask ruthlessly. Any irony or mockery in his comments came from the people themselves, in what they pretended to be and were not.

One of his acquaintances from earlier days was Constantin Ullmann, who frequented high society and called sometimes in the evening, dressed in his dinner jacket. But these visits soon stopped—he was no longer invited. It's been said that at one time M. Proust thought of making him his secretary but then decided M. Ullmann wouldn't have the patience necessary for the job. I never knew anything about this. But once M. Proust met him again by chance and asked me later what I thought of him.

"Too pale, monsieur, and, poor thing, so ugly!"

"And he thinks himself so handsome!" said M. Proust with a sigh. Then, after a short silence: "But Céleste, when you think of his airs, there must be days when he is very unhappy, looking at himself in the mirror. That is often why people are so nasty. They cannot forgive others for not being as ugly as themselves.''

He looked really sorry for the poor fellow. He didn't like to see people unhappy.

For example, one day when he'd sent me with a message to the Duchess de Clermont-Tonnerre and I told him I'd found her surrounded by a pack of women, he laughed at first, then said he admired the Duchess for her intelligence and sensibility.

"But what you don't know, Céleste, is that the poor woman has good reason for not being very keen on men. Her husband was a brute and made her life impossible. The things she had to put up with! And yet when you saw her she always looked as lovely and radiant as if she were the happiest woman alive. I can see her now, sitting in her drawing room with her hand stretched out to the fire— there was no hand so transparent.''

This didn't prevent him from making fun of the old Duke

Agénor de Gramont, the father of Mme. de Clermont-Tonnerre, and of one of his great friends, the Duke de Guiche.

"With his second wife's fortune—she was a Rothschild, of course, so you can imagine!—he built the château of Vallières, an enormous place at Mortefontaine near Senlis. Then La Rothschild died and he married an Italian princess. And believe it or not, Céleste, marrying a princess cured him of his jealousy of Countess Greffulhe, whose château was smaller than his but staffed with forty-five servants. To what lengths will vanity not go?"

He never forgave Count Pierre de Polignac, because when he married the Duchess de Valentinois, the natural daughter of Prince Louis of Monaco, who'd finally recognized her and made her a duchess, the count renounced his own title and became the Duke de Valentinois.

"A Polignac renouncing his own name in order to marry a washerwoman!" he said. "Everyone knows the Duchess's mother did Monaco's washing. I shan't see Comte Pierre any more."

Not only did he not see him any more, but one day when the Duke sent one of his books and asked him to inscribe it, M. Proust wouldn't.

"No, no. I cannot bring myself to write his name. If the messenger is still waiting, give the book back to him. If not, please return it by post."

He didn't believe in half-measures. One night he came home specially pleased with himself because, he said, he'd done a good deed. He'd persuaded a married friend of his, of whom he was very fond but whose name he did not mention, to break off what he considered an unworthy love affair. He handed me a sealed envelope.

"This is the letter he wrote under my dictation, breaking it off. To make sure, I said I would see that it was delivered. Please take it, Céleste, and deliver it personally today."

He asked me to wait while the lady read the letter. She wept in front of me. When I told him, he said:

"I know, Céleste, but there was no other way."

He didn't care for eccentricity, either. Once, after supper at Larue's, he recounted:

"Jean Cocteau was there with some other people, and when he saw me come in he jumped up and ran over to the table shouting, 'It's Marcel! It's Marcel!' Then he insisted on sitting beside me and telling me stories. He is very witty and amusing, but he tells such lies to attract attention! It is a long time since I have been as embarrassed as I felt this evening, with his showing off."

It was like this, more or less, every time he came back from an evening with Cocteau: for instance, the two or three times he let himself be persuaded to go to the Boeuf sur le Toit, a cabaret patronized by Cocteau that had become popular with artists.

"They are not serious," he'd say. "There is *boeuf à la mode*, but not as good as Félicie's. I feel out of place there."

Once, after an evening at the house of Princess Murat, who married Count de Chambrun, the ambassador to Italy, he said:

"She is one of the sharpest, most intelligent and amusing women I know—and I don't say that just because she speaks so well of my work. But because her first husband was a Russian, she thinks she has to be Slav in everything, including mood and laced boots. She must have them sent from Russia, and any moment you expect her to leap up and break into a Cossack dance."

Then there was Mme. Scheikévitch. When he first met her, at Cabourg in the early years of the century, he enjoyed talking with her about Russian literature, especially Dostoevski.

"She is a strange woman," he said. "She ruins herself giving grand parties she cannot afford. And the crazy things she does! She was unhappily married to a son of Carolus-Duran, the painter—so unhappily that one day she decided to commit suicide. So she went and asked the advice of Mme. Arman de Caillavet, a great friend of hers and of mine, who had tried to commit suicide herself because Anatole France was unfaithful to her with a dancer in America. Mme. de Caillavet was so jealous she had France followed by his butler, who sent her reports. She was so furious when she heard he was unfaithful that she tried to shoot herself—but missed. So poor

Marie Scheikévitch goes and consults her, so as to miss too! Later on she married a man with only one arm. But it was too heroic to last.''

One night after he'd dined with her in a restaurant in rue Daunou:

"She wore a white fox fur, and all the evening she was stroking my face with the fox's tail and saying, 'Marcel, I love you!' ''

He laughed as he thought of it, but then grew sad.

"It is terrible, Céleste. She is an absolute wreck, poor woman. And what makes it worse is that she used to think she was extremely pretty and attractive. She used to go around saying at the top of her voice, 'It is all natural! See these teeth? All mine!' ''

On another occasion she was one of his guests in a private salon at the Ritz:

"Do you know what, Céleste? At one point she went into a corner, let down her hair, then sat on the floor to make sure everyone noticed her! I didn't know where to hide.''

But that sort of situation amused him, really, because he always got something out of it. When I said Mme. Scheikévitch was a comedienne, he looked at me and said:

"Do you think so? I would say she is a character.''

His eyes sparkled—just as they did the night he came back from a party at Count Etienne de Beaumont's where the entertainment was provided by a hypnotist. Everyone had taken part in the experiment, including the host, who fell asleep and wanted M. Proust to try too. But the hypnotist wouldn't let him. "Oh no, not this gentleman!'' M. Proust was very proud of this as he had been of his encounter with the man during the air raid.

"He realized it wouldn't be the same as with the Count and the others. I am very fond of M. de Beaumont; he amuses me and interests me as a man. But he is one of those men who borrow what little wit they have from those around them. So the hypnotist didn't have much trouble influencing him. However, it didn't go very far.''

But he was never so pleased and talkative as when he'd met someone whose virtues outweighed his failings. I think he always distinguished between those he liked and saw because of his book and those he liked for themselves. Perhaps one of the people he admired most was the Abbé Mugnier.

M. Proust told me he'd been priest at Sainte-Clotilde's, in the fashionable Faubourg Saint-Germain, but had got into trouble for trying to help a defrocked curate. He was then demoted to chaplain to the nuns of Saint-François-de-Sales. M. Proust had met him at a dinner given by his friend Princess Soutzo, about whom I'll speak again later. He was fascinated by the abbé's manner and by his wit.

"He is not good-looking," he said. "He is ugly, really, with warts all over his face. But when you see him among all those people, in his threadbare cassock—for he is as poor as a saint—toying with a lock of gray hair and gazing at you with those childlike blue eyes, you would have to be a devil not to love him. And what brilliant conversation!"

Every time they met, M. Proust came home full of the things the abbé had said. The first time they were introduced, he asked the abbé, just to tease him a little, whether he had read Baudelaire's *Flowers of Evil*.

"You will never guess what he said. He patted his cassock and said, 'My dear fellow, I carry it about with me. Without the smell of sulphur, how should we appreciate the scent of virtue?' And afterward, as we were going out, still talking, among the rest of the guests, he stopped at the foot of the stairs and said, 'My friend, I wish our conversation could go on forever. But I absolutely must go home; my mystic hens will be waiting for me.'"

M. Proust was enchanted. "'Mystic hens,'" he repeated. "Have you ever heard anything so marvelous?"

At another dinner, on a Good Friday, both meat and fish were served so that the guests could take their choice. Abbé Mugnier was served meat but didn't say anything.

"Just as everyone was starting to eat," said M. Proust, "the abbé's neighbor leaned over and said, 'I wouldn't have thought you would eat meat, Monsieur l'Abbé, especially on Good Friday!' He pushed his plate away and said, 'What's this? But it wasn't with intention, madame.'"

If he didn't put this in his book, it was probably because he admired the abbé too much. The number of times he said to me:

"I would like you to meet him, Céleste. One evening I shall bring him home with me or ask him here."

And one day, I remember: "You will centainly meet him one day, Céleste. For I want you to promise, when I am dead, to ask him to come and pray at my bedside. And he will come, you will see."

I wanted to carry out his wish. On my insistence, Professor Robert Proust sent a telegram asking the abbé to come as M. Proust had asked. But alas, M. Proust was already dead, and the abbé was ill in bed with a terribly painful nasal complaint. But afterward he faithfully performed the memorial masses at Saint-Pierre de Chaillot.

Now, when my poor memory recalls those nights, and I almost can see M. Proust sitting on the end of his bed in the faint light of the room, telling stories and imitating one person after the other, with delight or sudden sadness, I realize I was the privileged spectator of the most beautiful theater in the world, and I understand why he enjoyed it too. His bringing home the drama of the outside world and unfolding it before me was an attempt to hold back time, to stop it from fleeing and taking his characters with it.

Most of them I never met. But those I did happen to see before or after he died seemed familiar right away, like people on television nowadays, whom you seem to know quite intimately from seeing them every evening on the screen.

Even before I met Jean Cocteau—he came to boulevard Haussmann a few times during the war—I could imagine him so well from M. Proust's description that one day when somebody mentioned him I blurted out, "That buffoon!" I could have bitten my tongue out, but I couldn't help it. I just saw him as M. Proust had described him jumping on the tables at Larue's.

"When I am gone, Céleste, that is what you will miss most—not having a little Marcel any more to amuse you, telling you about everything and bringing you home a salon full of people."

Another time when he was saying, as he often did|, how dull it must be for me to spend so much time alone at night, he went on:

"The least I can do is try to cheer you up."

But there was no need. I didn't mind living in the dark at all. When he came home, it was as if the sun rose.

Sometimes he would say, all of a sudden:

"Heavens, I am tired, talking all this time. It is strange how I enjoy chattering with you, but it does make me tired."

"Very well, monsieur. I'll go."

"No, no, I am sorry, dear Céleste. You only stayed because I wanted you to."

But I'm sure the real reason was, as I've said, that he liked to use me as sounding board.

There were times when, though he kept talking, I could see from his eyes he was suddenly far away. He had a strange faculty of vanishing, while his lips went on speaking. And then suddenly his gaze would come back and light on you again as if in surprise. Then he stopped speaking for a moment, as if trying to remember, and said:

"Oh yes, we were talking about . . ."

And the story would go on from where it had left off a moment before, only with another strange hesitation, as if part of him were again talking while the other part went away, and as if, when it returned, a few seconds were necessary for the two parts to join together again.

At any rate, whether he acted it for himself, for me, or for both of us, I just took his theater as it came. But he had the advantage of knowing all he was giving me.

One night—it must have been toward the end of the war, when I'd already been with him three or four years—he said:

"I wonder what you are waiting for to write your diary."

I laughed. "I can just see it, monsieur! You're teasing me as usual."

"No, Céleste, I am serious. No one really knows me but you. No one knows all I do as well as you do, or can know all I say to you. When I am dead your diary would sell more copies than my

128

books. Yes, it would sell as fast as the baker sells hot rolls in the morning—you would make a fortune. Better still, Céleste: You write it and I shall make comments on it as you go along."

I remember answering:

"There you are! You're always saying you haven't the time for what you have to do yourself, and now you talk about commenting on my diary too! I said you were kidding me!"

He sighed. "You are making a mistake, Céleste, and you will be sorry. You don't know how many people will come to see you, or write to you, after I am dead. And of course you won't answer them—I know you."

The worst of it is, it's all true. People came to see me from all over the world after he died. I still get letters, which I don't answer. But most of all I regret not having kept a diary, mainly because, if he'd made comments on it, I'd have had another weapon besides my own memory and my own word to fight against the untruths, well- or ill-intentioned, that have been told about him and his work.

129

12

HIS LOVE FOR HIS MOTHER

Eight years, day after day without a miss—that adds up to much more than the Thousand and One Nights. And in the silence of old age, when I close my eyes and think of all the characters streaming by in his stories, my head goes spinning.

Sometimes he would build his descriptions a piece at a time, as if he were putting a jigsaw puzzle together. Other times he would unfold before me a whole roster of society. But you always had the feeling that what really interested him were the fundamental relationships among people.

I think it must have been a family trait. I don't mean only heredity but also the example of all around him when he was a boy and a young man.

He talked to me a great deal about his parents, always stressing how close and affectionate they were until death came to separate them.

I remember how one night, when the conversation had been about them, he fell silent a moment. Then he went on and quoted some lines from one of Musset's *Nuits*. He recited these poems so often that I came to like Musset very much. Then he went on to a popular ballad he'd asked Odilon to sing to him so that he could write down the words; it was called "Lilac Time." After saying that everyone "mourns his friends or his loves," the song continues, "I think of the couples that last forever."

It was so beautiful I cried: "How lovely, monsieur! Do say it again!"

He was so delighted I should like it, he recited it again, then gave me the piece of paper on which he'd written the words—I still have it. Then he said, his eyes alight with feeling:

"If you think about it, Céleste, you will see it's true. At the beginning of a marriage, there is love. Then life takes over, and it is just an arrangement. But there are some marriages that last forever, out of esteem, out of an overriding need to stay together, through the great affection that comes from mutual understanding. And always remember, dear Céleste, that these marriages are indestructible whatever happens."

The harmonious combination of understanding, gentleness, and goodness he showed in everything, and the iron will and terrible determination in his work, must have come from the combination of the qualities of his father and mother.

"The men in our family have always been great workers," he once said to me. "My father was indefatigable. He passed examination after examination, but he could never know enough. He was a great researcher. He was always first, or in the top two or three, in all his exams. And he was a wonderfully brave and devoted doctor. For one thing, he was from the region of Beauce, and the Beaucerons have always been hard workers. And for another thing, he intended at first to become a priest—to understand him properly you have to remember that. Priest and doctor have in common the spirit of charity."

Then, smiling affectionately at the memory: "He had what it took to become what he did. A great man."

And this was true: Professor Adrien Proust was a leading figure in hygiene, inspector general of all the sanitary services in France and the colonies, or something like that. M. Proust's eyes would shine with pride when he told me his father had written many remarkable and well-known books about the problems of his specialty.

"It was he who halted cholera in France, in Marseilles, when people were dying by the hundreds. He not only looked after the sick himself and caught the fever himself, but he also discovered that the cholera virus was spread by rats on ships. He caused a diplomatic incident with the English because he put their ships in quarantine. They were so furious that their trade was brought to a standstill that they would have hanged him if they could."

As another example he gave me of his father's courage:

"He had to make long journeys of inspection, sometimes in climates that didn't suit him at all. I remember hearing him say that once when he was sailing through the Red Sea he suffered so badly from the heat and seasickness that he begged them to throw him overboard. Mother used to worry so much about these journeys that she insisted on going with him on one of them. I remember it because when she came back she was full of stories about riding on camels. But in spite of all this, my father wouldn't have changed his job for the world. And he didn't know what it was to rest: Ah Céleste, if only I were sure of doing as much with my books as Father did for the sick!"

His mother was quite different. She had the same devotion to duty, but it found expression in another way. According to what M. Proust said, the great understanding between his parents had a lot to do with his mother's taking charge of every household detail and her husband's financial matters so that he didn't have to bother about anything but his work. But at the same time, she had enough delicacy and diplomacy for two people. Whenever she felt that Professor Proust needed support, she didn't hesitate to accompany him to the Hôtel-Dieu hospital for a lecture or a lesson. But she was also very good at organizing the parties that had to be given.

"She always knew what she was doing," said M. Proust. "She made herself the ambassadress of Father's career, and she was marvelous for that."

He laughed.

"Imagine, Céleste, there was a time, when I was young, when we used to lunch regularly once a week at the Elysée Palace, at the table of the President of the Republic. And what a president—Félix Faure! Mother had been a close friend of Madame Faure for ten or twelve years, since the time when her husband was just a deputy. Their two daughters, Lucie and Antoinette, were part of the little group I played with among the trees in the Champs-Elysées. Lucie, the elder, was almost in flower then, but Antoinette was just in bud, like me. But with her gray eyes, she could have made me trot round and round just like the little donkeys we used to ride. Anyway, when the husband rose to the Elysée, Mother and Madame Faure used to go for a walk together almost every day in the Bois de Boulogne. Their friendship had ripened into confidence, and Madame Faure would tell Mother her troubles. These were as many as the President's lady friends, who were not few, as everyone knows. But Mother and Madame Faure still found the time for making plans. Oh yes, Céleste—one plan was to marry me to Antoinette's gray eyes. And then it all disappeared out of a back door with the lovely Madame Steinheil, after she screamed that the President had died in her arms at the palace. But I'm not sorry.''

Mme. Proust was an incomparable housekeeper, he said, and she needed to be, for both the household on boulevard Malesherbes and the one in rue de Courcelles, to which they moved in 1900, were kept up in style, partly out of social obligation but also on account of M. Proust himself when he grew up.

"Her eye was on everything in the house, from the attic to the ceiling. Everything had to be in order, in place, and spotless."

Nicolas, when he was still working for M. Proust on boulevard Haussmann, mentioned Mme. Proust two or three times—not more, for as I've said he was very discreet—in connection with the meticulousness of "M. Marcel" himself. He worked for her for years and knew her well. I gathered she must have been very firm with her servants and very exacting. "Everything had to be perfect," Nicolas said. There was one anecdote which showed at once how careful she was about everything, and how shrewd. She personally supervised the kitchen and saw that everything was kept clean and even kept an eye on what was simmering on the stove. One day there was a hot casserole keeping warm on the grate, and Félicie, the cook, took the cloth holder off the lid and said with a wink to Nicolas, "When Madame comes—we know her—she won't be able to resist taking the lid off," meaning she will burn her hand. Mme. Proust arrived, gave one look, then said to Félicie, "Would you mind taking the lid off that casserole for me, please?" Nicolas was still laughing about it: "If Félicie's face was red, it wasn't only from the fire!"

If everything had to be perfect for her husband and herself, it had to be more than perfect for the children, especially for her little Marcel, who was ill.

"You can't imagine how she spoiled us, Céleste, and how solicitous she was about me. Nothing was ever too good for Robert and me."

One night he showed me an old photo.

"What do you think of that little boy, Céleste?"

"A little prince, monsieur. How handsome he is, with his little cane. It could be you if his hair wasn't so fair."

"But Céleste," he said, laughing, "I was quite fair as a child, before I became dark, with a broken nose, as I am now."

He was clearly delighted about the "little prince." He told me afterward that their mother was very particular about their clothes, and they never went out without her inspecting them first.

"She thought of everything. In winter, when she sent us for a walk in the Champs-Elysées, she used to tell Félicie to bake some big potatoes in their jackets, which we put in our fur muffs to keep our hands warm."

"I loved my father very much. But the day Mother died, she took her little Marcel with her."

There was one area in which Professor Proust and his wife disagreed, and that was literature and the other arts. He had devoted himself too much first to his studies and then to science to have time for anything else. But Mme. Proust loved all the arts, was a great reader, and very musical. Quietly and unobtrusively she pointed out the new works to her husband so that he could be up to date. She even read aloud to him sometimes:

" . . . as she did to me, when I was ill," said M. Proust. "Poor Father," he went on with a smile, "there were days when he wasn't the slightest bit interested."

Mme. Proust must have inherited her artistic tastes from her own mother, a remarkable woman. When they were together, they were always exchanging quotations from Mme. de Sévigné. M. Proust adored his grandmother and spoke of her as a person of very superior intelligence and culture:

"Just the same as Mother, except that she always spoke as if she were reciting from a book. They were very funny together—they never stopped talking about what they had been reading. When Grandmother came to see us, which she did very often, they stayed in the salon, talking for hours, and when Grandmother got up to go, my mother would go with her. There'd be a first halt at the door, where they'd go on with their conversation. Then, still talking, they set off down the stairs. At the bottom they sat down on a sofa and continued sometimes for another half-hour. Then suddenly Grandmother would cry, 'Goodness, the time! I shall just see you back to the door, and then I must fly!' And they went upstairs and started all over again. They couldn't tear themselves away from each other."

They were so steeped in each other and in Mme. de Sévigné that if Mme. Proust had occasion to reproach her little Marcel when she wrote to him, she would quote the strictures of the Marquise to her daughter or her roguish son.

Of course M. Proust's grandmother adored him as he did her. It was almost with tears in his eyes that he said one day:

"When she was alive, the thought of her dying seemed so horrible I was sure I would not be able to bear it. And what happened? I was very upset but not as much as I thought I would be. Ah Céleste, if one died every time one thinks of dying!"

And he smiled so sadly I realized his tears were chiefly because, even if one doesn't get over one's greatest sorrows, one always survives them.

He possessed such lucidity about everything, which was always expressed with infinite delicacy and subtlety. For example, speaking of the loss of his parents, especially his mother, he would say:

"They spoiled me right up to the end by leaving me a fortune, with the freedom to enjoy it as I liked, without ever again having to ask anybody for anything. But even this freedom has never made up for losing them. And yet it exists, Céleste, it exists, and without it I never would have been able to do what I do. Even when she was alive, Mother did all she could to give it to me."

All her life Mme. Proust had been especially partial to her elder son, watching over his ideas as well as his health. As soon as he grew up she saw to it that his habit of going out or working at night was undisturbed. Life at rue de Courcelles was already, for him, what it would be later at boulevard Haussmann. When he got his freedom, he said, he merely perfected everything according to his own taste.

The domestics had strict orders from Mme. Proust not to make any noise while he was sleeping or resting. She herself wouldn't have disturbed him for anything in the world. Think of it—because of M. Proust's habits and the different lives they led, mother and son, living in the same apartment, sometimes communicated by letter!

Lecture him as she sometimes might, she in fact indulged his every whim. One day he decided to give a big dinner party and wanted the table arranged like a flower bed, with an electrically lit flower in front of each guest.

"But at that time, Céleste, most houses didn't have electricity. So Mother had a generator and accumulators installed in the courtyard. You should have seen the result—it was entrancing!"

It was his mother's special task to smooth out the difficulties with Professor Proust, for in spite of the father's love for his son, there were quite serious ones.

When he was still a child, M. Proust told me, he used to make scenes, especially after his asthma started. Taking advantage of the necessity for being very careful with him, he would refuse to go to sleep unless his mother came to kiss him goodnight in bed.

"That used to drive Father wild! But Mother always stood firm. Her gentleness in situations like that could be almost terrifying."

The father also reproached the son for his extravagance, which was generosity, really. There were two stories about this, which used to amuse M. Proust greatly.

One day, as a young man, he and his parents had taken a cab to go to see Mme. Proust's brother in place Malesherbes. When they arrived, he got out first.

"Being a nice, attentive young man, I helped my parents out, and then, since I had money, I paid the driver. When I turned round my father was staring at my hand and asked me how much tip I had given. I said five francs. He flew into such a rage! He wound up by saying, 'I warn you, Marcel—at this rate you will end up dying in rags!' He often predicted that. Poor Father! And to think that after he died, Mother told me one of his greatest desires was to leave me enough so that I shouldn't have to think about money."

The other story was about how Mme. Proust, too, was anxious about his extravagance and often scolded him, but never in front of his father. She would quote Mme. de Sévigné telling her daughter she lived in too high a style. But the whole thing began when he was only five or six years old, when she sent him and his brother to tea with a relative, Mme. Nathan.

"Mother dressed us up all neat and clean, and before we went, said, 'Here's a five-franc piece each. When you get there and Marie, the maid, opens the door, make sure you first of all wish her a Happy New Year, and then give her the five-franc pieces.' On the way there, in place de la Madeleine, I saw a shoeblack swinging his arms and stamping his feet to keep warm. I went up to him, asked him to shine my shoes, though they were already as bright as new pennies, and gave him my five francs. When I got home, Mother said, 'I hope you were good and didn't forget to give Marie the five francs?' I told her about the shoeblack. 'What did you do that for?' she cried in despair. So I explained: 'I saw him waiting in the cold for a customer, so I let him shine my shoes.' And she kissed me."

But what really worried M. Proust's father was his son's future, and here Mme. Proust played a decisive role. Professor Proust was determined that his son should have a career so that he would never be in need. The professor was backed up by all the men on his wife's side of the family, especially Mme. Proust's father.

"He was the most passionate of all," M. Proust said to me. "When he took up the question he would tear his hair. 'You will never make anything of that boy, he is much too spoiled! Or rather, though you don't seem to realize it, you will turn him into a good-for-nothing! If you don't lead him to some sort of profession, you will be the ruin of him!' Father would turn to my mother and say, 'You see? I have said over and over again we cannot let him become a dandy!' But Mother let it all flow over her. I can still hear her saying to Father in her gentle voice: 'Have patience, my little doctor. Everything will turn out all right.'"

At one time, I think it was when he was about twenty, M. Proust, to please his father, became assistant librarian at the Bibliothèque Mazarine, at the same time as he was studying law. He didn't receive any salary, but that was of no consequence. His father was pleased because at least he had a job.

"The only thing was," said M. Proust, smiling, "I was always on leave."

Needless to say, it didn't last. He left, and at about this time he wrote a long letter to his father saying it was all a waste of time— "time lost"—and that he thought his vocation was literature.

According to what he told me, there was a final showdown between his parents, at the end of which his father said to Mme. Proust: "Very well, I won't press the point. I shan't interfere any further in what he does. Make what you like of him."

"And my dear father kept his word. Not only that, but before he died he told some friends, 'You will see, Marcel will be a member of the Academy one of these days.'"

One night, much later on, I asked M. Proust if he was already thinking of his book and its title when he wrote to his father about "time lost." He smiled but didn't answer.

Knowing all that, one realizes what a shock it must have been to him to lose them both. All the more so as they died so closely together, the professor in 1903, Mme. Proust two years later, and both in circumstances that were painful—in the case of the father, especially so.

M. Proust was thirty-two when Professor Adrien Proust died. The younger brother, Robert, already a doctor, had been married a year, and his wife was expecting a child. The death of the professor and the birth of the child were combined in a single drama. I can still hear M. Proust telling me about it.

One day, after lunch, when the professor was due to give a lecture to the Faculty, he said to Mme. Proust: "I shall go a little early and stop at Robert's to see if there is any news about the baby." He found his son and daughter-in-law about to go for a short walk.

"Father was very tired," M. Proust told me, "and Robert was so shocked by how ill he looked that he took his wife aside and said, 'Marthe, I am worried. Would you mind going to your mother's and taking a walk with her? I think I ought to go with Father—I am sure he is not at all well.' Robert went with Father to the École de Médecine, and Father began his lecture. But after a little while he asked his students to excuse him a minute. When he didn't come back, Robert and some others rushed to where they thought he must be. It was awful, Céleste—I can hardly bear to speak of it. They broke down the door. He had had a stroke. Robert rushed him back to rue de Courcelles. My mother cried, '*I* ought to have gone with him!' But even in this sudden grief she was wonderful. Robert telephoned his wife: 'Father is not well. I have brought him home, but I cannot leave him for the moment. Please stay with your mother until I come to pick you up.'

"What happened next was worse still. During the night my sister-in-law gave birth to her little Suzy, but she caught puerperal fever, due perhaps to the hasty arrangements during the commotion of Father's death. She herself was between life and death.

"Of course she was not told about Father. They said, 'He is better, he will be over it in a few days. Just think of getting well again yourself.' But it all nearly went wrong on the day Father was buried. He was given an official funeral, and the procession had to go through avenue de Messine, where Robert's mother-in-law lived and where Marthe had given birth to the baby. Marthe's mother wanted to attend the funeral, so she said she had to go out on a little errand—Marthe would be all right with the maids, and her mother would be back soon. But when the procession went past, the music was so loud my sister-in-law couldn't fail to hear it, and asked the maid what it was. 'I don't know, madame; it must be some soldiers marching by.' 'No, no, it's a funeral march. Someone famous must have died. Who is it?' 'I don't know, madame; I haven't heard anything about it.' But they still managed to keep the truth from her for a while. When Mother went to see her, she took a brightly colored dress with her and changed out of her mourning clothes before entering her bedroom.''

He was even more reluctant to talk about his mother's death than his father's. Perhaps that shows that the wound was deeper. All he said to me was that when his father died he went on living with Mme. Proust at rue de Courcelles. As it was a very large apartment, they shut up part of it. And they never gave any more parties.

Every time he mentioned his mother in connection with that period he used the word ''wonderful.''

"I'm certain Mother lost all pleasure in life when Father died. But she never let us see it. She was wonderful.''

He used the word again when he told me about a little incident that occurred when people were filing past to pay their last respects to Professor Proust, lying in state. Mme. Proust came in just as an unknown woman was laying a large bunch of Parma violets beside the body—a gesture that could bear only one interpretation.

"Mother had the rare gift of not seeing what she didn't want to see. I remember when Robert was a young man, he had a motorcycle accident with a girl riding on the back. Mother rushed to his bedside. And there was the young lady. Mother not only did not look at her—she did not *see* her, Céleste! Well, that other time too, when Father was lying in state, I swear, she saw neither the woman nor the violets. Oh, she was wonderful!''

The same happened when she was ill. They operated in the end, but she never really recovered.

"You cannot imagine what a wonderful woman she was, Céleste! She kept her illness to herself, just as she had her mourning and her grief."

But he never commented on the nature of her illness or operation—though I've heard the operation was for a tumor—and I always had the feeling he didn't want to be asked about it. He was very reserved on the subject. Only by allusion, often his manner of communication, he gave me to understand that Mme. Proust died of an attack of uremia. Even after fifteen years, the memory of her death was too painful to talk about directly.

There have been all sorts of tales about how, on the anniversaries of Mme. Proust's death, he could scarcely breathe because of his asthma and had visions of a woman in black who looked like his mother. It's all nonsense. I would have known if it were true—he would certainly have told me.

In fact, he paid no attention to anniversaries. He didn't even think about them. I never saw him sad on any such dates, and he never talked to me about them or about his parents in any special way on those days. I know because he told me that at one time he would go every year and put a pebble in the vault of his maternal grandparents, who were Jewish: it was one of the customs of their religion. He did this out of loyalty to their memory and, I suspect, to please his mother. But I remember him saying, in connection with the flowers he arranged to have put on his parents' grave at All Saints':

"Flowers show friendship and love for the living. The dead have no use for them. It is the custom to put flowers on graves, so I follow it. But believe me, dear Céleste, I am no devotee of cemeteries. It is not there I find my beloved dead. My devotion is in memory."

When he spoke to me of his mother it was nearly always with a luminous smile full of affection.

"Mother often said, 'My poor little Marcel, where would you be without me?' Or 'My poor little pet . . .' Do you know what her last words to me were? 'My poor little canary, what will you do without me? But whatever you do, remain a Catholic.'"

And with his sweet, childlike smile he said, "Well, here he is, Céleste—your Catholic canary!"

The only opportunity I had to see how deep his grief was, was when he asked me to bring him his mother's photograph. If he said anything at all, it was to point out the details of her dress. But he very quickly laid the photograph down and asked me to put it away. Once he asked me to stand it on the corner of the mantlepiece so that he could see it from the bed. He kept it there for two or three days. Then he sent for me.

"Dear Céleste, I want you to put Mother's photo away. You see, one gets used to things, and habit stops one from really remembering people and objects."

One night when we were talking, I said—I don't remember what led up to it:

"I'm so fond of you, monsieur, I often think about what they say—that at the Last Judgment we shall all meet again in the Valley of Jehosaphat. How happy I shall be to see you! Do you believe it?"

"I don't know, Céleste—I would like to. But I can tell you one thing. If I were sure to meet my mother again, in the Valley of Jehosaphat or anywhere else, I would want to die at once."

13

THE CAMELLIA PERIOD

It was when he talked to me about his childhood and youth that I began to realize he lived only in and for the dream world of his memory. The image he retained of these two periods of his life was at once affectionate and full of wonder but without real regret or nostalgia, because to him to evoke them meant to be still living them.

From what he told me, he seems to have been in both periods as I knew him later—serious and reflective yet at the same time very outgoing, with a great desire both to know and to be known. For this purpose he used his charm, but not so much to attract attention, friendship, or affection as to be able to study others and enrich himself with the knowledge of them. He was a bee alighting unerringly on the right flowers.

Learning always came easily to him. He told me he never had any difficulty at school except in algebra, for which he often had to seek help from his younger brother.

"Robert used to say, 'All you have to do is what I do—work—and you will know the answers.' But I didn't want to. Algebra didn't interest me. Perhaps if I tried again now . . ."

But he made a wry face.

145

"As to other subjects, I didn't deserve any credit—I had no difficulty. People boast about being graduates and Ph.D.'s, as if they had conquered the Himalayas. I never prepared for any exam."

You could feel his naïve delight and wonder at not having had to make an effort.

His relationships with his schoolmates were equally effortless. The only thing that seems to have made him suffer was the physical inferiority, almost infirmity, caused by his asthma. But he had so many compensating virtues that the more intelligent of his schoolmates forgot it.

He said himself he had had a great luck with his classmates at the Lycée Condorcet in Paris. Even if he judged some rather severely for what they had become later, he admitted:

"When I think of it, Céleste, we were a nice little band."

He proudly listed names; all became well known or even famous since: Léon Blum, head of the Socialists, and his brother René, a celebrated lawyer; others who would become writers, like Henri Barbusse, Fernand Gregh, Robert de Flers, and Pierre de Lasalle; Leon Brunschvicg, who became a professor of philosophy; the future minister Paul Bénazet and the future ambassador Maurice Herbette; not to mention Jacques Bizet—"*Carmen*'s son," as M. Proust called him.

This little band met almost every day, when the weather was good, and in any case on Thursday afternoons to play amid the trees in the Champs-Elysées. There were some little girls too, like the Faure sisters.

"Our games were very bourgeois," he said. "Nowadays people would think us as stiff as people in their Sunday clothes."

And then at Illiers there was the place belonging to his father's family, where he went for the holidays and which he made into Combray in his book. You could see he had marvelous memories of this—like a cloudless sky, a paradise where everything began.

"I think it was there, Céleste, that I got into the habit of observing things."

He spoke about this like someone who has gone blind but who

had so treasured and guarded in his memory all the details of what he saw before that he can bring them to life again better than a medium. He used to tell me about the family garden in Illiers, named the Pré Catelan after the little park in the Bois de Boulogne in Paris. In the garden was a stream with a pretty little bridge over it. He told me about the trees and plants, the path by the hawthorns; how transported he was when, about Easter, the hedge seemed just one bush covered with flowers; about the village, the peasants, the church, the colors, the scents.

"You had to go through Chartres to get there," he said, "with the great plain all around and the cathedral like a clock face without hands. It had no need to show the hours. It measured eternity."

The two things he liked best were going for drives with his uncle in his gig and shutting himself up in the little pavilion in the Pré Catelan to read or write. It was there, he said, that he started to sketch out his first book, *Les plaisirs et les jours,* which he published nearly fifteen years later, in 1896, when he was twenty-five.

He was twelve or thirteen when Professor Proust decided that the climate of Illiers didn't agree with his son's asthma, that he needed a more bracing air. After that he spent his holidays in Dieppe or Cabourg with his maternal grandmother, the one who spoke like a book.

One day when I asked him if he'd been back to Illiers since, he said:

"No, never."

"Why not, monsieur?"

"Because the only place where you can regain lost paradises, Céleste, is in yourself."

I think one of the first times he referred to his youth was early in the war, when he told me about his military service as if it were a good joke. It amused me too:

"How on earth did they come to take you, monsieur? It's hard to see you as a recruit!"

"They didn't *take* me, Céleste; I volunteered. If you volunteered before your year was called up, you had to do only a year. The Chamber of Deputies had just then passed a law abolishing voluntary service, which meant I would have to serve three years. But I anticipated the law, before it was put into effect.''

He didn't conceal the fact that his father's connections had helped. This was in 1889, when he was eighteen. He was drafted into the infantry at Orléans.

"It was not too bad on the whole," he said. "But I admit my life as a soldier was rather unusual. Surprisingly enough, I kept quite well and felt no ill effects from the drill—though it is true I was exempted from the most tiring and violent ones. But I did ride on horseback. I didn't sleep in the barracks; I had a civilian billet despite the regulations. I used to be invited to the prefect's house. One evening I was dining with a captain and he offered to put me up for the night. When I got into the guest room I found the bed hadn't been made up—there was just a pile of sheets and blankets. I was annoyed because I had never made a bed, and I got myself all entangled with the sheets. I ended up sleeping on the bare mattress.''

When he left the army his mother put his uniform carefully away in a box, which he still had in the wardrobe. He asked me to get it out and showed me the uniform, made to measure and very smart.

"You must have looked just like a cadet from Saint-Cyr!" I said.

He was delighted.

Long before entering military service he had already begun the social life that so displeased his father and that he afterward resumed with more enthusiasm than ever. He called it his "camellia buttonhole" period.

From what he told me it was clear he wanted to make his entry into a different world, a world both intellectual and elegant, and this was partly out of a desire to win friends and use his charm and partly because he was already anxious to observe people.

"The people my parents knew were one thing," he said. "With

my father in the position he was, it was the circle of an eminent doctor and his eminent colleagues, together with prominent patients. But I wanted to get to know society people, the cream of what was called the 'Faubourg Saint-Germain.'"

His schoolmates at the Lycée, who included noblemen and sons of upper-middle-class families, were a great help to him and no doubt influenced his taste in this.

"The main thing is to gain admission," he said. "After that it just builds up on its own."

When he was still quite young he was introduced into the salon of M. and Mme. Alphonse Daudet and made friends with Mme. Daudet and her two sons, Léon and Lucien, who adored him and remained his friends forever. He thought Mme. Daudet very refined and cultivated.

"Like my mother, she was in a way an ambassadress for her husband. She was also a marvelous nurse: he was dying of a disease of the spinal cord. Alphonse Daudet himself used to grumble into his beard: 'My dear, your little Marcel has too much influence on our sons—he has too much influence everywhere he goes.' He didn't mean it too seriously; he just thought Léon and Lucien admired me too much, which was quite flattering. I was told he also said, 'That Marcel is a demon. He always has an answer.'"

He was very proud of his admission into the salons because he managed it all on his own.

"Even Mother couldn't have introduced me into that sort of society."

For him, it was a series of victories.

He was very conscious of his charm and said that his eyes and complexion, together with the winning and attentive manner of a young, cherubic page, captivated the ladies. And he didn't conceal that he was a little in love with all of them too. It was natural, at his age, but I think a stronger reason still was the need to know he was able to please.

I listened as if to a fairy tale. It was only later, when he let me into the secret of his characters and portraits, that I began to realize that he had been storing material up for years, first as a child and even more as a young man. It was as if he had a presentiment that all this would be the material for his work.

At first I didn't see this genesis. He gave me the clue to it later, bit by bit, as I shall show. All I saw for the moment was the story.

When he talked to me about this period, he did so sometimes in his room and sometimes in the small salon. In both rooms he kept souvenirs: in the bedroom, photographs and all sorts of objects in the chest; in the small salon he kept books.

Sometimes, when he came home, instead of asking me to go into the bedroom he'd say:

"Let's go into the small salon, Céleste. Not for long—just for a moment."

Of course we stayed for hours.

On one wall of the salon was the portrait of him by Jacques-Emile Blanche, dating from the "camellia buttonhole" period. The portrait exercised a sort of fascination over him. Often, as he was talking to me, he would look at it as if seeing himself in a mirror as he was then. The first time he showed it to me he said:

"Do you notice anything strange about it?"

"I don't know, monsieur. All I see is the pearly complexion and the look of a young Oriental prince."

"Well, once I introduced you to a Marcel Proust with untidy hair and no beard, and now I show you him with no beard and no legs either."

Laughing, he told me it had started off as a full-length portrait, but Jacques-Emile Blanche had asked him to lend the picture for an exhibition, and when he sent it back the legs were gone.

"He must have thought that I would show more wit that way!"

When we went into the small salon I didn't remain standing, as in the bedroom. He would sit in one armchair, in front of the bookcase so as to have the books within reach, and I'd sit in another, a little to one side. He would take a book and read me a passage, leafing through the pages and stopping only at what concerned him at the moment. From the way he summarized what came afterward I could tell he knew their contents inside out. The readings always had to do with some idea he was developing or the wish to summon up some memory. I was just an excuse for him to speak his thoughts or his memories aloud and try them out on me.

For example, one day he took down the works of Renan, author of the *Life of Jesus*. He ran his fingers over the covers, shook his head, and said, sighing:

"When I think of it, Céleste—I was still hardly more than a boy . . ." (as far as I can gather, he was about eighteen) " . . . whatever could have made me set off with my *Life of Jesus, Apostles,* and *Origins of Christianity* under my arm and go and ask the old priest to sign them for me?"

He did an imitation of himself with the three books under his arm, his head flung back and his eyes full of daring. Then he opened the books and showed me the dedications.

"This is his writing. What do you think of it?"

"Those huge letters—it's like a child's."

"There is something in what you say, Céleste. There was that element in him. Anyway, he was very nice to me and seemed pleased and almost proud of my youth. That old Breton in his cassock! Do you know why he gave up the frock? He was defrocked by then. He did it because he no longer believed in what he had to profess. He had come to wonder who Christ was, and even if he ever really existed. He had gone to the Holy Land with his sister, who loved him almost like a mother, and she caught some illness there and died. Perhaps that had something to do with his coming back and saying he didn't believe in all he had seen. But listen to what he wrote, Céleste. Even if he had lost his faith, this is what he wrote about death: 'Teach me to understand it more so that I may fear it less.' That is the sort of thing I would like to have written, and I think that must have been why I went to see the old unbeliever, still wrapped in his cassock."

He always re-created the scene when he talked about people, and then added his own comments.

151

I remember the portrait he drew of Mme. Lemaire, who had a very popular salon during La Belle Epoque and was one of his models for Mme. Verdurin in his book, who also has a bourgeois salon. She lived in rue Monceau, in the same part of Paris as the Prousts. All the most prominent aristocrats thronged to Mme. Lemaire's salon because many of her friends were artists and it was fashionable then to rub shoulders with them. She was a painter herself.

"I wish you had seen her, Céleste! She was charming and imposing at the same time. She painted mostly roses, so many of them and so fast that Count de Montesquiou said, 'The only one who has painted more roses than she has is God.' And she was always dressed informally, with her hair barely combed, as if there was no such thing as a day of rest for her."

She looked on "little Marcel" almost as a son, as the brother of her daughter Suzette, who was very pretty and sweet but terribly tyrannized by her mother, according to M. Proust. Mme. Lemaire had a beautiful country house, the château de Réveillon, at Seine-et-Marne, and she entertained there as well as in Paris. M. Proust said he had spent two of the most marvelous months of his youth there, with Suzette, Reynaldo Hahn, and others who came to Mme. Lemaire's parties.

She was inclined to be domineering. According to M. Proust, when she held a concert in her studio among the palms and the flowers, real and painted, you almost expected her to climb on a chair and call for silence. She wouldn't put up with the slightest noise. M. Proust agreed with her about this, but laughed at her method of keeping her guests quiet. She was a woman of decision, too. I remember one night—it must have been toward the end of the 1914 war—he asked me to fetch her to help him verify some detail for his work. I pointed out how late it was, but he said:

"Don't worry, Céleste; she will come right away, you will see. You will find her in a negligee as usual, but she will leap up immediately, and she will put on some lipstick when she is in the cab. But you will see what a great lady she is!"

It turned out as he had said. I found her in her home in rue Monceau, sitting in the dark in front of the fire with Suzette, and no sooner had I delivered the message than she jumped up, and said, "Come along, quickly!" And she made herself up in the cab.

One of the earliest salons he frequented, apart from that of the Alphonse Daudets, was Mme. Arman de Caillavet's in avenue Hoche. She was the jealous and possessive mistress of Anatole France, and her husband, when he came into the room unexpectedly during one of her receptions, would shake hands with the guests and say, "I am not Anatole France, I am only the master of the house!" M. Proust was more severe than M. de Caillavet on Anatole France:

"He was selfish and supercilious. He had read so much that he had left his heart in other people's books, and all that remained was dryness. One day I asked him how he came to know so much. He said, 'Not by being such a handsome young man as you. I wasn't in demand, and instead of going out I studied and learned.'"

But I think the most important of these ladies for M. Proust was Mme. Straus, who had been the widow of Georges Bizet. After all, he put her into his book as a duchess—there's much of her in the character of the Duchess de Guermantes, even if she wasn't the only model—and Mme. Lemaire and Mme. de Caillavet only appear as members of the bourgeoisie.

Between Mme. Straus and M. Proust there was a friendship that lasted till death. On M. Proust's side, when he was a young man, and even later, before I knew him, there was more than friendship—there was a great affection, although he was too delicate to say anything definite about it. But I could tell from the way he used to ask me to bring him her photograph out of the drawer. It showed her in her widow's weeds, before she became Mme. Straus. He would look at it for a long while.

"Heavens, Céleste, how beautiful she was beneath those veils!"

She was much older than he was, of course, being the mother of Jacques Bizet, who'd been at school with him. But he had an immense devotion and admiration for her, and one could guess what he must have felt for her, first as an adolescent and then, more strongly, later. This was plain from the sadness with which he used to give me back the picture:

"Heavens, how she has changed!"

From what he said, she had a rare esteem and admiration for him too, even when he was a boy, and she was very fond of him. But she never lost sight of the difference in their ages.

He went to her dinners and parties as much to see her as for the pleasure of meeting writers, painters, musicians, and members of the aristocracy. Among her guests were Paul Bourget, Charles Gounod, Jules Renard, the designer Jean-Louis Forain, and Degas—and also Countess de Chevigné and Countess Greffulhe, who helped to inspire his Guermantes, and Charles Haas, who is partly Swann.

"Ah Céleste, Charles Haas! He was the son of a stockbroker. And because of his heroism in the war of 1870, the only Jew apart from the Rothschilds allowed to become a member of the Jockey Club. He seemed to put everything—money, time, thought, yes, everything—into the art of pleasing the ladies. And naturally he had his reward. They adored him. But what distinction, what brilliance! And what a dandy! I can see him now with his gray topper lined with green!"

As well as going to her dinners and receptions, M. Proust often used to call on Mme. Straus and spend evenings with her by the fire. M. Straus was usually there, muttering unpleasantly. It irritated him to hear his wife talking about Georges Bizet, with whom she'd been very much in love—all the more so as her father had done—unsuccessfully—everything he could to stop them from marrying. M. Proust irritated him still more, and from what he said I could tell the feeling was mutual.

"You should have seen him when we were sitting by the fire. He couldn't bear his wife to call me her 'dear little Marcel'—when she wrote to me, her letters always began, 'My dearest little Marcel.' He would fidget in his chair, get up, walk about, sit down again, pick up the tongs and poke at the fire, then throw them down with a clatter. Madame Straus would say, 'Emile, please!' and he would grumble, 'My dear Geneviève, you will tire yourself talking and sitting up so late.' Then I would start to get up. 'Forgive me, madame, the pleasure of your company makes me take advantage of your kindness. I really ought to go.' But she would say, 'Please, my dear little Marcel, don't take any notice. Emile, leave us alone!' And all Monsieur Straus could do was bang about with the tongs again."

As far as I remember, M. Proust saw the Strauses much less frequently than earlier during the years I was with him. But he and Mme. Straus wrote to each other very often—long letters. I delivered several of them myself.

"Don't forget to go in if it is convenient for her to see you, Céleste. Then you can tell me how she is," he would say.

She called several times at boulevard Haussmann while I was there, when she came to see Dr. Williams, the American dentist on the next floor. She'd ring at the bell and ask me how M. Proust was. But she never came farther than the hall, and M. Proust never had her in—she never asked to come in, either. She was still immensely attractive, although her features had somewhat thickened and were sagging and her face twitched with nervous tics. I'm almost sure the reason they saw each other less frequently then was M. Proust's sigh: "Heavens, how she has changed!"

Countess Greffulhe was another lady M. Proust greatly admired. But between the Countess and him there was never the same remarkable intellectual intimacy as he had with Mme. Straus. With Countess Greffulhe it was mainly a question of encounters in public and the satisfaction of the eye. She was a Caraman-Chimay, who to save her family, which was almost ruined, had married the Count for his huge fortune. Her guests included the cream of the Faubourg Saint-Germain and of the Jockey Club and diplomatic corps, and when M. Proust talked about her it was mainly in terms of the relationships between princes and princesses, dukes and duchesses, and parties and receptions such as have never been seen since the 1914 war and never will be. He spoke of a whole society and way of life that was disappearing then and is now gone forever.

He told me of the incredible luxury, the servants, flowers,

paintings, chandeliers, gowns, jewels, and how all the streets were full of carriages letting out or waiting for guests.

"It was unbelievably magnificent, Céleste. But sometimes, what eccentricities . . .!"

He would evoke it all, though there were some things he didn't approve of.

"One evening a man came to one of Mme. Straus's dinner parties with a pet monkey in a stiff shirt and complete evening dress. Apart from the fact that I don't care for animals, it was in extremely bad taste. And once at a costume ball at Mme. Greffulhe's, four of her forty-five servants, in full livery, drove around in little carts drawn by two lion cubs. I thought that was going a bit far too. And although the lion cubs were supposed to be tame, that didn't stop them from chewing up the concierge's arm the next day."

But there is no doubt that he had a very soft spot for Mme. Greffulhe.

"I can admit it now, Céleste," he said one night. "I believe I was conquered the very first time I set eyes on her. She had such breeding, such class, such presence, and such a marvelous way of carrying her head. The way she wore a bird of paradise in her hair. Unique!"

His nimble hands imitated the graceful pose of the bird on the piled-up coiffure.

"It was innate in her, and in her alone," he said. "I don't know how many times I went to the opera just to admire the way she went up the staircase. I just stood there and watched for her. To see her pass by, with her graceful neck and the bird looking as if it had alighted on her head by itself, it was sheer pleasure."

But apart from some receptions to which he was invited at her house, and various meetings at parties and weddings, he didn't see much of the countess. This was largely due to the jealousy of the count, who made no secret that he disliked M. Proust and did not wish his wife to see him.

But M. Proust had his revenge, and in a way that highly amused him.

It so happened that Count Greffulhe flung himself at the feet of another lady, Countess de la Béraudière. She, with the most honorable of intentions, was at the feet of M. Proust and didn't know what to do to make him interested. What happened came much later, at a time when I was already at boulevard Haussmann. It was revenge served up cold, so to speak.

You should have heard M. Proust coming in one night and saying to me, with an ironical gleam in his eye:

"Come here and listen, Céleste. I have solved the mystery of Count Greffulhe."

His comment was:

"How could anyone with a queen like Countess Greffulhe at home go off to see someone like Madame de la Béraudière, who has none of her refinement, nobility, culture, elegance, or beauty. And yet that is what he does. Apparently he is crazy about his Béraudière. How amusing!"

Knowing him as I did, I could tell he wouldn't leave it at that. And sure enough, all of a sudden one day he had no time for anybody but Mme. de la Béraudière. Whereas for years, I gathered, he'd more or less been fending her off, now he wanted to get to know her. He asked me to telephone to see if he could visit her, and she agreed. Then one night he came home delighted. He'd got what he'd wanted.

"Come in quickly, dear Céleste. . . . As you know, I was at Countess de la Béraudière's this evening. Well, who do you think was there? Count Greffulhe! You should have seen him writhing in his chair when I was shown in!"

He allowed himself that pleasure several times, over two or three months. He told me again and again, laughing, how charming Mme. de la Béraudière had been to him. And then, when both his desire for revenge and his curiosity were satisfied, it was all over— he didn't see her again. But when he told me the result of these evenings, his eyes sparkled, and he still seemed to be manipulating people just as he wanted to.

Strangely enough, although I saw him now as a recluse, I had no difficulty imagining him at the time of the camellias: he enjoyed himself so much, and became young again, as he told me about it. But when he talked about the Club in rue Royale, where all the dandies met, and then I went to open the door to the Duke de Guiche or the Duke d'Albuféra, instead of finding the brilliant, amusing, carefree young men he'd described, I was shocked to see them with gray hair. The others had grown older, while he had not.

But I remember that when he told me about a duel he'd had at that time with the writer Jean Lorrain, over a malicious article Lorrain had written on his work, I couldn't help saying:

"I can't believe it, monsieur! I can't see you shooting at someone with a revolver!"

"Why not?"

"You seem so timid and gentle."

"I could not get out of it, Céleste. It was the thing to do."

"Like flowers at All Saints'?"

He laughed.

"I know you don't like disagreeable remarks," I said, "just from the stern way you throw out your chest when you tell me about them. But from that to guns and swords! Don't tell me you actually went."

"Of course I did."

"And did your mother know?"

"Yes."

"She must have been terribly upset!"

"Yes. Poor Mother! She didn't want me to go. Nor did several other ladies. But I had been insulted, and no one had prompted me—it was I who wanted the duel. Jean Lorrain was jealous because of a preface Anatole France had written for *Les plaisirs et les jours*. Lorrain claimed it was just a polite gesture to a young man-about-town with literary ambitions. We exchanged bullets in the forest of Meudon early in the morning. It was only serious in theory."

Then he added ironically: "Everyone said I had been 'very brave,' though I had been foolish enough to say in a letter that I had wept in the hours leading up to the duel. Of course I also wrote, but I am not a coward."

At the time I knew him, he was at a point where, rejuvenated though he was by his memories, he spoke with a certain nostalgia about that period.

"Ah Céleste," he sighed, "all that is crumbling to dust. It is like a collection of beautiful antique fans on a wall. You admire them, but there is no hand now to bring them alive. The very fact that they are under glass proves that the ball is over."

Often, after he'd been talking about something, a sudden sadness would extinguish the pleasure of remembering. It was like that the time he told me a story about the writer Georges de Porto-Riche, who was a frequent visitor at Mme. Straus's.

"He was a very eager ladies' man. Once he was so proud of being in love with a young dancer, he went for a pedicure and then proclaimed to anyone who cared to listen, 'How pleased she'll be to see my little feet tonight!' The dancer was not the only one. Madame de Porto-Riche knew about it too, and she, in her turn, told everyone, 'I won't have had my husband young, but I shall have his old age.' In those days, Céleste, I laughed like all the rest. But now—I must admit it makes me sad. I think, 'Poor woman, she never had her husband either young or old.'"

13 Monsieur Proust (on the right) and his brother Robert. He kept this picture in his room and he would say to me, "Doesn't it look like I'm protecting my little sister?"

14 Proust's father, Professor Adrien Proust.
Photograph by Paul Nadar.

15 Madame Proust.

16 Madame Proust's mother, Adèle Weil, the grandmother who, according to Monsieur Proust, "spoke as if she were literature."

17 Madame Proust's father, Nathée Weil.

18 His childhood vacation house at Illiers. His bedroom window is behind the tree.

19 This is him, "a little prince," which is what I said to him when he showed me this picture and then gave it to me. This picture was his grandmother's favorite. She was the one who had it framed in "the fleur-de-lys of renown," as I also said to him.

20 Left: Monsieur Proust, wearing the boater, at the parc Monceau with Antoinette Faure, the daughter of the future president of the Republic. They remained friends all their lives. Madame Proust and Madame Faure at one point discussed their getting married.

21 Below: Monsieur Proust in his philosophy class at the Lycée Condorcet (1888–89). He's the first on the left in the second row.

22 Friends on a country outing, including Monsieur Proust, standing in the middle wearing a boater, and his father, professor Adrien, seated at right in the bowler.

23 Top left: Monsieur
Proust during his mili-
tary service in 1890,
in his handsome
uniform cut, as I told
him, in the style of
the military academy
at Saint-Cyr.

24 Top right:
Madame Proust and
her two sons, Marcel
(left) and Robert. They
are in mourning after
the death of their
father.

25 Monsieur Proust at 21.

26 The "camellia
boutonniere" period,
when Monsieur Proust
went out to the salons
all the time.

27 The last photograph
of him alive, age 51 in
1922, on the day when
he went to the Orangerie
to see "Vermeer's little
section of yellow wall"
one more time.

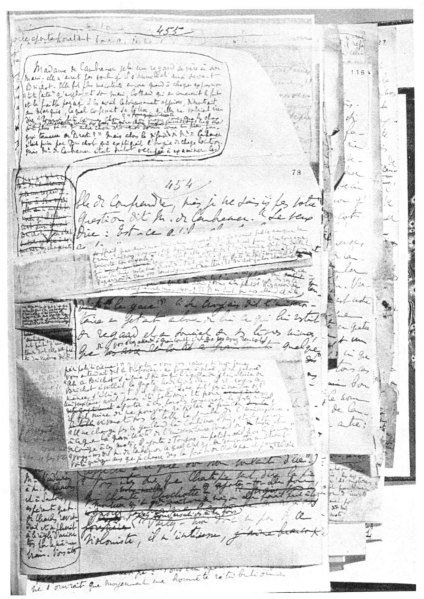

28 The manuscript of *Sodom and Gomorrah*. When the margins were full, the only thing to do was to paste on little slips of paper. It was my idea. It even got so I could read his handwriting backwards!

14

THE FAMILY

If, during those last years that I knew him, he wasn't very eager to see the *haute monde* again, the explanation really was that, like his childhood at Illiers, it was a lost paradise which he knew he could find again only within himself.

There was the same sort of distance between him and his family. All his affection was in memory. There were some cousins at Illiers—three, I believe—who sometimes sent his brother, Robert, fruit from the garden of the house where they spent their holidays. But M. Proust never saw these cousins. Once I was bold enough to say:

"I can't make it out, monsieur. All your father's family came from there and you used to be so fond of them all. Even if you did have asthma at Illiers, your cousins are not going to bring it with them."

"I can't, Céleste," he said. "I am ill and my life is too complicated. You know very well I don't see anyone."

"That's exaggerating a little, monsieur!"

"Yes, but why should I see them? They are very nice. Robert sees them now and again. He told me just the other day that one of them had looked in on him to say hello. But I have neither the time nor the strength."

I could see it was a subject he preferred to avoid. As always in such cases, the explanation emerged indirectly. Gradually I came to realize that the two sides of the family had drifted apart. There was no quarrel or decisive break or even discussion about it; the two sides just grew apart, covering the fact to avoid any clash. The various deaths only made the separation wider.

I have a very clear recollection of how one day, when he'd been telling me about the marvelous sympathy and understanding between his mother and father, he said:

"Father adored Illiers, and Mother was not the sort of woman to stand in the way. She went because she loved him too much to let him think for a moment that it bored her, still less that she disliked going at all. But he loved her too much not to suspect the truth, though he didn't let on. So one year the air at Illiers suddenly became very bad for my asthma. Father said so, and we didn't go there again."

From other things he told me I gathered that the mother's and the father's families were very different, and this was one of the factors in their drifting apart.

You might suppose at first it was a matter of the difference in religion. Professor Proust's father and mother, and his sister Elisabeth—the one who became Tante Léonie in the books—were devout Catholics. As I've said, the professor himself nearly became a priest. And Mme. Proust's family, the Weils, were Jews. But that wasn't the real problem. The Prousts weren't intolerant, and they had raised no objection to their son's marriage. As in many such cases, it was merely agreed that the children should be brought up as Catholics, and that's how it was for both the sons. M. Proust was taught his catechism by an abbé. He often told me about it, with amusement.

"Mother used to take me herself and be present at the lessons. Sometimes she thought the abbé was a little too exacting, and then she would say, 'I think that will do, Monsieur l'abbé. Don't forget he is only a child.'"

Both he and his brother took their first communion, but he referred to it just with a vague gesture. Although he was usually so fond of describing how people were dressed, he never told me what he or his brother wore to their first communion, or whether there was a reception, or whether Félicie made a special cake. And he only went to church on public occasions, whereas his brother went regularly. One day he said, with a look that held a sort of distant astonishment:

"When Robert was here just now he said, 'Last Sunday at Saint-Philippe-du-Roule . . .' He still goes to Mass regularly. Isn't that strange?"

"Do you think so, monsieur?"

"I don't know. There are very devout people who do things *you* would never do, I am sure. What matters is loftiness of mind, conscience, honesty. And the greatest of virtues is charity. If only everyone's heart had charity!"

It was, then, a question of background rather than religion that separated the two families. Professor Proust's parents had kept a grocer's shop in Illiers and had worked their fingers to the bone to pay for their son's education. The mother was just as devoted as Mme. Proust was to her two sons later on: when the boy got a scholarship and went to study in Chartres, she went too, to look after him. The father died early, without knowing of all his son's successes, just like Professor Proust himself. When he had become a doctor and gone up in the world, the mother sold the grocery and retired, though she still lived in Illiers. Her daughter, Elisabeth— "Tante Léonie"—also lived there; she had married Jules Amiot, a local wine merchant. It was at the Amiots' house that Professor Proust and his wife and their two sons used to stay during the children's holidays. Jules Amiot was very rich and owned much land in Illiers and round about. But his wealth was nothing compared to that of the Weils, on Mme. Proust's side. And then the Amiots came from Illiers, a village in the provinces, whereas the Weils lived in Paris, the well-to-do Paris which became the Paris of Professor Proust too, with important connections, names, dinner parties, the theater, the high life.

In a nutshell, the Illiers family felt awkward with the Paris family. From what M. Proust told me about how his father's mother didn't attend her son's wedding to Mlle. Jeanne Weil, I could tell it wasn't because she disapproved but because she would have felt uncomfortable among the society people. The same applied to the Amiots and everyone else on the Proust side. They may have been wealthy in the country, but their life had nothing in common with the life the professor lived, any more than their house at Illiers could compare with the luxury of the big apartment in rue de Courcelles, or the villa at Auteuil belonging to Mme. Proust's uncle.

Mme. Proust probably had stronger family feelings than her husband, too. Not that he was lacking in filial affection. On the contrary, when his mother retired it was he who rented two rooms in Illiers, one of them a very fine room over a porch, near the church, so that she wouldn't have far to go to Mass. And he remained very attached to his sister, Elisabeth.

It wasn't for nothing M. Proust turned his Aunt Elisabeth into the Tante Léonie of his novel. She had been very important to him. It mustn't be forgotten that the entire *Recherche du temps perdu* starts with the memory of the madeleine she used to dunk into her lime tea and it is that that sets all the memory in motion.

"She was a character," he used to say.

You could tell from what he said that she was an ideal subject for his book. She married very young, and although she had three children he had never seen her except in bed.

"She was worse than I am. She didn't even get up and walk about the room any more."

She'd taken to her bed years before and never left it again. People thought she was a *malade imaginaire*, until she had an operation and died, and then it was evident she'd known she was ill and hadn't exaggerated. But M. Proust was very discreet about any illness in his family. Rebellion against the small-town life of Illiers might perhaps have been at the root of his aunt's illness. But he never talked about it.

Whether it was example or heredity or both, who knows. What's certain is that there was a great similarity and attraction between aunt and nephew. They were very fond of each other, and he made no secret that he was fascinated too.

"She was very pretty," he said, "but with a tyrannical compulsion to supervise everything from her bed. On Sunday, before going to Mass, you had to parade before her to show how you were dressed. She was always saying her rosary and reading her missal. And there was a little altar in her room, with a picture of the Virgin Mary. She was extremely devout and insisted that everyone else be devout too. She was exacting about everything. Her whole life was organized in that bedroom, right down to the visits of the curate. He would not dream of not coming on the appointed day and hour. But once he was there, she soon got tired of his conversation. Her nourishment consisted of a few medicines and some Vichy water, which she kept on the bedside table. The only other thing was the madeleine she dipped in her tea in the afternoon. I took part in this sacred repast. To see her there in bed you'd have thought she was a princess waited on hand and foot."

"Well, monsieur," I said. "I know a prince waited on hand and foot who likes to rule over everything from his bed."

He laughed. "Yes, but I don't tell my beads."

At Illiers he had the room next to his aunt's, and he used to spend hours with her.

"She made a great fuss over me. She sent for books, and we looked at them together. She bought a magic lantern too, and we would close the shutters and pull the curtains, and I felt as if I were in an enchanted castle in a fairy tale. I often used to stay in her room and listen when people came to see her. She had a regal way of complaining."

Once he said: "If I think of my mother on the one hand, and Aunt Elisabeth and grandmother Weil on the other, I see that the women of the family have played a very important part in my life. They all loved me, and I owe much of what I am now to them, mentally as well as in my habits."

The Weil side of the family was quite different.

"Mother's was a very united family. For the six years that my grandfather, Nathée Weil, lived on after his wife's death in 1890, my mother took the utmost care of him. She was in and out of his house all the time, and if he didn't lunch or dine with his brother, my great-uncle Louis Weil, he came to us. The bond between all of them was so close that when Great-Uncle Louis died in 1896, my grandfather followed him hardly over a month later; one went May 16 and the other on June 30. And when Mother left us in 1905, her brother Georges died of grief almost immediately afterward. He adored his sister and used to discuss everything with her, even his domestic affairs. He was a great reader and used to bring her books. When he realized Mother was dying, a strange thing happened: he disappeared and didn't come back until after the funeral. He didn't tell anyone he was going away, or where to. Obviously he couldn't bear the thought of losing her."

He asked me once what I thought of it and if I would be capable of such a thing.

"I don't know, monsieur. I think it is beautiful."

"Yes, but strange, don't you think? He lingered on for a year. Yes, it is very strange; they all departed like that because they couldn't bear the idea of being without one another."

He didn't talk very much about his grandfather Nathée, who was a stockbroker and lived in boulevard Poissonnière, except to say he was a character too—very bossy but very kind, despite his tyrannical insistence that his grandson should have a profession. He couldn't bear his little Marcel to be unhappy.

"I wish I were as infallible on the Stock Exchange as he was," M. Proust once said, laughing.

But the real character on that side of the family was Great-Uncle Louis, who was as infallible in business and industry as his brother was on the Stock Exchange. He, too, had amassed a large fortune, but he enjoyed it while he was alive, whereas his brother tended just to withdraw into his wealth.

The first time M. Proust mentioned his great-uncle to me was when I admired some cuff links he was wearing.

"They were left to me by my great-uncle Louis. He made them

himself in one of his factories. Do you know he had representatives all over the world?''

"Uncle Louis," as they called him, had a house at Auteuil, which was then on the outskirts of Paris. It was a big house with a large garden, which he had bought fully furnished from an artist.

"Everything was very expensive but rather ugly," said M. Proust. Uncle Louis liked things gaudy and ostentatious; as long as they were that, art didn't bother him.

One day, talking about this, M. Proust said: "That is rather Jewish, you know." He also told me: "He was as proud of his gig as if it were a coach. He had an extraordinary coachman called Auguste, who was also his valet and his butler and had to be impeccable in everything. When the carriage was waiting, Auguste had to sit still as a stone with his whip across his lap. And you can't imagine the way the table was set and the service! Just like the Grand Hôtel. But Auguste got his revenge in his own way. He tyrannized over Uncle Louis, too. Auguste's wife was the linen maid, and they had a daughter, and they were all so devoted to one another they couldn't bear to have anyone else around. But of course there had to be a cook. Every time my uncle engaged a cook, everything would be perfect for the first week. Uncle would help himself to something and say to Auguste with a wink, 'I think we've got a treasure this time.' And Auguste would answer, 'Yes, monsieur, I think so.' But after a week things would start to go wrong: too much salt, too much pepper, the roast mutton lukewarm, the gravy cold as ice. Uncle Louis would be furious. "Auguste, I'm going to send her packing, this can't go on!' 'No, monsieur. Monsieur is quite right. It can't go on.' Mother, with her shrewd eye, discovered what was happening. Auguste either dawdled as long as he could on his way from the kitchen, so that everything got cold, or deluged it in salt and pepper, which he kept in his pocket for the purpose.

There was tenderness in M. Proust's amusement when he told me these stories. You could see he'd been fond of Uncle Louis and that Uncle Louis had been fond of him.

At Auteuil, Uncle Louis kept open house and lived in high style. At first, from the stories M. Proust told me, I assumed he had never been married. Then one day, when I'd been tidying up the unused dining room at boulevard Haussmann—it contained, among other things,music sheets that had belonged to Mme.Proust and large frames piled against the walls, some of them with portraits. I told M. Proust I'd been intrigued by one of these portraits because I didn't recognize in it any of the people he'd told me about.

"If you don't mind my asking, monsieur, who is the lady in the big frame?"

"She was Uncle Louis' wife."

And he told me she had been rich and of German origin. Louis married her in Hamburg, and she died young, leaving him all her money.

If it hadn't been for that, I'd have thought from what I heard that he was a bachelor, and a very gay bachelor at that, not to say a rake. The luncheons and dinners at Auteuil were famous for the naughty and frivolous beauties one could meet there.

The Prousts went often to Auteuil, and Uncle Louis welcomed them with open arms. He was captivated by Mme. Proust's intelligence, the politeness and charming ways of "little Marcel," and by Professor Proust's fame. Mme. Proust was so fond of her uncle that she turned a blind eye where necessary; she wouldn't have given up those visits for the world.

"On the way home," M. Proust told me, "my parents used to laugh about Uncle Louis and his pretty girl friends. Sometimes, on the way there, Father would say, 'I wonder which cocotte he has found this time.' It was usually Father who joked. Mother, as always, gently played things down. And she knew well that Father didn't dislike it all as much as he would have people believe, and that I too, even as a child, and all the more so later, used my eyes."

You could see from his smile that his memory of all this was both ironic and affectionate.

But, like everything else, it was only a memory.

"It was a kind of perpetual gaiety. There was money, ease, joy of living, love of show. And then they started to die. It was all over. The curtain fell."

He pointed to the big blue curtains, which had belonged to Uncle Louis, and his hand dropped.

For M. Proust, all that was left of his family was his brother, Robert. The affection between them was still the affection of two boys, which their mother had cultivated. I know it's been said that M. Proust was jealous of his brother as a child and even later, because he usurped part of their mother's affection. I don't believe it; and even if it were true at a certain time, he wouldn't be the only one. I never saw any trace of jealousy in what he told me. At the most, like all children, they quarreled sometimes and threatened not to lend each other toys. And they soon developed quite different tastes: M. Proust had his very personal way of studying and his interest in society and literature; his brother preferred science and physical exercise and was very fond of sport.

What they had in common, inherited from their father, was an indefatigable capacity to concentrate and work. They merely chose different paths.

I think it took Robert Proust longer to appreciate M. Proust than it took the elder brother to be proud of the younger's scientific successes.

"You wouldn't believe what a clever student my brother was," M. Proust used to say. "He was a professor when he was thirty-two. During the war it was he who arranged for ambulances to be taken up to the front, so that the wounded could be operated on right away instead of dying from loss of blood. He is as devoted as my father was—you can't help admiring him. Even now he still goes on working. When he has finished his round he is half dead with fatigue, but his nurse just brings him a glass of water and a biscuit and he carries on. When he gets back from the hospital he eats when he has the chance, often alone, while writing, or with his books in front of him. He has put his heart and soul into his career. He lost a lot of blood when he was wounded at the front, and he was weak for a long time afterward. But he wouldn't stop. He said, 'My patients must not suffer because of what may happen to me.' "

But there came a time, well before the end, when Professor Robert did become very aware of his brother's merits. M. Proust told me more than once:

"Robert said, 'I saw so-and-so the other day, and he was talking to me about you. He wouldn't stop. He thinks your work is marvelous.' "

"And has your brother read it himself?" I asked.

"Dear Céleste, his patients have more time than he has. You can't live two lives at once. It is enough that he thinks, as dear Father used to do, that I may be a member of the Academy one day."

But they didn't see each other often. It was always Professor Robert who came to us. As soon as I said he was here, M. Proust would exclaim:

"Well, let him in!"

Once they had an appointment M. Proust would never ask me to give the excuse as he did for other people—that he was too tired. I have seen him put down his notebook with regret when his brother came, but a moment later he was pleased to see him.

Although M. Proust never spoke of it, I think it was chiefly the memory of their mother that still brought them together. She had implanted in them so deeply the feeling that they were brothers that it was as if she'd implanted the warmth of her own love, which sprang forth whenever they were together. I wasn't present at their conversations, but I heard about them afterward. They were generally long, and about memories which I suspect M. Proust wanted to verify. It was always, 'Do you remember, Robert?' and 'Do you remember, Marcel?' In a dedication for his brother in one of his books he wrote: 'In memory of the lost time of our childhood, found again each time we meet.' "

It was lovely to see them together, happy and laughing. Sometimes M. Proust would seek information on present-day matters; he asked his brother a lot of questions about the war, for instance, and

I'm sure they must have discussed medical problems. Professor Robert wrote books, like his father, and M. Proust read them. Similarly, he once asked his brother if he could visit his hospital. He was still very shaken when he told me about what happened. He'd gone by mistake into a lecture room.

"I saw legs on one side and arms on the other! And that table! I shut the door and rushed away."

One thing characterized their relationship: for his brother, M. Proust had to a certain extent taken their mother's place. He made it plain he was the elder. But how skillfully he did it! He had the wisdom never to run slap into things; he was so careful at leading up to them. He would examine a situation without seeming to, and then, when the right moment came:

"Why do you see that man so often? For your work? For company? Do you really think that's the sort of person you ought to be mixing with?"

Almost every time it ended with: "Do you think Mother would approve if she were here?"

And afterward he was so pleased to be able to tell me: "Robert admitted I was right."

He had his own way of running things. For example, Professor Robert was crazy about his daughter Suzy, who is now Mme. Mante-Proust; and when he came he used to talk to M. Proust about her. M. Proust would take the opportunity to ask about how she was being raised:

"Do you think she is being brought up as Mother would have wished?"

And I remember that on one of their visits to Paris the Schiffs were very taken with Suzy too and wanted to take her with them to England. M. Proust had great respect and friendship for the Schiffs, but he intervened.

"The Schiffs are very nice," he said to me. "But I don't see why my niece should go to stay with them. She is still too young to travel or to live with strangers."

In matters of education, he was for the old methods of authority tempered with mildness. The same day he said:

"Mother was sweetness itself with us. But I assure you when she said something she meant it."

He was very fond of his niece but saw little of her. His timetable could hardly be made to fit in with that of a child. He saw her most during the war. Sometimes she came with her mother in the evening after dinner, when Mme. Robert Proust had news of her husband at the front. Suzy was then twelve or thirteen. Even when she was older and we'd moved to rue Hamelin, he never saw her again in his own place. But he wrote her very affectionate letters, and I remember one day he wanted to give her a present. He sent me to a well-known jeweler's in the Faubourg Saint-Honoré to get her a sewing box. I can still see it—a pale blue case. The present was a great success.

The fact is he didn't care much for children—which is strange when you think how he had an almost religious feeling for his own childhood.

"I like looking at children," he used to say, "but not spending time with them."

And about his niece: "She is very pretty with her curly hair, and she is dressed simply. I like that."

When I think now of the desert all around him, and I hear again the echo of those nights, I think, "What loneliness! And what strength of mind to have chosen it, and, having chosen it, to have endured it!"

15

FIRST LOVES

Sometimes in the depths of the night I'd ask him:

"How is it you didn't get married, monsieur? You'd have made such a kind husband, so sensitive and thoughtful, and your children would have been so clever and well brought up."

"My dear Céleste," he'd say, "you know very well I am not clever. And anyway, cleverness doesn't help. They say clever people have stupid children."

"How can you say such a thing, monsieur? Your father certainly wasn't stupid, and his two children are far from being so!"

He would laugh as if pleased. One night he said:

"It is strange that you of all people should say I ought to have married, for you know and understand me better than anyone. So come, my dear Céleste, you must realize I am not made for marriage. I ask you: What would I have done with a wife who wanted to go to tea parties and dressmakers'? She would have dragged me everywhere and into everything: I wouldn't have been able to write. No, Céleste, I have to have peace and quiet. I am married to my work. All that matters is my writing."

Another time he joked: "I would have needed a wife who understood me, and as I know only one woman in the world who does, the only person I could have married is you."

"What an idea!"

"Yes, but you are best still at replacing Mother."

Yet another night, when he was talking to me for perhaps the hundredth time about the harmony that existed between his parents, I asked him if he made a distinction between platonic and physical love. He gazed at me intently, then answered:

"I don't know what you mean."

I saw that was all the answer I was going to get.

But I remember one evening when Jacques Porel called in to say hello on his way home. He was the son of the famous actress Réjane, M. Proust's great favorite and the rival of Sarah Bernhardt. M. Proust himself had only just come in. Jacques Porel had his young wife with him. She was very pretty and wore a deep décolletage which left her back almost bare. Her husband insisted on her twirling around in front of M. Proust to show off her beauty.

"I don't understand Monsieur Porel," M. Proust said to me after they'd gone. "He admires his wife, but he wants everyone to know it and to see how pretty she is. Making her show off her back like that! It wouldn't take much for him to exhibit her naked. If *I* admired a woman I wouldn't talk about it and want others to admire her too—no, I would keep her to myself."

And I remember saying to him, another time: "You're so kind and loving and affectionate in your ways, you must have been able to choose anyone you wanted. It's impossible not to love you."

"Perhaps I was too demanding," he said. "Or too spoiled."

And after that, silence.

As a matter of fact, I don't think he had ever really been in love with anyone. He went too deeply into people's souls, including his own. He saw all their facets too clearly; none was ever left in the dark.

But he never forgot anything. The chest of drawers contained not only photographs of his mother and of friends and relations but also pictures of women he'd known and sometimes admired, and various souvenirs, including some pieces of jewelry. He often asked me to get them for him. But it was chiefly in his memory that he rummaged. Then you could see that his thoughts were following a kind of underground track, as if he were organizing everything into images before putting them into words. His eyes became motionless, and I said nothing, waiting for him to return from his internal journey.

There were certainly some memories he didn't want to stir up, perhaps because when I knew him they'd already been buried too long or perhaps because he'd finished studying and sorting them out. I think this applies to some of the romances of his youth.

For example, he didn't seem keen on talking about Marie de Benardaky, a Polish girl, though he told me he'd been very much in love with her when he was about fourteen or fifteen and still used to go and play in the Champs-Elysées. She was slightly younger than he was, with masses of black hair; in winter she wore a fur toque that was very becoming. I don't know if he ever had a photograph of her; there wasn't one in the chest of drawers. It may be that at the time he built a whole adolescent romance about this fancy, for he told me:

"I was madly in love with her."

But he said it with a smile, not sadly. Even if, as has been said, he was in such despair when Mme. Proust decided they shouldn't go on playing together that he thought of throwing himself off his parents' balcony on boulevard Malesherbes, his feelings were very different now, and the memory seemed quite peaceful. I gathered, too, that at the time he himself hadn't been too keen on his young friend's parents: the mother was reputed to have a weakness for adventures and champagne. Even if Marie de Benardaky contributed something toward the young Gilberte Swann in the book, he also added traits belonging to many others for whom he'd felt the natural impulses of youth, or whom he'd observed in later years, such as Antoinette Faure, for whom he felt no more than friendship, and the Lemaire girl, with whom, at the most, he flirted a little, as they say nowadays.

About his youthful romances he himself said: "It was rather a case of fluttering from one to another."

One of his school friends, Horace Finaly, who came from a family of wealthy bankers, had a sister Marie who was very pretty and intelligent, with sea-green eyes. She was one of the young girls in flower M. Proust used to know when he was about twenty and studying law in Paris, and they all used to meet at the seaside in Normandy in the summer and visit village churches or go for drives through the fields and orchards. There was certainly affection between the two of them—he told me he used to recite Baudelaire to her: "I love the green light of your long eyes"—but as far as I could make out it expressed itself chiefly in talk about ideas and literature. Later, Marie Finaly married, but he never spoke about this as if it were painful to him. When she died in the Spanish influenza epidemic toward the end of the war, M. Proust was very upset but mainly because his Horace was so grieved. As for saying, as some have, that it was she who furnished the character of Albertine—there again, it was a mixture: a bit of this one and a bit of that, and the rest M. Proust was quite capable of imagining without help from anyone else.

His "fluttering" included one of his mother's maids, another Marie, who was very pretty, he told me, and by whom he was greatly smitten. It was she who made the red satin quilt which he never used and which he asked me to give to Céline to keep Nicolas Cottin warm in the hospital during the war. I believe he thought it was hideous—for himself, at any rate.

"Poor Marie," he said. "She put all that work and care into it— 'I know how easily chilled you are,' she said sweetly. But Mother had her suspicions—nothing escaped her—and dismissed her. Yes, poor Marie—she was actually very sweet."

He remembered her with affection, and the feeling was reciprocal. Even in my days she went on faithfully writing to him, and although he never said anything about it I think he was so touched by her devotion all those years that if I'd left, or he hadn't found me, Marie was marked down in his memory and he would probably have sent for her.

Another thing that strikes me when I think of him and the way he used to say "I was madly in love with her" is the tremendous energy he must have put into these romances. No doubt that's what he meant when he said he was "too demanding." As in everything else, he had to have immediately whatever he wanted, like a spoiled child. I remember how surprised I was when he told me how one day he looked through a shop window and saw a very pretty girl working in a dairy. Without the slightest hesitation he went and bought some flowers, gave them to her, and asked her outright if she'd go out with him that evening.

"I was snubbed," he said, laughing. "She wouldn't hear of it, and I was very angry and disappointed. But I left her the flowers!"

I was so astonished, thinking of how respectfully he always treated me, I couldn't help exclaiming:

"You did that, monsieur? You are always so distant!"

He laughed all the louder. "Ah yes, Céleste, but I could be impulsive once!"

From what he told me, there was one time when he really thought of getting married—actually *wanted* to, for here again I'm sure there were other fleeting impulses. But in this one case, he told me, it was really serious.

Many books about him have embroidered on this, talking about a "mysterious girl" who was supposed to have always haunted him.

He was very reticent about this subject but didn't hide the fact that he'd very much wanted to marry this girl and that his mother had been absolutely against it.

"I was very taken with her," he said, "and finally I told Mother. She reacted violently. 'Marcel! Please! Not *her!*'"

I gathered that Mme. Proust's main objection was that the girl wouldn't make a good housekeeper, at least as Mme. Proust understood it. Be that as it may, M. Proust ended his account by saying:

"Whether Mother was right or not, Céleste, at least she wasn't wrong."

He never mentioned the girl's name, and I never knew it. Nor were there any photographs of her in the drawer. But as usual I was able to unravel the mystery gradually, through allusions. One day he said:

"Her grandfather was an officer." And another time: "We used to see each other at Uncle Louis', at Auteuil."

177

Putting two and two together—and I know him, I know he enjoyed setting riddles for me, so I'm not betraying his confidence in saying all this—I finally worked it out that the girl was a cousin, the great-niece of his great-uncle Louis Weil.

Grandfather Nathée and Great-Uncle Louis had had a brother, Abraham Alphonse Weil, who retired from the army as a major and died in 1886. He was the only one of the Weil brothers who wasn't rich. He left a daughter who was very extravagant and who would have had great difficulty making ends meet if it hadn't been for Uncle Louis.

"Her husband was an excellent man," M. Proust said, laughing, "but she was beyond everything."

Great-Uncle Abraham Alphonse's daughter also had a daughter, and this was the mysterious girl M. Proust met at Uncle Louis' house and found "very pretty—beautiful even." It must have been the influence of the mother's extravagance that Mme. Proust was afraid of. Uncle Louis was kind enough to give the mother an allowance before he died, and as M. Proust became his great-uncle's heir after Mme. Proust died, he was bound by the conditions of the will to continue the allowance. Once, the money was held up and the lady wrote and made inquiries and M. Proust asked me to take the money and deliver it personally. So I saw the mother, but either the daughter wasn't there or she didn't appear.

One day I asked M. Proust if he was sorry the marriage hadn't taken place. All he said was: "No. No regrets."

Amid Ruskin and the rest in the big black bookcase in the small salon there was one book he often showed me. He handled it very carefully. It was a luxury edition of a novel by Paul Bourget—*Gladys Harvey*, I think—covered with flowered silk brocade. The first time he took it down he told me as he turned the pages that at the time—the "camellia period"—everyone, that is to say everyone in certain circles, knew that the heroine was based on a woman M. Proust himself had known very well. It was she who had given him this special edition. The silk of the binding was from one of her gowns.

"She was one of those women who used to exist and will never exist again," he said. "They were as famous for their beauty as for their blue-blooded friends, for whom they vied with one another as to quality, quantity, and money, of course. But the woman we are talking about was also extremely intelligent and cultured. While others swallowed up whole fortunes yet never had a penny, she was clever enough to use some of the money to reassure her friends of their own generosity and to keep enough to thank them for setting her up. Some of the friends are dead, yet she still lives with their furniture." He told me that her name was Laure Hayman:

"She had beautiful pale blond hair and black eyes, which could look like contrasting flames when she was angry or pleased."

Afterward he often talked to me about her, either in the small salon with the book, or in his room asking me to get the photographs out of the drawer for us to look at.

"She dressed almost like a duchess," he said, "and she had more wit than some princesses. She was descended from a famous English painter."

Without ever admitting the truth, which wasn't difficult to guess, he said she was a "constant visitor" at Uncle Louis' villa in Auteuil. But she also had a charming little house in Paris, and her salon was frequented by writers and artists.

"She started with a German prince," he said, "and he was followed by all the grand dukes of Russia."

He had met her at his great-uncle's when he was eighteen and she was thirty-seven or thirty-eight, and it was easy to guess, too, that she was one of those on whom he "used his eyes." He said, a smile lurking behind his reserve:

"Uncle Louis was only too happy to give Laure Hayman anything she wanted. I admired her very much and spent such ruinous amounts of money on flowers for her that she told my father. He scolded me for my extravagance—I was very young. But he admired her too, for her wit and intelligence, and for that reason he rather encouraged me to be friends with her."

And another time: "They said she could initiate even the most stupid man into the ways of the world."

There was one thing he especially respected her for. He told me about it one day, comparing two photographs. In one she was wearing a magnificent gown; in the other she was dressed almost like an old woman and had a child in her arms.

"Would you say they are the same person?" he asked.

"No, monsieur."

"But they are both she. It is a beautiful story, Céleste. She had a son whom no one ever saw or heard of, because she sent him far away to be brought up by Jesuits, so he would never know what she was and that he was illegitimate. The only concession she allowed herself was to go to see him. She watched over his upbringing and education with the utmost love and unselfishness."

He was very moved. He put both the photographs down.

"And a frightful thing has happened, Céleste. You remember I told you the other day I was very upset by a letter I had received from her? It said her son had been killed at the front. I went to see her this evening. She has great dignity."

Later, but still in the "camellia period," there was the actress Louisa de Mornand, who was the very close but by no means exclusive friend of the Duke d'Albuféra, one of M. Proust's associates from the Club in rue Royale. He spoke of her as a fashionable person in whose company it was agreeable to be seen and with whom it was not difficult to be intimate. Looking at her photo, I said I thought she must be a great actress, but he laughed.

"Oh no, Céleste. It's true she had a few very good parts in the boulevard theaters, but the fact was that by spending a lot of money they just managed to make her a bit player."

Nevertheless I gathered she was one of those he had been "impulsive" about.

In such situations he was terrible; he wouldn't allow any resistance. There was the famous business of the gloves, over which he had lost his temper with his mother. He still talked about it with a mixture of amusement and remorse.

"I was smitten with a demimondaine who lived by the Bois de Boulogne, and after many unsuccessful attempts I'd at last managed to arrange a meeting with her. I was so excited I wanted to appear in all my splendor, and I had asked Mother to buy me a new tie and the most elegant pair of cream-colored gloves she could find. She came back with a very nice narrow tie, but about the gloves she said, 'I'm sorry, my little Marcel, but I couldn't find the kind you wanted anywhere. So I thought you would like these instead.' They were gray! I suppose Mother thought cream gloves were rather unsuitable for the occasion, and she was right. But I flew into the only real rage of my life and looked around to see what nasty thing I could do to spite her. We were in the salon, and there was a fine antique vase, a present from someone, which I knew she was very fond of. So I took it and dashed it to pieces on the floor. . . . Céleste dear, I can still see her now. She didn't stir. She just said, in the quietest voice in the world, 'Ah well, my little Marcel, it will be like a Jewish wedding. Your breaking the vase will make our love all the stronger.' I rushed to my room and wept and wept for hours at having hurt my mother—her answer told me how much. But the joke is that I went off to my rendezvous, and when I got there with my tie and my gloves and bouquet, do you know what I found? The bailiffs, who had come to seize the lady's property and were already moving the furniture out! Terrific!''

To go back to Louisa de Mornand, there must have been some sort of attachment between them, for I remember one evening at boulevard Haussmann when M. Proust was already dressed to go out and he asked me to take an urgent message to her house. I found her all ready to go out, too. I can see her now in a sheath dress of black satin, still young and beautiful. When I said I came from M. Proust, she exclaimed:

"Oh, Marcel, Marcel! How lovely—give it to me quickly!''

She practically jumped for joy as she read the message, which was an invitation to dinner for the same evening. She dropped everything to go. As far as I know, M. Proust never saw her again after that. She came once, after he died, to the little hotel that Odilon and I had bought in rue des Canettes. There in front of me was a very old lady in a sort of little concierge's hat, asking:

"Don't you recognize me?''

"Yes, I do believe I've seen you before, madame or mademoiselle."

"'Madame.' I live with a gentleman on rue Lauriston."

She told me who she was and stayed for a long time, slumped on a chair, talking to me about "Marcel." She didn't say anything particularly interesting, except about the great friendship between M. Proust and the Duke d'Albuféra, and how it had ended in an estrangement for reasons I'll come back to later. But I could easily see that the memory of M. Proust had never left her.

He must have been difficult for many to forget, just as he himself forgot nothing. But when I knew him his only attachment to the people of his youth was in terms of the memory of "time lost."

He now seemed completely detached, even in the case of the girl he probably loved most before he was grown up and after Marie de Benardaky. Her name was Jeanne Pouquet, and she belonged to the little group that played together. They saw each other in the Champs-Elysées and at tennis. There's a famous photograph, often reproduced, that shows her standing like a queen on a garden chair and M. Proust, among the rest, kneeling at her feet and strumming at a racket as if it were a guitar. They were still at the age of romantic love.

"I was as much in love with her as it's possible to be," he said.

"And what did you see in her, monsieur?"

"She had magnificent fair hair."

"But was she clever, at least?"

He never answered that. He said:

"I couldn't sleep. When we went to play tennis, in the morning, I took lots of sandwiches and all sorts of little cakes. I couldn't do enough to please her. I bought her presents and flowers; I went to endless trouble. When I was going to see her, I didn't walk, I ran! I loved watching her fair hair fly when she was playing tennis. The other boys were jealous of my pretty speeches and sometimes got their own back by hitting the ball into my boxes of *petits fours*. Of course, I couldn't shine in the same way they could."

When I asked him if Mme. Proust knew about his feelings, he said no.

First Loves

He had met Jeanne Pouquet before he did his military service—
that is, when he was about eighteen—at the house of Mme. Arman
de Caillavet, whose son Gaston was then one of his greatest friends.
From what he told me she made fun of his advances, though they
tickled her vanity. All the boys were in love with her, but in the end
it was Gaston de Caillavet who won and married her. I believe they
became engaged when M. Proust was in the army at Orléans, or
soon after. The tennis parties went on for some time before they
were married. One night when we were talking about it I said:

"Being in love like that, you must have been very upset that
your friend took her away from you?"

He remained silent at first, looking at me, his face impassive.
Finally he said: "No."

From the way he said it I had the impression that her marriage
showed him her true self and that from then on he stopped loving
her. But I don't think he hated her. She merely ceased to attract
him. He saw the two of them very little after that, except occasionally in society, and one evening when he wanted to see what
Simone, their much-praised little girl, looked like. But that was
nearly twenty years later. He went to their house. The daughter was
naturally in bed—it must have been midnight at least. He asked
them to find out if she was asleep.

"But Marcel, of course she is! And I am not going to wake her
up to come down at this hour," said Mme. Caillavet.

"Please, madame! I need to see her."

Finally the daughter came down, not at all pleased at having
been awakened.

He looked at her for a moment, then said: "Thank you, mademoiselle."

And then he went.

Then came the war, and, as I said, Gaston de Caillavet died, not
at the front but from a serious illness he seems not to have fought
against. Then a strange thing happened. I had just lost my mother
and was at Auxillac, but M. Proust told me all about it when I got
back.

He'd received a letter from Mme. de Caillavet asking him to see
her so that she could tell him something her husband had made her

swear, before he died, to tell M. Proust. As soon as he received the letter he sent a cab to fetch his old friend's widow. She came, and when he told me of this he was still shattered by what she told him.

Although he was married, Gaston de Caillavet had fallen madly in love with another woman—a dancer, if I remember rightly—but finally he gave in to his wife's protests and broke the affair off, but he never got over it. That was what he'd made Mme. Gaston de Caillavet swear to tell. And that was what had shattered M. Proust.

"Poor Gaston!" he said. "She ought never to have made him break it off."

About her, all he said was: "I still thought of her with fair plaits. But I saw before me a woman with white hair."

This was in 1915. He mentioned her again only a couple of times, except in connection with his memories of youth—once to tell me she'd lost no time in getting married again, to a cousin of hers whom M. Proust used to know; and then, much later, to say he'd seen her again, and even sat next to her at a soirée given by Mme. Hennessy.

It was right toward the end, in 1922—the last big soirée he went to. As the guests began to leave she said:

"Well, goodbye, Marcel, I must go."

"Oh, but I must see you, madame. May I escort you home?"

"No, not this evening, if you don't mind. We'll meet another day."

"Very well, madame. But if you won't see me today, then goodbye, for we shan't ever meet again."

That was the conversation as he told it to me when he came home. He was exhausted. He didn't say whether it was because he didn't wish to see her again or because he felt that death was not far off.

What is certain is that he spoke of her, as a woman, with indifference now. But one night, talking about her when he was young and felt so much for her, he said:

"After her, it was only passing fancies."

16

"OTHER" LOVES

I said I didn't think M. Proust had ever been really in love. That
doesn't mean he was incapable of it. But I think that even when he
was quite young he already had too much ambition for his work to
become attached to people for other reasons than what he later
called his "search." He realized very early that he would make
demands which, together with those imposed by his health, would
be difficult to ask of people. I am sure that when he saw that for me
every demand he made was a pleasure and easy to accomplish, he
became attached to me.

Of course people have said that in his youth he met with nothing
but disappointment in love and that because of this he turned away
from women to seek other kinds of love.

On this point, I'd like to repeat that I've vowed to tell only what
I know from having seen or heard it. Or, at the very least, from
having sufficiently understood it through M. Proust's allusions so as
to be reasonably sure of not making a mistake.

Therefore I can only say what I know about what happened
before I came. And if I now say M. Proust never told me anything
that showed him in the particular light some have alleged, I don't
want anyone to think that what I claim to know is the absolute truth,

185

and still less that I intended to paint an idealized portrait of M. Proust. Good heavens, why should I? Nothing could alter his charm.

What I want to make clear is that I loved him, put up with him, and enjoyed him just as he was. I don't see what good it would do him if I tried to make of him a plaster saint.

But there are two things I can say, and they are important for what follows. On the one hand, as I have said, he told me everything, and I don't think the fact that I was a woman would have stopped him from confiding in me on this particular subject—which was nothing compared to some of the things he told me, as we shall see. On the other hand, no one ever came into the apartment of boulevard Haussmann, or later at rue Hamelin, without my letting them in and out. Not only did M. Proust not have a key or know where the keys were kept, but he would never have lent one to anybody. What's more, because I was always on the alert for any call from him, I'd have heard any movement in the apartment, even in my sleep—I had soon developed a sort of sixth sense for it, and it never failed me. At the slightest sound I was awake and up. And again, every time anyone came to see him, he would tell me about it afterward.

That still leaves his going out. Of course I didn't go with him. But all the time he drove him, Odilon always told me that "I took him here, or there, and waited." Odilon was a man of integrity and considered that what his customers did was no concern of his. But I knew, because, again, M. Proust told me all about his evenings.

Take, for example, the young men I showed into the apartment at one time or another—they were almost all writers, or admirers of his work, and nothing like the sort of person some people imagine. To say the opposite would be pure invention on my part. Apart from there being very few of them, they certainly didn't come for *galanterie*. I remember the critic Ramon Fernandez. M. Proust told me he saw much of Mlle. d'Hinnisdaël, a young lady who belonged to the aristocracy. I remember it because M. Proust thought the family ought not to allow such insinuations, though he was full of praise for Ramon Fernandez's intellectual qualities. And then there was

Emmanuel Berl, who tells himself how he came to talk to M. Proust about the problems of being in love with three women at the same time. (My apologies to M. Berl—I don't remember having seen him.)

There was only one who was different, and that was a young Englishman, the friend of a wealthy M. Goldsmith or Goldschmidt who persecuted M. Proust with invitations to dinner. M. Proust didn't like going; he said M. Goldsmith was boring and it was a waste of time. But also—and this is a proof that he didn't mind talking to me about such things—he made no bones of the fact that his would-be host belonged to the "Sodom party." M. Proust never invited nor received him. He said:

"I couldn't receive him lying in bed. He is much too formal. It would have to be dinner jacket or tails."

But he was fascinated by the way the young Englishman dressed, and particularly by his waistcoats. (I knew him only as Charlie.) That was the only reason he allowed him to come to the apartment twice—to study his dress, for the book. After that he never saw them again, either the young man or his older friend.

A lot has been said, too, about his secretaries, and his seeming preference that they be men. There is no doubt in my mind that this was connected with the enormous respect he had for women, and with his modesty, as an invalid nearly always in bed. Even with me he was very reticent in what he said about anything concerning women. When he touched on the question of love between members of the opposite sexes he always spoke indirectly: you could guess what was meant, but nothing was actually said. I remember one day, when he was talking of his curiosity about people, he told me that one day, during the "camellia period," he had asked Duke d'Albuféra:

"Louis, would you do such a thing with your wife?"

"Oh, Marcel, one would never ask that of one's wife!" answered the duke.

M. Proust laughed at the thought of how he'd scandalized his friend. But he never said what he meant by "such a thing."

That he had two male secretaries didn't stop him later, when he felt at ease with us, you might almost say at home, from asking my niece Yvonne to come and stay at rue Hamelin to type part of *La Prisonnière.*

I myself knew only one male secretary who lived in—Henri Rochat, whom he'd found at the Ritz, where I think he was on the staff of the manager, Olivier Dabescat. And M. Proust—this was a typical example of his kindness and generosity—had taken him in largely out of charity, because he was touched by the young man's aspirations.

He was a young Swiss, rather surly and silent, with the air of superiority Swiss often have. He wanted to be a painter. If he played the part some people have alleged, M. Proust certainly made a good job of keeping it from me. But how? That's what I'd like to know. We weren't at boulevard Haussmann then, but in rue Hamelin, where the layout of the apartment was almost the same. M. Proust lived at one end, Rochat at the other. Between their two bedrooms there was a boudoir and a sitting room. My own bedroom opened onto the hall and was a sort of combined cockpit and listening post commanding the whole apartment. No coming and going could have escaped me.

Rochat had only one thing in his favor: he had beautiful hand-writing. Apart from that:

"He thinks he is painting," M. Proust used to say.

He soon got tired even of the beautiful handwriting. Sometimes, at the beginning, when he'd had his coffee, toward the end of the afternoon or in the evening, he asked me to ask Rochat to come to work, and he dictated to him for a while. But then he stopped asking for him. Rochat stayed in his room daubing at his painting, or else he went out. We hardly saw him. M. Proust said·

"As far as work goes, he tires rather than helps me."

Charity turned into pity. He kept him a little over two years, torn between the desire to get rid of him and the reluctance to leave him without a roof over his head. Finally he asked his old school friend, Horace Finaly, to get Rochat a job abroad, which was what he wanted—but it was a good, secure position, a job in a bank in

Buenos Aires, not in New York, as some people have said. It was a branch of the Banque de Paris et des Pays-Bas.

Rochat was more or less engaged to a girl who lived in rue des Acacias and visited him in his room in rue Hamelin. When he went away he just left her in the lurch, and after he'd gone M. Proust went to comfort her. For Rochat himself he never expressed any regret. His only comment was:

"Here we are, Céleste. Peace and quiet at last."

It mustn't be forgotten that M. Proust was tremendously loyal to anyone who worked for him and had a great sense of responsibility.

One of the cases about which most ink has been spilt is that of Agostinelli, who'd been one of his regular taxi drivers at Cabourg before the war, along with my husband. He belonged to the famous company run by Jacques Bizet. I'd say he was an unstable young fellow who wanted to rise above his station, like Henri Rochat. Though I myself had very little to do with him, Odilon knew him well. They'd worked together almost from the beginning, in Monaco and Cabourg.

"He's a nice chap," Odilon always used to say. "He's never given me any cause for complaint."

But he was obsessed by the desire to be something other than what he was. In the end he asked M. Proust to make him his secretary. He had left the taxi company and gone back to his native Monaco, where he'd met his friend Anna and found a job but lost it. Again out of kindness, M. Proust agreed to take him in. Both he and Anna stayed in the apartment, and actually there is some of his handwriting to be seen in the manuscripts of that period.

It was in 1913, just after I married Odilon. I remember clearly one Sunday when, at Agostinelli's suggestion, we had a picnic in the forest of Fontainebleau. I was horribly bored. The two men were quite happy swapping stories about their taxi driving days, but I only had the girl, who was disagreeable and ugly—my husband called her "the flying louse." I can see her exactly as she was that day, with her straight black hair merging into the black monkey collar of her pony-skin coat. And I can still hear Agostinelli saying, "Are you coming, Anna?"

But actually, as far as Agostinelli himself goes, I have only a very vague memory, which is not enough to judge him by. Odilon told me he was mad about mechanics and that this enthusiasm was transferred from cars to planes. He talked so much about it to M. Proust that in the end, with his great kindness, M. Proust let him attend a flying course at Buc aerodrome near Versailles. As Agostinelli no longer had a car, Odilon drove him there, and M. Proust paid the fare with his usual generosity. That's what I mean by his loyalty. Like the time when Agostinelli, out of a job in Monaco and not having yet suggested becoming M. Proust's secretary, asked to be taken back as chauffeur. But M. Proust said straight out that it was too late; it would have meant being unfair to Odilon, who'd become his regular driver and in whom he had complete confidence.

"You will understand that all the better, as he used to be your colleague and is still your friend," he said.

It was also Odilon who told me Agostinelli took himself very seriously as a secretary. He certainly was conceited. M. Proust bought a typewriter for him to use (he sold it later to the manager of Larue's; I saw it on the cashier's desk when I went to collect some food). I don't know whether it was a coincidence, but I remember that while Agostinelli and his friend were staying at boulevard Haussmann, Céline had one of her bad moods and left. I remember, too, that though the couple lived in the apartment, they had their meals out.

And then one day, suddenly, Agostinelli left again for the south of France. I think Anna's influence had a lot to do with it.

She didn't like Paris. He wrote to M. Proust from Antibes, where he was still taking flying lessons. He was a wheedler. From what I gathered afterward, his idea was to persuade M. Proust to help him buy his own plane, which he said he would call "Swann," after the chief character in the book M. Proust had just published. Agostinelli was reckless too. Just after he got his license, only the second time he went out as a real pilot, he disobeyed orders and flew out over the sea. He never came back. His body was found a week later, the eyes eaten away by the fish.

Agostinelli was killed on May 30, 1914. The tragic thing was that he'd written a long letter to M. Proust, full of joy at having got his license, and the letter didn't arrive until after his death. Of course M. Proust was shattered. He showed me the letter and read it out to me later. It was a very nice letter, full of gratitude and overflowing with pride. Then came a flood of messages from the Agostinelli family, begging M. Proust to help finance the search for the body, which he did. When it was found, on June 7, he sent flowers to put on the grave, and he did the same the following year for the anniversary of Agostinelli's death. He also helped Anna and the brother. It's even been said that the brother came to Paris to be M. Proust's secretary for a while. This is strange, for I can't remember it; and yet I would have known, as I was already living in. The only person I remember acting as secretary, apart from Henri Rochat and my niece Yvonne, was Agostinelli, before what's been called his "flight" to Antibes. At that time I was the "courier," and I saw him two or three times in the kitchen with Anna.

All sorts of stories have been woven around M. Proust's grief at Agostinelli's death and the feelings he had or was supposed to have had for him. Some great intellects, or small ones, I don't know, have even discovered that Agostinelli was to some extent the Albertine in the books, with whom the "Narrator" is in love. To my mind that's ridiculous. To begin with, Albertine existed in M. Proust's mind and in his notebooks long before Agostinelli. And then I'm sure, from the way M. Proust used to talk to me about him, that it was the same with Agostinelli as with Henri Rochat. M. Proust took an interest in him, first because he was pleasant company as a driver (Odilon always said that), and second because Agostinelli wanted to improve himself. And as he was far from being stupid—his letters were very nicely written—M. Proust was induced by his own natural generosity to help him. If M. Proust was angry and hurt by the "flight" to Antibes, it was partly because it seemed like ingratitude after he'd offered to let the couple stay at boulevard Haussmann and had paid for the flying lessons at Buc, and partly because, knowing of Agostinelli's recklessness, he was afraid he'd do something foolish. I shouldn't be surprised if he actually foresaw the tragedy, with that faculty he had for looking into people's souls. And having been very fond of someone, who wouldn't be grieved to see adverse presentiments come true?

To say he tried to keep Agostinelli "prisoner" of his feelings, like Albertine in the book, is more absurd still. At that rate, Odilon was as much a prisoner as Agostinelli. And what about me! Anyone who worked for M. Proust was in a sense imprisoned by him and by his work.

Another relationship, which has often been used as evidence that his tastes excluded women, was his acquaintance with Albert Le Cuziat, who in the book is one of the models for Jupien and the keeper of a house of ill fame for men. Here I know what and whom I'm talking about, for apart from the fact that M. Proust talked much to me about him and kept me informed about what was happening, I saw him with my own eyes. I'll say straight out I didn't like him and made no secret of this to M. Proust. But as he agreed with me, I don't think my dislike taints the impartiality of my judgment.

He was a bean-pole of a Breton, slovenly, fair, with cold blue eyes like a fish—eyes that matched his soul. The precariousness of his profession was in his face and look, a hunted look, which was not surprising, seeing that his place was frequently raided by the police and that he often did short spells in jail.

He had started out as a footman in great Russian houses—at Count Orloff's, Prince Radziwill's, and elsewhere—where, according to M. Proust, he had had some curious experiences. Prince Radziwill—the father—was well known for his peculiar tastes. As for Count Orloff, Albert had told M. Proust a story which both amused and shocked him. Right in the middle of a big dinner-party, the count sent for his chamber pot and relieved himself in front of the guests. "Worse than the royal close-stool of the old days," said M. Proust.

As far as I can recall, M. Proust must have met Albert at the Radziwills'—one of the sons used to go to the Club on rue Royale. Later, Albert gave up domestic service to set up on his own as a hotel keeper. He began with a place near the Bourse—he was there in 1913 when I started to work at boulevard Haussmann—and then kept a bathhouse on rue Godot-de-Mauroy, a street near la Madeleine, which still has a highly dubious reputation. Lastly, about 1915 or 1916, he opened a kind of male brothel in a little house on rue de l'Arcade.

M. Proust is supposed firstly to have helped him set himself up there, with furniture and money, and secondly to have visited the place.

Although it's all malicious gossip, since it has been said, let's deal with it. And before the explanation, there are these facts.

It is true that M. Proust did give Le Cuziat some furniture, but this was long before the famous house in rue de l'Arcade—it was when he took over the bathhouse in rue Godot-de-Mauroy. M. Proust told me about it himself. As I've already said, with the furniture he inherited from his parents and the things that came to him from his Great-Uncle Louis, he had far more of it than he could use. The dining room was crammed to the ceiling, and I had to pick my way through it as if I were going through a forest. And there was another shedful in the courtyard. So when Le Cuziat told M. Proust he didn't have enough money to buy furniture for his own bedroom on rue Godot-de-Mauroy, he let him have the key of the shed and told him to take what he wanted. He only took a green half-length chaise-longue—a sort of reclining arm chair—and one or two other chairs and a pair of curtains.

As to money, yes, M. Proust did give him some, under definite conditions I shall come to later, but certainly not to set him up in business. In the first place, he didn't strew his money around like that; and secondly, if Albert needed help, he had protectors much richer than M. Proust. It has also been said that when we lived on rue Hamelin, M. Proust wanted to sell some furniture and carpets to give the proceeds to Albert, who had appealed for help. It's not true.

M. Proust no longer had anything to do with Le Cuziat then; and if he thought of selling some things, it was only to help Mme. Scheikévitch, who was in difficult circumstances, but who proudly declined his offer.

And now the explanation. I'm sure, from what he said to me, that M. Proust gave away the furniture in just the same way as he gave away so many other things. For example, he used to tip by the handful. If proof is needed, I can still hear the pent-up anger and distress in his voice when he told me how he had found out what use Le Cuziat had put his furniture to in rue de l'Arcade.

"The scoundrel once asked me to give him that furniture for his own room in his bathhouse in rue Godot-de-Mauroy. And what do I see in rue de l'Arcade? It's being used for disgusting purposes. I would never have thought him capable of such vile behavior. My God, Céleste, what a fool I was!"

I can remember it all the more clearly because he was just back from that place when he told me about it. And I could see he'd never forgive Albert.

Lastly, if he gave him any money it was never much.

It, too, was a sort of tip for the information Albert brought him, or which sometimes M. Proust went to get himself, for the book. You only had to look at Le Cuziat to see he never did anything for nothing. He might run a house of his own now, but he still had the soul of a servant. M. Proust also paid Olivier Dabescat, manager of the restaurant at the Ritz, to keep him informed of such details as who dined with whom, what dress Mme. so-and-so wore, and what sort of etiquette was observed at the various tables.

Of course, the stories Le Cuziat supplied were a strange brew. But M. Proust never concealed any of them from me, any more than he tried to hide the fact that Albert himself had very special tastes, whether by nature or because of his past experiences. He told me the names of people who used to frequent the house in rue de L'Arcade—they included politicians and even ministers. Albert supplied details about their vices. It amused M. Proust, but usually he would end on a note of sadness, saying he didn't understand how people could sink so low.

When he wanted any information from Albert he sent for him, usually after he'd had his coffee, toward the end of the afternoon. Le Cuziat didn't stay long, just long enough for a brief chat; he was always in a hurry to get back to his rue de l'Arcade. It's been said that when Odilon returned from the war it was he who went to fetch Albert in his taxi. No. I always took a message. I never went beyond the hall—I remember the house had a double exit. M. Proust always said:

"And don't forget, Céleste, ask for him and give him the letter personally. And whatever you do, see that he *gives it back to you.*"

So when people say Le Cuziat had lots of M. Proust's letters which he is supposed to have sold later, I can't help wondering where he could have got them.

The precaution about delivering notes personally was wise because one could never be sure Albert wasn't in prison. Several times I didn't find him there for that reason; there was only a young fellow who lived with him—André, I think his name was—and looked after the place in his absence.

"I don't like to stay there too long when I go," M. Proust used to say. "You never know when there will be a police raid. I shouldn't like to see myself all over tomorrow's papers!"

I shan't waste time on the stupid things that have been said, and repeated in a book, about incidents that are supposed to have taken place in an establishment more or less resembling Le Cuziat's: some story about rats with pins stuck in them, which M. Proust, supposedly, watched die, and another about his showing photographs of his mother to those people to make them laugh and to give himself the pleasure of committing sacrilege. How dare people print such nonsense? M. Proust always had a holy terror of rats—so much so, he told me one day in passing, that he couldn't even bear the sight of them. As for the photographs of his mother, they never left the chest in his room, except when he asked me to get them out to look at them or show them to me—always with love and emotion. As a matter of fact, he never took anything with him out of the house; and apart from eating, washing, and dressing and using his notebooks and pen, he seldom did anything with his hands. Strange as it may seem, he used to call me in to hand him the least thing, and the idea of his opening a heavy drawer and sifting through photos, putting the photos in an envelope and the envelope in his pocket, and then bringing them back and going through the process in reverse, is unthinkable to anyone who knew him as I did. The only thing he ever took out with him was sugar, which he had me do up in a parcel to give as a present to my sister-in-law, Adèle Larivière, when it was rationed during the war.

In any case, I can vouch for the fact that he never lived in the house of rue de l'Arcade and didn't go there any more often than I knew of through messages, Odilon, or what he himself told me. And I don't think that could have been more than five or six times in four or five years. And once his need for information was finally satisfied, he never set foot there and never saw Le Cuziat again.

The strange thing is that every time he came back from rue de l'Arcade he would talk to me about the visit just as if he'd come back from an evening at Count de Beaumont's or Countess Greffulhe's. What interested him was the spectacle he'd seen, nothing else. When I said, with my usual forthrightness, that I couldn't understand how he could let Albert come to see him, still less go there, he said:

"I know, Céleste. You can't imagine how much I dislike it. But I can only write about things as they are, and to do that I have to see them."

I shall always remember the night he came home after having, in fact, seen something he describes in his book. He came in with his hat cocked, which meant he hadn't been wasting his time. He called me into his room right away and told me all about it, sitting on the edge of the bed. In answer to a message, Albert had told him to come that evening and he would be able to see something Albert had told him about.

"My dear Céleste, what I have witnessed this evening is unimaginable. Le Cuziat told me there was a man who goes there to be whipped, and I saw the whole thing from another room, through a little window in the wall. It is incredible. I didn't believe him when he told me—I wanted to see for myself. Well, I saw it. It is a big industrialist who comes down from the north of France specially for that. Imagine—there he is in a room, fastened to a wall with chains and padlocks, while some wretch, picked up heaven knows where, who gets paid for it, whips him till the blood spurts out all over everything. And it is only then that the unfortunate creature experiences the heights of pleasure."

I was so horror-struck I said: "Monsieur, it's impossible, I don't believe it!"

"It is true, Céleste; I didn't make it up."

"But how could you watch such a thing?"

"Precisely because no one could make it up."

And when I said I thought Le Cuziat was a monster, he answered:

"I don't like him, Céleste, either, believe me. You are right; he is a bad fellow, disgusting. But I learned something this evening."

"And did you have to pay a lot of money to see it?"

"Yes, Céleste. But I had to."

"Well, monsieur, you say that awful man spends most of his time in prison. What I say is he ought to die there!"

He started to laugh.

"And to think he can't praise you highly enough! The other day he asked if it was you who polished my silver salver so beautifully. He was in raptures!"

"I don't want compliments from a brute like that, thank you!"

"Yes," he said. "It is true what you say about him. But there is something you ought to know, incredible as it is in a monster, as you call him. He loved his mother dearly and did all he could to make her happy. She died, and when I heard about it I sent him a simple little note of condolence. And, do you know, Céleste, he wrote back a long letter, talking about her in a way that was deeply touching. It is almost one of the best letters I have ever read about the death of a mother. So that proves he has a heart somewhere, despite his objectionable way of making a living. You can't help feeling sorry for him."

197

Anyway, we talked about the horrible flagellation scene for hours that night, I still horror-struck and he going over it as if not to forget anything, and no doubt thinking aloud, as usual, of what he was going to write.

17

POLITICS

The enchantment wasn't only at night. It began as soon as he was really awake, after he'd had his coffee. He gradually emerged from his sleep and started to come alive again.

At the first ring of the bell I'd take in the little silver tray from the hall with the mail on it, as well as the coffee and the croissant and the milk. That was part of the ritual. He didn't look at the mail until he'd finished eating. When he picked it up he did so in a very comical manner, very delicately, almost with the tips of his fingers, as he did with everything he touched. He would examine the envelope or the writing, trying to guess who it was from. He always opened his letters himself, just tearing open the flap, without the aid of a paper knife or anything. Sometimes he'd put a letter down for a while without reading it and go on to others. When he first woke up, everything was done in silence—I wasn't allowed to speak either until he gave the signal—but as he read his letters he gradually grew more and more animated.

He liked sharing his mail with me. While he usually didn't read everything out loud, he'd give me the general drift and then explain about the bits that were most interesting or amusing. Only on occasion would he read me a whole letter from the first line to the last. This often was so with letters from Count Robert de Montes-

199

quiou, for example, because there was nearly always some sarcasm between the lines which M. Proust emphasized as he read and explained to me laughing. His comments on the letters were accompanied by remarks about the people who'd written them.

I soon got so used to his ways that I could guess his reaction to a letter even before his comments and remarks. I could tell whether he was going to invite people out or to the apartment or whether he was going to accept someone's invitation. From the very tone of his voice I could follow his thoughts and tell whether he was interested or indifferent. If there were persons, even persons he knew quite well, that he didn't want to see for the moment, or suddenly didn't want to see at all, I could tell at once that they were going to be put on the black list. I was never wrong. The persons in question were just fading out of his interest. Their names would disappear from the list of telephone calls; no more messages would be delivered to them; their names were no longer on the envelopes I put in the letter box.

Then he would give me an idea of what his reply was going to be, and this always confirmed my previous impression. He'd say:

"I shall write to so-and-so and say we will meet soon."

But he hardly ever fixed the day and the time immediately. He had to mull it over—decide whether they'd meet alone or with other people, and if so, with whom and where. He was very careful and precise about this.

"Dear Céleste, I would like to invite Countess de Noailles with Madame X and Monsieur Y. Do you think that will be all right? There are certain circumstances . . ." And he'd tell me about the people's current relationships.

His social doings were very carefully weighed and hedged with precautions. He never answered at random, nor for the mere pleasure of writing or expressing emotion. There was always a definite object—either some information he needed—part of his research— or to get someone to arrange a meeting for him with someone again, for one of his characters; or to meet people interested in his work; or to arrange to meet others and make them interested.

Anyway, whether he was receiving letters or sending them, the post provided him with some of his favorite moments. The enjoyment with which he read me Montesquiou's letters and his own replies! He'd say:

"Listen, Céleste, I shall read you the key passage. Listen for the hatred he breathes out between each word. He is terrific!"

And he'd laugh as hard as he could.

Sometimes he'd say, in a depressed voice, running his hand impatiently over the envelopes strewn on the bed: "When I think of all the letters I shall have to write, and I haven't even time for my book!" But it was only a manner of speaking. He really adored writing letters. He'd say:

"Oh well, I suppose I shall have to answer this one . . ."

But once he got started it just flowed on and on.

One of the things he worried about toward the end was having spent too much time on correspondence. He often talked about it; it became an obsession.

"You will see, Céleste, I shall hardly be cold and everyone will start publishing my letters. I did wrong; I wrote too many, far too many. Because I was ill, my only contact with people was through writing. But I should never have done it. Still, I shall take what precautions I can. I shall see to it that no one has the right to publish my letters."

This tortured him; he kept referring to it; he even talked about it to other people. One night he came home very depressed after spending the evening with the playwright Henry Bernstein. He'd mentioned the matter to him, and Henry Bernstein said he didn't really see what he could do about it. M. Proust then consulted his friend Horace Finaly, the banker; not much hope there either. Finally he fell back on his lawyer, who was also a friend. He came home shattered.

"He said, 'My poor Marcel, you are just wasting your time trying to forbid publication. Every one of your letters that is in the possession of the person it was written to is his property, and he can do what he likes with it.' How could I have been so careless, Céleste! Those who don't publish them will sell them. I have given all those people arrows that will be turned against me!"

For him it was a disaster that darkened the last months of his life. But he went on writing and answering letters just the same. True, as he saw fewer and fewer people, it was practically his last means of contact.

Toward the end of his life, too, he adopted a peculiar attitude about letters arriving from outside. His fear of germs had become greater than ever. He began wearing gloves in bed when people came to see him whom he knew too well or not well enough to be certain about their health. And he would keep his gloves on until the people went, for fear the visitors might pass on germs when they shook hands. Someone advised him to get a box and put formol in it. Then the letters were placed in the box both before and after they were opened. He told me how it worked and why he used it:

"You see, Céleste, in the state I am in, someone with scarlet fever or measles or any other contagious disease would only have to write to me and I would catch the germ in no time. So it is best to disinfect all the letters."

It was very ingenious, so much so that after he died his brother exclaimed over the idea and took the box away. He said it would be very useful.

Besides the letters, every morning he read the newspapers. There was a kiosk in the street, opposite the house from where they were brought up to us. Reading them was part of the routine and he didn't let a day go by without going through them carefully. Although he was so sensitive to odors, that of printer's ink and paper didn't seem to bother him.

He read chiefly *Le Figaro, Le Journal des Débats, Le Temps,* and the financial papers, and reviews such as *Le Mercure de France, La Revue de Paris, La Nouvelle Revue Française, L'Illustration,* and many others. Sometimes he sent me to fetch other papers so that he could read opposing political points of view.

He always kept up to date with the news. As in other matters, nothing escaped him. I remember that when Jacques Bizet committed suicide, his mother, Mme. Straus, sent a servant round immediately, before M. Proust was awake, to ask me to hide that day's

Figaro, which reported her son's death. She didn't want M. Proust to learn of it through the papers. I explained that it was impossible, I couldn't do it. If the paper had been missing from among the others M. Proust would have complained and asked me for it immediately.

He followed everything in the papers: politics, the Stock Exchange, literature, and the other arts. An article by a critic on a book could make him want to meet him; and then the maneuvering would begin to bring this about.

Almost every day he gave me a commentary on the main events—"for the good of your education," he said. At that time *Figaro* carried drawings by the cartoonist Forain, which he admired very much. He used to show them to me, explaining what they meant, because I wasn't always able to understand the allusions. He did the same with the articles on politics and made commentaries on them just as with his letters.

I remember his saying to me during the war:

"Céleste, with the censorship there is only one paper now that is well informed and that is *Le Journal de Genève,* because it is neutral. Will you take it regularly from now on, please?"

He disliked extremes. For instance, if he read *L'Action Française,* the monarchist paper, it was chiefly because he found most of the literary articles very good, and also, for old times' sake, because of the articles by Léon Daudet. Daudet had become one of the leading royalists, together with Charles Maurras, whom M. Proust respected for his literary work without—far from it—sharing his politics. About Léon Daudet he said:

"There's extraordinary talent in his articles. It is a pity he is so eccentric in everything and so excessive in his ideas. I wonder why the government lets him get away with what he writes. Maurras, too, for that matter."

Once when I went to deliver a message from M. Proust at Léon Daudet's house I was told he wasn't in, so I waited outside. He arrived eventually in a cab, but it was obvious that, after seeing me standing here, he made the cab stop farther up the street. Then he came back, keeping to the wall and then disappearing into the house like a flash. I went up after him, and finally he had me shown in, apologizing for not having recognized me and saying, "These are troubled times."

"My poor Céleste," said M. Proust when I told him. "He thought you were a suspicious character. He's convinced he is going to be assassinated. He is not very stable, you know."

But he did add that a lady supporter of *L'Action Française* had been murdered during the previous week.

He also admired the feeling and intelligence of another friend of his youth—Léon Blum, one of the luminaries of the Socialist party. But he never said a word about his articles. On the other hand, I remember that he was shattered by the murder of Jean Jaurès.

"He was a great man," he said, "and a brave one. The only one who could have saved us from this stupid war."

For he never liked or approved of the 1914 war, though he wanted France to win it. As long as it lasted he often said how sorry he was that France and Germany had come to this conflict. In his opinion it would have been natural for the two countries to get on well with each other.

"And to think that all that was needed was for them to get together. If Germany and France could come to an understanding, Europe and the world would be at peace for centuries."

He hated the Kaiser Wilhelm II for his responsibility for the war, but he said we'd asked for it, too. And once he made a comparison between France and Germany in their attitude toward their great men.

"The awful thing is that we don't help our scholars and artists— sometimes we even let them die of starvation. But Wilhelm II at least had the intelligence to give any great scholar or talented writer who was brought to his attention whatever help he needed. But look at poor Branly, here in France. He's a genius, but he has to struggle against poverty, without a penny for his laboratory and his discoveries. I don't know why I don't get up a petition for him!"

There was a phrase he liked very much and quoted often, which he'd seen in an article written by a German in *Le Mercure de*

France. I think it was Wilhelm II who was supposed to have said it: "I don't want France to take off her hat to me. I want her to shake my hand."

"And that is what will happen, Céleste, you will see."

Among French statesmen, his favorites were Georges Clemenceau because of his energy, Aristide Briand because of his eloquence, and Joseph Caillaux because of his efficiency, especially in finance. When Mme. Caillaux shot Calmette, editor of *Le Figaro,* because, in order to damage her pro-German husband's reputation, he was going to publish love letters from Caillaux to another woman, M. Proust said:

"I don't know whether she did it out of love for her husband or out of ambition, but all she did is to prevent Caillaux from coming to power. And that is a disaster, because France won't replace him easily."

When he explained that sort of thing to me I'd sometimes say:

"It is a pity, monsieur! With the shrewdness and clear-sightedness you inherited from your mother, you'd have made a marvelous minister or ambassador. You'd have had no difficulty managing *your* portfolio!"

It always delighted him to hear that, and he always laughed.

The Dreyfus affair had been very important to him. You might have expected him to be timid, to be anxious to keep out of such conflicts, but he told me how he threw himself into the struggle and went to all the court hearings. He extolled Emile Zola and all those who defended Dreyfus for their courage.

"Do you know, Céleste, I even brought books to the Cherche-Midi prison for Colonel Picquart, who had been jailed for trying to clear Dreyfus and bring the truth about the 'Affair' to light."

It was clear that, as always, what had disgusted him most was what he had seen at once—the deceit and injustice of the trial and the sentence.

"It was terrible," he said. "All France was divided in two. On one side was the enormous majority trying to believe what wasn't true, and on the other was a handful of people who fought back.

Mme. Straus, for example, was as enthusiastically for Dreyfus as I was; but I quarreled over it with some of my friends. Even Father was an anti-Dreyfusite, and we had a row. I didn't speak to him for a week."

He never told me what his mother, who was Jewish, thought about the matter. But I'm sure it wasn't the Jewish blood that spoke up for Dreyfus in him. It was just his humanity and his great love of truth.

He was scathing enough about some kinds of Jew, though never out of racial or religious prejudice.

"Have you ever been to the Marais," he said, "—the Jewish commercial district?"

"No, monsieur."

"You haven't missed anything, Céleste. The ugliness and meanness! On the other hand, it would have been an interesting experience for you. Fortunately they are not all like that—far from it. You don't have to be a Jew to have those faults, or many others. But those merchants! It is not surprising Christ drove them from the Temple!"

I think that, finding himself between the two religions, he didn't want to choose either. But there was one incident that had struck him very much when he was a boy. His maternal grandfather, Nathée Weil, who was a stockbroker, followed the Lenten sermons every year at Notre-Dame.

"And do you know what he said to me? 'They are far better than us.' He said it at the table, in front of Father and Mother and everybody."

We never talked much about religion. I never heard him oppose any faith. Just once he told me he strongly disapproved of the separation of Church and State—he had even written an article about it, called *La Mort des Cathédrales*, in *Le Figaro* in 1904. He still deplored it, but he said his main concern had been fear that the beauty of the cathedrals and churches of France was doomed to slow destruction.

But did he believe or didn't he? He never told me. There were

always two points that seemed crucial to me in this connection—
two questions to which he alone knew the answer, and he took the
answer with him into the grave.

I don't think there's any point in talking about the anniversary
masses he had celebrated for various people—dead friends, Agostinelli, even members of my family. I think these were intended as
gestures—a way of using traditions to express affection. The two
questions I'm referring to are, first, his wish, which he expressed to
me many times, years before his death, that Abbé Mugnier should
come and pray at his deathbed. This wish couldn't be fulfilled, as
I've already said. The second concerned the rosary he had received
from Lucie Faure, the younger daughter of President Félix Faure,
whose elder sister, Antoinette, he once had thought of marrying.

He had remained friends with her much more so than with
Antoinette. She was very religious and had brought back a rosary
for him from a pilgrimage to Jerusalem. As soon as he started to
make me search through the memorabilia in the drawer of the chest
and asked me to bring them over to the bed to look at them and show
them to me he told me about the rosary.

"Look, Céleste," he said, "the cross has got 'Jerusalem'
carved on it. How I would have loved to go there! But still, I have
the rosary and I am very fond of it. And one day, Céleste, when you
close my eyes—yes, yes, it will be your beautiful little hands that
will close my eyes—I want you to wind the rosary round my fingers.
Promise you will, Céleste."

And this, contrary to what has been said, was not an idea that
just came to him at the end, like with those people who think,
"Might as well call the priest. You never know." He talked to me
about it as early as during the 1914 war, and I don't know how often
he repeated his request during those eight years. And it wasn't that
he wanted to take the memory of Lucie Faure with him into the
grave. He always told me he'd never loved her. So?

I knew him well enough to be sure that if he didn't say anything
about it, it was because he didn't think the answer to the question
was anyone's business but his own. The only indication he ever gave

me was the phrase I mentioned before, about meeting again in the Valley of Jehosaphat. I said, "Do you believe in it, monsieur, you who know everything?" And he said:

"I don't know, Céleste."

I personally wouldn't try to draw any conclusions from that.

18

TYRANNICAL AND SUSPICIOUS

In the end, I don't think there are many things I didn't understand about him, or know about him, or that he himself left unexplained for me. That was part of the spell he cast. By dint of watching and listening, I must unconsciously have acquired a fraction of his powers of divination and analysis. There was a sort of mutual understanding between us, which enabled me to anticipate his thoughts and wishes. Sometimes he himself would be surprised:

"Dear Céleste, how did you know I was just going to ask you to hand me another sweater?"

I could interpret his faintest expression. I could foresee the movements of his hand, his impatience about this or that. Perhaps this was because I wasn't anxious about keeping my job; I was completely disinterested, and never considered the life I led with him either as a job or as any kind of servitude. He didn't treat me as a servant. That he sensed right away that I was captivated and would stay of my own free will was probably the reason he wanted to keep me, and why there was this marvelous understanding between us.

For it must be admitted that anyone who stayed for money or an easy life wouldn't have stayed long. Félicie had gone; Céline would have done the same eventually; even Nicolas, who was the most devoted of them, wouldn't have been able to stick it out beyond a certain point. In any case, M. Proust wouldn't have asked it of them. With me he didn't have to ask; or if he did ask he knew I would do whatever he wanted with alacrity. When I started to wait up for him and be ready for the door of the lift at night, it wasn't at all out of duty; it was still less because he demanded it. It was simply for the pleasure of seeing him again and hearing him talk. He used to thank me, but really I don't think he was at all surprised. He'd seen through me too well not to suspect that that was how it would be.

When I said, earlier, that I bore with him, it was true. One day after his death his niece Suzy, who became Mme. Mante, said:

"He couldn't always have been very easy to live with."

"Yes, very easy," I said, "at least for me. It didn't matter that he was a tyrant. When you knew the reasons behind it, you loved him for it."

For there was grace even in his tyrannies. And yet, God knows, he was demanding! Everything he wanted, everything he needed, had to be there right away. It was the same even with Odilon, who wasn't entirely on tap as I was. When he ordered the car, Odilon had to be there waiting downstairs before he went out, and once he'd got hold of him he didn't let go. Sometimes he'd ask him to wait after he came home, in case he decided to go out again. Or at two in the morning he'd fancy a cold beer, which had to be fetched, as I've described, from the Ritz. As soon as I'd shut the door behind him and knew he was safely downstairs—he never had to come back for something he'd forgotten; everything was so meticulously organized—I bustled about doing the housework so that everything would be ready for him when he came home. If I left him at eight or nine in the morning I usually had a list of errands and messages for the evening that had to be attended to right away—letters to be delivered, phone calls to make, a table to be reserved, a private room to be booked at the Ritz. And as soon as he woke up, not only was there the coffee and the preparations for his dressing room, but his round of details would also begin. Once he was dressed he would send for me and walk about the bedroom dabbing at his face with a towel.

"What is the time, Céleste? Did you remember to telephone? And you won't forget the other messages when I am out? I don't know when I shall be back, but I hope everything will have been done. And you won't forget to tidy up here and air the room?"

Or: "Now let's see, Céleste. I had decided not to go out, but I think I would like to see Princess Soutzo. We will have to telephone to find out if I can go. What do you think? I am very tired."

"If you like, monsieur, I'll telephone."

"All right then, but quickly. And could you warm my underwear and send for the barber? And you will have to order a cab for . . . just a minute while I see . . ."

He would decide how long it would take to heat the footbath and warm the underwear, how long it would take him to dress, and how long it would take the barber to shave him, and then he'd tell me exactly when he would want the cab. And I'd start to rush around.

Even when he had confidence in someone, he was still very much on his guard. He observed you all the time, and every so often put you to the test.

But he was only careful about what interested him. Money, for instance, didn't interest him. He knew he had enough for what he wanted to do, with what he'd inherited from his parents, and, through them, from his Great-Uncle Louis. This didn't prevent him from being extremely meticulous in the management of his fortune—he told me he got this trait from his mother.

Every morning he read the financial pages of the newspapers. In the evening, too, we sent out for *Les Débats, Le Temps,* and the reports from the Stock Exchange. If Odilon was there, after he got back from the war, he often sent for him, late, to discuss the stock market. He appreciated Odilon's good sense. He gave him advice, too. I remember once he urged Odilon to buy shares in Shell; he said they'd rise, and they did. He had an introduction from someone called Neuburger to the Rothschilds, the bankers. He also had an account at the Crédit Industriel, and a financial adviser, Lionel Hauser, who lived near the Observatoire. M. Proust had great confidence in him, though he never saw him, only wrote. Even if it's true he told other people he was "ruined," I never saw him short of money, except at Cabourg at the beginning of the war, when all the banks had moved to Bordeaux. And I never saw him worry about the future in this respect. I think his laments about money were just another way of excusing his semi-retirement from society. Just once he lost what was then a large sum of money—eight hundred thousand francs—speculating on the Stock Exchange. This was before the war. It was something to be upset about, and he was upset. It was when he was telling me about this that he said:

"Father said I would die in rags. And I believe he was right."

But he laughed as he said it, and he didn't tell me he was "ruined." His main feeling was fury with one of his brokers, who had led him into the venture.

"He's a prize idiot," he said, "and I have told him so."

I think he even wrote him a letter.

If he sold some furniture three years before he died, it wasn't through shortage of money but shortage of space. He didn't know what to do with all his furniture when we moved from boulevard Haussmann, and so far was he from being in difficulty that he intended to give the proceeds to his old friend Mme. Scheikévitch.

What I'm trying to say is that while he took a normal interest in the state of his financial affairs, so as to be sure he'd never be short of money, he didn't concern himself at all with actual expenses. Odilon used to write down his fares in a notebook, but he never presented it until, from time to time, he was asked for it. M. Proust would then pay without any discussion and without looking at anything but the total.

I would often go three or four months without being paid. M. Proust gave me a hundred francs a month, which was reasonable at the time, the equivalent of perhaps a bit over a thousand francs today. I paid the household expenses out of that, and he paid me back when I gave him the account book. He never looked at the bills I gave him at the same time. If there were any change he rounded the amount out, always in my favor.

Just once he commented:

"*Café au lait* comes dear, don't you think, Céleste?"

As I would always have charged him a penny too little rather than one too much, I snapped:

"What do you mean, monsieur? Do you think I have listed things I haven't bought and paid for?"

"Come, come, Céleste, I was only joking."

It was plain he wanted to see how I'd react. He didn't do it again. But at first, during what I might call my "apprenticeship"— for he really educated me step by step in his ways, his tastes, and his needs—he used to take soundings, just to see.

One day he came into the kitchen, a thing he rarely did. I was just washing up the few dishes used for coffee. There were some magnificent white linen towels with red borders, and I washed the bowl carefully and picked up a towel to dry it. He watched me, then said:

"My dear Céleste, you're drying that bowl, but the water from the tap is much cleaner than your cloth."

I reared up. "Monsieur, I've just got it out of the cupboard. It couldn't possibly be cleaner. It's just back from the laundry. What am I supposed to do? I can't give you a bowl that's sopping wet."

"Very well."

And he turned on his heel without another word.

Another time, when I picked up a glass from his tray to take it into the kitchen, I put my finger in it.

"Céleste, you should never put your finger in a glass even if it's been used."

I went scarlet and apologized, his voice was so severe. Ever since then whenever I've seen someone put his finger in a glass I've felt a sort of repugnance.

And then there were the sheets. He never went to bed twice in the same pair; every time he got up I changed them. One night he came home, and as he'd gone out the day before and I'd put clean sheets on then, they seemed all right to me and I didn't see any need to change them. So he went into the bedroom, and I followed. He looked at the bed: all was ready, the hot-water bottles there, the woolen sweater and the pajamas wrapped round them. Suddenly:

"Céleste, you haven't changed the sheets."

"They're not dirty, monsieur. I thought . . ."

"You thought! Let me tell you what I think. I think they may be damp—there is always some dampness and a little sour smell after they have been used. You don't realize it, but what you have done is awful. You know I can't have it. Even if I go out every day, the sheets have to be changed every time."

"I'm sorry, monsieur."

"You must have known it is the sort of thing I can't stand. So why did you do it?"

I changed the sheets; I'd learned my lesson. I all but stammered out, like a little girl who's been naughty, "I won't ever do it again."

At the beginning he used to say: "When I go out, don't forget to open the windows and air the room as usual."

And he'd say for how long, depending on the weather and time of year.

"Right, Céleste?"

Then he'd come back.

"Everything done, Céleste?"

"Yes, monsieur, and I left the windows open just the time you said."

"I know. I came by and saw they were closed again."

He'd driven by on purpose to inspect.

Once I said: "You trust me as far as you can check me."

He laughed but didn't answer.

He was terrible when he wanted to anger or wound. He didn't waste many words, and every one struck home, as he used to say his mother's did, and you were left mortified. I remember once he wanted something instantly and I said:

"It's impossible, monsieur."

"My dear Céleste, that word doesn't exist."

"I was taught it, monsieur."

"Well, you were taught wrong. What you ought to learn is that the word 'impossible' is not French."

One day when I'd done something clumsy I said, "Oh dammit!"

He looked at me severely.

"Céleste, you forget yourself."

I didn't say it again.

Another time I had a very long list of chores and I forgot one of them. He always checked everything, and I was so upset when he noticed that I told him: I was humiliated enough without his reminding me.

"Monsieur, I'm so sorry," I said. "Please forgive me. But I haven't got your memory, and I forgot."

"My dear Céleste, you're always telling me you do everything you can to please me. Well, when one does everything one can to please, and when one likes doing it, one does not forget. Memory is like everything else—it must be cultivated. If you want one you can have one."

I was so hurt by his tone that I never forgot anything again in all the time I was with him. And he trained me so fast that, after the very beginning, he didn't have to reproach me once for saying or doing anything I shouldn't. It's one of the things I'm most proud of.

He was most tyrannical and mistrustful about the telephone and telephone messages, because these made up his whole life; they governed his comings and goings, which were almost all connected with his work, and apart from his letters, which took longer, they constituted his main link with the outside world.

When I first went to boulevard Haussmann I'd never used a telephone and didn't know how it worked. During my first few months there, before he had it disconnected, there were several extensions in the apartment, each with a little switch for transferring the call into the room required. There was even a line to the concierge, so that if necessary he could take messages during the day and relay them to M. Proust when he woke up.

Once I started living there, he taught me to use the phone, first how to make calls and then how to receive them. One evening after he awoke he asked me to switch on the extension in his room and then to ask for a number. Then he said:

"Will you take the phone and speak, please?"

I didn't get very far with the message. I was shaking like a leaf.

215

He was behind me. I just said "Hello?," no doubt so awkwardly that he snatched the receiver out of my hand and spoke himself. When the conversation was over he turned to me.

"There is no need to be afraid, Céleste. It is very simple. Just imagine you are talking to someone."

Then he gave me a whole course, teaching me to make sure I'd got the right person and how to address them:"Do I have the honor of speaking to Monsieur le comte de A, to Monsieur B, or to Madame C?" He told me the titles, if any, beforehand. I gradually got used to it. Soon I knew nearly all the most familiar names and numbers by heart. I also made myself a little card with a complete list of his closest friends, and if I was in any doubt I checked. When I had to go down and phone from the café d'Anjou, I checked with the card beforehand. A fine thing it would have been if I'd made a mistake and the message had been delayed! It wasn't only that he couldn't bear waiting; I myself liked to do things quickly and in the way he wanted them.

At first he used to make me repeat messages carefully, but soon there was no need. I became so much his tape recorder that people used to take me for him and say, "Hello? Marcel? How lovely to hear you!" One lady even complained to him that he shouldn't let me imitate his voice. Of course this was completely unconscious on my part; in a way, I carried his voice about with me. He used to tell me, laughing as if at a good joke, what people said about it. Some were annoyed that they could never speak to him directly on the phone: "Céleste, always Céleste! Every time we have to go through your Céleste!" He pleaded his illness as an excuse, but with me he laughed about it. But most of the time people were very kind to me on the phone, just as they were when I delivered messages to them. You could see that most of them adored him and that a word from him was manna from heaven even if it came via a third person.

But even when he knew he could count on my words repeating his words faithfully, he still went on checking up, though indirectly. I'd be there in his room and we'd be talking about this and that. He would seem to be chatting quite freely and gaily. And then suddenly

216

he'd pause, as if about to plunge into thought; and then he'd come to life again just as suddenly, and out would come the question:

"By the way, Céleste, before I start work—and it is about time!—could you tell me again the answer to that message you delivered?"

Or: "Dear Céleste, I am sorry, but the other day we were talking about something and . . ."

"And what, monsieur?"

"Do you remember? I asked you to phone Gallimard's with a message for Madame Lemarié . . . or was it Monsieur Tronche?"

"It was Madame Lemarié, monsieur."

"Ah yes, I thought so. But, you know, I can't quite remember what I asked you to say. Would you mind telling me, reminding me what the answer was?"

On some occasions he didn't look at me when he spoke, which was very unusual for him. He'd listen to me saying it all again, and when I'd done he'd turn to me with a sweet smile and say:

"Thank you. That's it. Please forgive me for asking. I am so tired I had almost forgotten."

But I understood very well. In spite of all his confidence, he'd had a misgiving. And he couldn't set his mind at rest until I'd recited my lesson.

One thing that still amazes me is the freedom with which I spoke to him. With my natural spontaneity I was absolutely unconscious of this, but it was certainly there. I generally behaved as if I were absolutely docile, and I certainly was—but in my own way: by my own free will, and because it pleased me to be so. So when I got on my high horse, I did so quite naturally. And also I think I loved him too much to be afraid of him.

In the copy of *Pastiches et Mélanges* that he gave me he wrote: "To the Queen of Pastiche . . . to the Queen one would like to be a little less imperious, a little more majestic and mild Queen . . ." On the other hand, on one of the photographs he gave me he wrote: "To Céleste, from her hated tyrant" (he burst out laughing when he showed me); and on another: "To Céleste, affectionately, from her old Marcel." That's enough to show that my bossy ways couldn't have weighed on him too heavily, just as he knew very well that his tyranny wasn't really hated.

I said what I thought, that's all, but I kept to my place. Sometimes I would be carried away in my opinion about someone, for example, as with Le Cuziat. He saw I was launched, and said laughing, and referring to my parents' house:

"There goes the stream rushing under your mill!"

If he saw I was upset because he'd said the coffee or the stewed fruit was awful that day, he would correct himself gently:

"Dear Céleste, don't take it like that. You have misunderstood. I only said it tasted awful to me; I didn't say it *was* awful."

When he saw I disapproved, either because he was overtiring himself or because I couldn't see why he was making a friend of someone who didn't deserve it, he would give me a searching look and break off the conversation:

"Leave me for a while, please, Céleste."

"Just let me say what I was going to say, monsieur, and then I will."

"Céleste, I am tired, I need to be alone for a little while."

And I'd go, sensing or knowing he was probably afraid he might show impatience or say something disagreeable. But I also knew he'd come back to the subject by himself. Either he'd call me in again later, when he'd finished working, or else when he came in that night he'd say:

"I didn't want to discuss that before because I was tired. But we must clear it up."

And if he decided I was wrong but was being obstinate, it wouldn't end there. He might come back to it two or three days running, and each time I didn't give in he'd break off with "I am tired, please leave . . ." Or he might bring the subject up again several days later. It was as in his books: He came back again and again to the same point, always with a different explanation; and yet the matter did not repeat itself, it progressed until it was bared and finally "cleared up." And of course in the end, even if appearances had indicated otherwise, he always turned out to be right.

But he never gloated, he would never have said, "You see, you were wrong, Céleste." He just had a strange way of lowering his eyelids and then suddenly raising them again like a judgment. Then there would be a caressing look to thank you for having understood. He lowered and raised his eyes in the same way if anyone paid him a compliment and he felt at once that it was sincere.

At any rate, you couldn't help forgiving him. If he was suspicious it was because of his desire for perfection or because of his health—he was continually trying to stave off an attack of asthma. And if he was tyrannical it was because of the pressure of time and of his work.

To tease me he'd say:

"It's funny, Céleste—everyone says 'How lucky you are, Marcel, to have such a gentle, agreeable person to look after you.' If they only knew! I don't know any torrent or waterfall that rushes on faster than you!"

But then he would make up for it:

"All my friends know you through me. I tell them what you are like, and they are all very fond of you. You'll see. . . ."

And, in fact, every time I took a message I was received with warmth and kindness, not just as an errand girl but in the light of the kind things he'd said about me. People would talk to me about him and myself, and about his esteem for me. Some of his friends would stop by to see me while he was still asleep and chat with me for a moment in the kitchen.

I always hurried as fast as I could when he sent me on an errand, because I knew the time would drag for him until I got back. I never stopped for anything else. As soon as I got home I would make my report, and when he saw me come in he'd say:

"Goodness, Céleste, back already? You *were* quick! Well . . .?"

I remember one evening he was ready to go out and he suddenly

219

changed his mind. So I had to rush and telephone. I ran down to the little café, and he was so impatient that, for the only time in all those years, he went out on the balcony. Of course he was dressed to go out. My sister, Marie, was with us at the time, and she followed him out and pointed down into the street.

"Here comes Céleste, monsieur!"

"Impossible! She hasn't had the time!"

When I came back, breathless, his face shone with pleasure and affection.

"Look at her, Marie! She doesn't walk, she flies!"

His smile, as it always did when he paid one a compliment, refreshed me immediately.

Sometimes I'd go in with the coffee in the afternoon and he'd suddenly say:

"Goodness, how pretty you look this morning, Céleste!"

"You're making fun, monsieur."

"Not at all. You look like Lady Grey."

And he explained that she was a famous English beauty. Other people told me he said the same thing about me to them.

Once, for the wedding of one of my nieces, I had a dress made for myself—black lace over yellow silk. And, at his suggestion, bought a boa at the luxury branch of the Samaritaine department store. I also had a cape made—black satin with a yellow lining like the dress, with a fringe of bird-of-paradise feathers all round. He said:

"Don't forget to come in and see me when you are dressed."

He made me parade around the room and complimented me on the effect.

"I am proud of you, dear Céleste. You have very good taste."

If ever anything was bothering me I tried to keep it to myself. But though I was quite sure I wasn't letting it show, he always saw immediately.

"What is the matter, Céleste?"

"Nothing, monsieur."

"Yes, there is. Something is upsetting you. You look different."

220

"I assure you there's nothing the matter, monsieur."

"Come now, you are anxious about your husband's health—I know. Don't you worry—I shall talk to him."

His powers of observation were constantly at work, screening. He was never taken in. And always, with his kindness, he found just the right thing to say.

"Ah, monsieur," I once said to him, "if all tyrants were like you, the world would be a paradise!"

Grande, fine, belle et maigre,
Tantôt lasse, tantôt allègre,
Charmant les princes comme la
                              pègre
Lançant à Marcel un mot aigre,
Lui rendant pour le miel le vinaigre,
Spirituelle, agile, intègre
Telle est le nièce de nègre.

29 He wrote this little poem and gave it to me, which led me to tell him, "Well Monsieur, you have certainly dressed me up!" We had a good laugh over that.

30 This is me in the dress that I made to wear to a family wedding. He thought it very pretty.

Paris, 10 décembre

Monsieur et cher confrère

Nous avons l'honneur et le plaisir de vous annoncer que vous avez été désigné aujourd'hui pour le Prix Goncourt pour votre livre : *à l'ombre des jeunes filles en fleur.*

Veuillez recevoir, Monsieur et cher confrère, l'expression de nos sentiments dévoués

Elémir Bourges   Gustave Geffroy

J. H. Rosny aîné
                    Léon Hennique
Léon Daudet

          [signatures]

31 The letter from the Academie Goncourt, announcing that he had won the prize in 1919. He got six votes out of nine. His strongest advocate was Léon Daudet.

32 My favorite picture, because it has everything: the rebellious fore-lock that would stray away on its own, the glance, and the position of the hand. He looked just like this when he spoke to me from his bed.

33 A manuscript page from *Swann's Way*. He'd show me a page like
this and say, "Take a look, Céleste, haven't I been working hard!"

34 These are the printer's proofs of his books, after he corrected them. He was never satisfied. If he hadn't died no doubt he would have gone on revising his work.

Marie dir à mon frère,
car avant d'avoir pris mon café au

d' autruche faraut Quand je

Cafés au lait. appeler Céleste

mon café au lait bien tôt, et d'igno
venait du plaisir de faire, et des gram c
tandis que je n'ai pas fait un seul feu
V eut à ce qu'elle se souvienne d'autres tout ça,
s'offrir pas.

_____

J'écrais entendre fa fer an

_____

Céleste voilon paut faut et
dans 10 minutes ! et rentrer vers 6
approchez de moi la chaise .

35 When he was tired and didn't want to talk, to save his breath and his strength, he'd write his wishes on little slips of paper. These are three which I picked up from his bed after his death—some of the last he wrote. On the one at the bottom, there's a stain from a cup of coffee that he tried to get down, saying, "This is to make you happy, you and my brother." That was around 7 in the morning. He died at 4:30 in the afternoon.

36 The painter Helleu, one of his friends, came to do this drypoint
etching after he died and before Dunoyer de Segonzac and the photographer Man Ray showed up. Helleu made two prints, and Monsieur
Robert Proust gave one to me. After that Helleu destroyed the plate.

19

FRIENDS BUT NO FRIENDSHIP

In an article published after M. Proust's death Prince Antoine Bibesco, who'd known him for more than twenty years, said that in his view M. Proust had only really loved two people in the world—his mother and me. It's certainly true about his mother, and from the tributes I had from him I'm inclined to think, without being vain, that it's probably true about me too. Prince Bibesco said in the same article that he doubted whether M. Proust had had any great and profound friendships. And there again I'm inclined to agree.

I don't remember, for example, our ever having had any conversations about friendship in general. Looking back now on how he was then, my impression is that he must have let, or even made, a lot of people think he felt affection and friendship for them, whereas in fact—it was a thing that always struck me—he could do without all of them with the greatest of ease.

Of course I'm talking about the time I knew him, when he had enough in his memory not to need the actual presence of people. And of course I did see him mourn the death of various people and hear him say, "My friends, my friends." But all the same . . . From his way of talking about them, and judging the mere tone in which he spoke of them, I sensed it was a matter of acquaintance rather than friendship. How many times did he say to me:

"Here is a letter from X. He says he will call. If I am awake and not working when he comes, I may see him."

And how many times did the "may" become: "Say I can't, I am too tired"?

And yet the visitor would be on the list of friends. And goodness knows what they wouldn't all have done to see him. They even accepted the times that suited him—ten or eleven at night, sometimes one in the morning.

This is quite apart from all the people who considered themselves his friends while he was alive and called themselves such after his death, only because he had decided to cultivate in them some elements of one of his characters, or to get some information or a favor, or simply to satisfy his curiosity.

I think many people were misled this way. It wasn't that he intended to deceive them. But they often met his politeness and charm more than halfway and deceived themselves. If they'd heard his comments during our nightly conversations, or even if they'd been able to see the flicker of his eyelids, they'd have kept their claims of friendship to themselves after he was gone.

Apart from the new acquaintances he made through the publication of his books, practically all that were left during my time were a few old intimates from among those he'd known best in the early days. He didn't really say much about the others. Some were already dead: Gaston de Caillavet (whom he mentioned in connection with Jeanne Pouquet), and Bertrand de Fénelon, whose death at the front was a great sorrow to him. The day the papers confirmed Fénelon's death, he spoke to me of his courage and integrity. But I've often wondered if he didn't mourn as much the loss of his chief model for the Knight of Saint-Loup in his novel as the loss of what really was in this case an old and real friend.

One of those from the old days who remained close to him right up to the end was Mme. Straus. If I may express an opinion, I'd say she was probably the only person for whom he kept, right up to his death, the sort of affection and admiration that's closest to friendship. But this hadn't prevented him from cutting himself off completely from her son, Jacques Bizet, who had been one of his friends and companions ever since they were at school together at the Lycée Condorcet. When I first knew him, in 1913, they no longer saw or even wrote to each other.

The other people he saw most—still among the "old ones"—were the Duke d'Albuféra, the Duke de Guiche, Count Robert de Billy, Lucien Daudet, Prince Antoine and Prince Emmanuel Bibesco, Frédéric de Madrazo, and Reynaldo Hahn. This was the "old guard" from the Club in rue Royale and the salons and receptions of the old days.

A significant thing is that when I glance over my memories I don't think I remember ever hearing M. Proust address one of them with the familiar *tu*—not even Reynaldo Hahn, to whom he'd been very close for twenty-five years.

I never met the Duke d'Albuféra; as he didn't come to the apartment M. Proust used to see him elsewhere, with his friend Louisa de Mornand. He said:

"The Duke's intelligence is equal to Mademoiselle de Mornand's talent. If only they were both as gifted as he is rich!"

I remember seeing the Duke de Guiche once at boulevard Haussmann during the war. He was on leave and came to see M. Proust in captain's uniform. M. Proust was very attached to him because of his style and wit.

Count de Billy was one of those who came most often. One reason was he was in the diplomatic service and so had plenty of just the sort of story that delighted M. Proust. And then he was very intelligent and had an enormous admiration for M. Proust's work, which M. Proust himself said he could discuss with great insight. His visits used to last three or four or five hours, right into the night. I can still see him sitting in the chair beside M. Proust's bed. He was one of those men by whom you could most easily measure the passage of time: he was fat and aging and looked more than fifty beside M. Proust, who still looked thirty. M. de Billy spent most of his time abroad as ambassador, but he visited every time he was in Paris. I was never present at their conversations, except briefly, if I was sent for something. Then they always looked gay and animated. M. Proust always said the count was "fascinating."

Lucien Daudet visited quite often too. M. Proust preferred him to his brother Léon, the politician. Lucien was extremely sensitive and put much feeling into being a devoted admirer of M. Proust. He was perhaps one of the few people M. Proust was fond of for themselves, without thinking whether he might be useful as a character in his book. But it might have been that he wasn't a striking enough personality for that.

Besides Mme. Straus and Robert de Billy, his only friends from the old days were the Bibesco brothers, Frédéric de Madrazo, and Reynaldo Hahn, whom he saw with the greatest pleasure and whom he loved dearly, if the word "love" can be used in this case. What is certain is that he was tremendously loyal to them. But he saw things too clearly. By dint of analyzing himself and others I think he'd left himself with nothing but motives and explanations.

Still, he did have a great affection for the Bibesco brothers and an enormous respect for Emmanuel, the elder of the two.

"Céleste," he once said, "you ought to read Dostoevski's *Brothers Karamazov*—they are the Bibesco brothers. Emmanuel is without any doubt the more intelligent of the two. Antoine is crazy and charming, but his brother has an extraordinary delicacy of feeling. Although it is a burden to him, he has taken on all the administration of their land and money in Rumania so that Antoine can be free of material worries and enjoy a more brilliant life. Fortunately, Antoine understands, and adores his brother."

Antoine, like Count de Billy, had entered the diplomatic service, and when I met him he was working at the Rumanian Embassy in London; Rumania was our ally. Every time he came to Paris— and this was true after the war too—he immediately sent a *pneumatique* to M. Proust, announcing his arrival. They were always whirlwind visits. I remember him coming once when he was engaged to the daughter of the great English statesman Asquith. I showed him in and he said, jokingly:

"Céleste, I love you!"

"Crazy as ever, I see, Prince!" I answered.

"But I do love you, Céleste!"

M. Proust laughed, of course, but said: "Now, now, Antoine, don't be silly. Leave Céleste alone. She doesn't like that sort of thing."

Not long afterward he came again, this time with his fiancée. M. Proust was in bed, and supposing the girl wouldn't be allowed in, the prince left her on the landing and came in on his own.

"May I go into his room?" he asked.

"I'll have to go and see," I said.

I went, but while I was doing so the prince picked up his fiancée like a doll and followed me into the room with her. He was the only person who would have dared to do such a thing, knowing how much M. Proust hated any woman but me to see him in bed. I can still see his expression as he lay with his face in the shadow and his hands folded over his jumper and the sheet. He was horribly embarrassed. He turned to me and said, letting one hand fall back on the sheet:

"You see, Céleste? I told you he was crazy!"

Prince Antoine was a marvelous raconteur, always full of gossip about society people and the literary world.

"He sounds like a concierge sometimes, and his stories may or may not be true," M. Proust said, "but he is so funny!"

Alas, Antoine's favorite brother, Emmanuel, hanged himself in his room at the Ritz in London because he was threatened with general paralysis. I shall never forget his last visit, in 1917 I believe, when he came with Prince Antoine. He didn't come up. His brother came and told M. Proust that Prince Emmanuel was waiting downstairs in a taxi. M. Proust went down, and when he came back he said:

"Céleste, I have just seen something terribly painful, but it was wonderful too, because it shows how the two brothers love each other. When I got downstairs I found Emmanuel huddled up in the back of the taxi, as if he were hiding in the shadow. I said, 'I shall sit on the tip-up seat,' but Antoine stopped me and said, 'No, I shall sit there, you sit beside him, Marcel.' So I did, and all the time we were talking I could only see Emmanuel's profile, and I realized Antoine wanted to spare Emmanuel my seeing him so changed. For it is the other side of his face that is paralyzed. He knew it would be painful for me, but above all he knew how much it would grieve his brother. And that was why he put up that screen of love."

He was still shaken. People have said I saw him weeping all that night. But it's not true. Perhaps a tear or so. But M. Proust didn't cry as easily as some people say, or as he himself sometimes suggested in his letters. Although he was grieved to learn of Prince Emmanuel's suicide later, he didn't mourn. He didn't speak to me about him again.

As far as I remember, M. Proust had met the two brothers in their mother's salon long before the war—Princess Hélène's salon was one of the most brilliant in Paris. They in turn introduced him to their cousin, Princess Marthe Bibesco. I fear she spoke about him after he was dead much more than he spoke about her when he was alive, though he did think her beautiful and intelligent.

"But with her, intelligence is just another form of coquetry," he said.

I saw Princess Marthe after M. Proust was dead, and she was kindness itself to me.

I'd met her only once before, one evening when she called at rue Hamelin after the theater and asked if she and Princess Elisabeth, Prince Antoine's wife, could see him. The prince wasn't with them. M. Proust asked me to say that much to his regret he was unable to see them. This incident gave rise to the elegant phrase that's been attributed to me: "Monsieur cannot stand the perfume of princesses." I'm afraid it's a piece of embroidery; neither I nor M. Proust ever said it.

The one M. Proust had the greatest affection for in the Bibesco circle, apart from the two brothers, was Countess de Noailles, the poetess, who was related to them through another Rumanian family, the Brancovans. Her esteem for him dated from the Dreyfus affair. She, like him, had thrown herself bravely into the Dreyfusite camp and had suffered many insults because she wasn't French. He would sometimes recite her poems to me in the little salon—*"Le Coeur innombrable"* and *"Les Vivants et les Morts"*:

> Having honored all, setting and rising suns,
> Death too I have loved. . . .

He found her capricious and a little crazy, like Prince Antoine. She told him in detail about her husband's infidelities, and this enchanted him.

"One day she said, 'My little Marcel, you and I are the only two who are intelligent. Look—if I pull back my hair, we look alike.'" He imitated the movement and the voice, including the accent, and added: "Ah, she knows the poetry of gesture as well as of words!"

He went on seeing her, as well as her sister, Princess de Chimay, whom he admired for her cleverness and wit.

Although he saw him less than before, he was also still very fond of Frédéric de Madrazo, a wealthy dilettante who was a close friend of Reynaldo Hahn. Scandalmongers said there was "something" between Hahn and "Coco," as everyone called Madrazo, but M. Proust never said anything about this to me. M. Proust and Frédéric de Madrazo had met when they were very young, in the salon of Mme. Lemaire, the one who had painted as many roses as God. "Coco" was a painter himself, and a musician, too. But more than his pictures and his music, M. Proust remembered the way he talked about painting. It was with him and Reynaldo Hahn that he'd visited Venice with his mother when he was young. He had wonderful memories of that journey. It was in 1901 or 1902, during the two or three years when, he told me, he'd made three of his most important intellectual discoveries: the English writer Ruskin; the cathedrals, especially Amiens and its angel; and Venice and Venetian painting. He was truly grateful to Madrazo, for it was because of his insistence that he had seen Venice, and it was he who helped him understand it. He still thrilled to think of it, and he once said:

"You will see Céleste. When I have written 'The End' on the

last page of my book, I shall take you to Venice, and I shall go to see the angel at Aiens again with you, and Chartres. . . ."

That and Vermeer's painting—the little patch of yellow wall, which came later.

Madrazo was also immensely kind. So great was his respect for M. Proust's work, and his concern for his health, that he would often call to see how he was without even asking to see him. He would come up the service stairs when he knew he was most likely to find me in the kitchen and cause no disturbance. We'd talk for a moment and then he'd go away, asking me to give his love to M. Proust. Like Prince Emmanuel, though later, he too had a tragic death. There was a time, M. Proust told me, when he had had a very nice house on boulevard Berthier. But he lost all his money and was seriously ill with an ulcer. One day he was found dead in his bath, and there was no means of knowing whether it was an accident, a heart attack, or suicide, M. Proust was very upset. He talked about it for a long while, first with Reynaldo Hahn and then with me.

Of all M. Proust's intimates, Reynaldo Hahn was the only one who was always allowed in when he came, provided M. Proust was awake. He often called in without warning. I'd open the door, and if M. Proust was awake and had finished his fumigation, Hahn walked straight in. Otherwise he asked how M. Proust was, then left. But usually he came late, when he was sure to see him. He was the only one, too, that I didn't see out afterward. He would sneak out on his own—there's no other word for it—and leave a draft behind. As no one was allowed to slam doors because M. Proust couldn't stand the noise, M. Proust sent for me nearly every time after Reynaldo Hahn had left.

"Dear Céleste, did Reynaldo shut the doors behind him properly?"

For while doors mustn't be slammed, they had to be properly closed because there mustn't be the slightest draft. And Reynaldo Hahn nearly always left all the doors open. So as soon as I knew he'd gone—and nothing escaped me—I used to check. One day, to excuse his friend's carelessness, M. Proust told me the story of the scholar Henri Poincaré, who stopped on the quai de la Mégisserie to look at the birds in the pet shops. But all the time he was really thinking about his mathematical calculations, and he walked off with a cage full of birds in hand. The shopgirl ran after him, and he apologized and handed the birds back—it had never entered his head to buy them. I remember answering:

"Yes, but he had the excuse of being an important scientist. But Reynaldo only *wants* to be important."

"You *are* severe, Céleste. He is so nice!"

In fact, he had Reynaldo Hahn sized up perfectly.

"It is a pity he didn't just remain a singer," he said, "instead of wanting to compose songs himself. When I met him at Mme. Lemaire's there was no one like him. All the salons wanted him, and he got very good fees for singing. One day I shall engage him to come and sing '*Si mon coeur avait des ailes*' for you, just as he used to. It was marvelous, there was nothing like it! But unfortunately, now, he wants to be Saint-Saëns. I wish you had heard him when he came with his mother to see mine!"

For there had been a close bond between their mothers too, and also with Reynaldo Hahn's cousin, Marie Nordlinger, who introduced M. Proust to the work of Ruskin. But after the war, and in particular after the publication and success of M. Proust's second book, *A l'ombre des jeunes filles en fleurs*, the relationship between M. Proust and Reynaldo Hahn cooled off, and perhaps there was a certain amount of acrimony on the part of the latter.

"We were very close once," M. Proust told me. "We used to go see the great equinoctial tides at Pointe du Raz together. We both spent one summer at Mme. Lemaire's, at the château de Réveillon; our common ground was the intellect and our mutual esteem. Then the war came. Reynaldo had to go into the army, and although he kept up his correspondence, he had the impression that I was succeeding while he was left out. It is a funny thing, Céleste, but he is jealous of me, you know. I realized it when he came home on leave from the front. He is jealous of me because people talk about my books in literary circles, whereas he has to content himself with a minor success. He says: 'Everywhere I go people can talk of no one but you and of nothing but your book.' Isn't it strange!"

Once after Reynaldo Hahn had been to see him he called me in. "Dear Céleste, I do feel depressed. I asked Reynaldo why he hadn't been round lately and if anything had happened to annoy him. And do you know what he said? 'My dear Marcel, I haven't either your money or your success. You have everything you want. Nowadays, one can't do anything without money. It used to be called "cash." Now they cal it "dough." Well, I need dough.' I said, 'My dear little Reynaldo, do you want me to give you some money?' He said, 'You don't understand, Marcel. I don't want your money. What I mean is I have to earn some. That is why I haven't the time to come to see you.' He looked very sad, and as I listened to him I couldn't help thinking how sweetly he used to sing in the old days."

If M. Proust was depressed, it was much more for Reynaldo Hahn's own sake than for the anger and envy in what he'd said. The proof is that he was delighted, shortly before his death, to learn that Reynaldo Hahn had had a success as a composer. This was the famous operetta *Ciboulette* (Chives), for which he'd written the music to the words of Robért de Flers and Francis de Croisset, the son-in-law of an old acquaintance of M. Proust's, the Countess de Chevigné. The operetta had its real success in Paris at the Théâtre de Variétés, after M. Proust's death. But when it was first performed in the South of France it had a good reception, and I can still see M. Proust turning to me with his hands clasped on the sheet and saying with that luminous smile:

"Dear Céleste, how glad I am that Reynaldo's had some success at last!"

I also remember his telling me he'd been very worried about Reynaldo Hahn because of an unhappy love affair. Hahn had been in love with only one woman in his life:

"It was Cléo de Mérode, the famous demimondaine—you know, Céleste? It was about her they said, 'A hungry belly has no ears,' because she was greedy and because she combed her hair in bandeaux to hide the one flaw in her beauty—her ears. She was very bad for poor Reynaldo, who was petrified by her. She led him on with no rewards and caused him great sorrow. It may even have affected his talent."

Anyway, the friendship between Hahn and M. Proust was too old for them not to overlook things when necessary, and they remained loyal to each other right up to the end; but perhaps it was more as young brothers than as friends.

So there were the old acquaintances, but despite what has been said, there were not many new visitors either at boulevard Haussmann or later rue Hamelin. But I don't want to wound people's little vanities; I'd rather smile at them, as M. Proust would certainly have done if he'd been able to read some of the articles published after his death.

He mostly saw people outside, and since he was much sought after—usually for dinner parties at Larue's, the Crillon, or the Ritz, unless he himself invited people to a party in a private room—he still saw an enormous number of people. But he related everything to his work, and many of them just amused him in passing, without really interesting him.

For example, I remember that one evening Prince Antoine Bibesco, who was always very much up to date, called to take him to one of these dinners with the object of introducing him to Picasso, who was beginning to be talked about. It was at the Crillon, not, as has been said, at the Ritz—but that's of little importance. On the stroke of two in the morning, all three of them went to Picasso's studio to see his paintings. M. Proust told me about it when he came in.

"He is a Spanish painter who has started to paint what is called cubism."

He gave me a short description of what the pictures were like, and I commented that the Picasso faces must be a funny sort. He laughed and said: "I must admit I didn't understand it much."

It was clear he didn't really care, and he never spoke about Picasso's painting again. It's been said he dined with the writer James Joyce, together with others, but if he did, it didn't leave any impression on him, and he didn't even mention the name.

There was a banker, Henri Gans, whom he liked very much because of his refined manners and his understanding of M. Proust's work. He was one of the few people who came to dine once or twice in M. Proust's room at rue Hamelin. There was a close bond between them, and sadly enough on the Saturday after M. Proust's funeral, which was on a Wednesday, Henri Gans, who was out shooting, was accidentally killed by a charge of buckshot from one of the huntsmen.

But the principal newcomers during the time I knew him were the writer Paul Morand and Princess Soutzo, who later became Morand's wife.

Paul Morand captivated M. Proust at once with his subtle comments on his work and by the brilliant and amusing stories he brought back from his travels. For he, too, was in the diplomatic service, and having made friends with Prince Bibesco in London, he was introduced by him to the court of M. Proust.

After the first time Paul Morand came to boulevard Haussmann, M. Proust asked me in the course of our nocturnal conversation what impression he'd made on me.

"He seems very nice," I said. "A bit Chinese."

He laughed, and I was rather annoyed.

"What did I say that was funny, monsieur? I meant I thought his face looked rather Chinese."

He went on laughing. "Yes, Céleste, but he is as subtle as a mandarin too."

Paul Morand, in turn, acted as ambassador for Princess Soutzo, whom he had met through the Bibescos. The princess was also Rumanian. She was a banker's daughter, very rich, and already married; but not much was seen of the husband. She had had a beautiful house on avenue Charles-Floquet, near the Champs-de-Mars, but had shut it up because of the war and the consequent servant problems and gone with her maid to live in an apartment at the Ritz. It was about this time that Paul Morand introduced her to M. Proust.

She was a very intelligent woman, very interested in literature and the other arts, and had the laudable ambition of making herself a name in Paris by attracting the best people of those days, even though many of them had been scattered by the war. She continued with this ambition after the war when she had moved back into her own house, where M. Proust, too, visited her.

I don't know whether the idea of meeting M. Proust was her own or whether it arose out of what Paul Morand had told her about him. Anyway, Paul Morand told M. Proust she was a great admirer of his, and he agreed to meet her and dine with them.

I can clearly remember his asking me to send for the barber.

"Get everything ready as soon as possible, Céleste. I must hurry. Monsieur Morand is calling for me to dine with him and a Rumanian princess at Larue's. He is anxious for me to meet her."

At about ten o'clock Paul Morand came, accompanied by his other guest. I went to tell M. Proust.

"Ask him to come in, please."

"There's a lady with him."

"Yes, she is the one I told you about—Princess Soutzo. What is she like?"

You couldn't lie to him, so I said what I thought.

"Rather small, with a very straight neck and a little hat with strings. She's in black, as if she were in mourning. I wouldn't swear to it that she isn't a bit older than he is." (Paul Morand wasn't yet thirty at the time.) "If you don't mind my saying so, she isn't exactly elegant, but she looks a charming little doll."

These descriptions of people always amused him.

"Well, we shall see!" he said.

So I fetched Paul Morand, and they chatted for a few moments while the princess waited in the hall. Then they all went out together. When he came in I could see that M. Proust was pleased with his evening, and he told me so himself.

Almost immediately after that he began to see the princess very often. This developed into his Ritz period. He dined there often. The restaurant stayed open very late in spite of the war. He also used to visit the princess in her apartment. I'd telephone to ask if he could call, and she was one of those who mistook me for him.

"Is that you, Marcel?"

"No, Princess, it's Céleste."

She was also one of those who thought I dressed too well. After she'd had a minor operation M. Proust asked me to take her a big bunch of flowers, and when she saw him later she said:

"Céleste is impossible. Not only does she talk like you on the telephone, but she's much too elegant. You oughtn't to put up with it."

"It is funny," M. Proust said, when he told me. "I'm exactly the opposite. Even with people I don't know I can tell what they are like just by looking at the person who opens the door. I know one house where the maids wear Alsatian costume, which is very pretty though perhaps going a bit far. But they have holes in their elbows— their employers are trying to make themselves out richer than they really are."

He added that I mustn't mind the princess' little oddities, as she came from a country that was still rather feudal. I think he enjoyed analyzing her, and she for her part did all she could to please him. If he mentioned someone's name and said he'd like to meet him, she'd say:

"Nothing could be easier, Marcel. Whenever you like. Tell me the day that suits you, and I shall invite him to dinner."

He was very aware of her usefulness.

One night, coming in from the Ritz, he laughed and said:

"I do believe the princess has got her eye on me. I said to her today, 'But you are married, madame.' And do you know what she answered? 'That doesn't mean anything.' I do believe she wants to marry me!"

All he wanted to do was study her. I always thought he guessed she'd in time marry Paul Morand. More than once he told me he knew Paul Morand was in love, very much in love, with her. He was happy for Paul Morand's sake, and I'm sure he gave them his blessing from above. He knew very well Paul Morand had no reason to be jealous of him but that he probably was a bit jealous just the same. He would laugh as he told me about his visits to the princess:

"Behind the sofa in her salon there is a big screen, and, believe it or not, Céleste, every time we sit on that sofa and talk I can't help thinking M. Morand is behind the screen, listening."

"What an idea!"

"I really wouldn't be all that surprised!"

He was quite delighted with the princess' pursuit of him. After all, he was only human and therefore susceptible to the interest people took in him, especially if that interest was connected with his work. I remember a young attaché—Truel, his name was—who adored his book so much he deluged him with letters and requests to be allowed to come and see him. When I said, "You're tired enough without that, monsieur," h'd say, "Yes, Céleste, but he is so nice!"

Anyway, I could tell from what he said, and from his voice and look, that it was the same with Princess Soutzo as with so many others. In the last resort M. Proust's friendship consisted in thinking that a person deserved his analysis, which was accorded in proportion to the interest that a person represented for him.

One of the most touching things he ever said to me was to admit that his first opinion of Paul Morand had been wrong. It was during the week before his death, and Paul Morand had just paid him a long visit. He sent for me and said:

"Céleste, I have a confession to make. I thought M. Morand was egoist and all the affection was on my side. But this evening I realized he was very fond of me, perhaps fonder than I of him. And do you know what made me think that? It was because he couldn't bring himself to go. He just sat on in the chair looking at me and talking. He saw how ill I was, and he was so kind, so tactful! I was wrong before, but now I can tell you with certainty the M. Morand was very fond of me."

Only when his words came back to me, together with the echo of his voice, did I realize that he spoke already in the past, and that his confession was a form of grateful farewell. For he added:

"You won't forget to tell him, will you, Céleste?"

20

THE PURSUIT OF CHARACTERS

Admittedly, in the society he knew, friendship must have been a fairly rare thing, often disappearing behind easy manners or formal elegance. It might have existed in certain people, and if M. Proust, who was perspicacity personified, didn't discover it, that was perhaps because he didn't bother to look for it. What interested him in people, at least during the time I knew him, was the material they might provide for his book.

Yes, the more I thought about it afterward, the more I remember him ready to go out, with his coat on, his smile, his hat shading eyes already lit up by the hope of a "good evening," and then coming back either beaming or tired and vexed over time wasted, the more it seemed to me he never went out except with his book in mind.

When he set out it wasn't at random but always with a definite objective—for he was a hunter of details, a pilgrim in quest of his characters.

His characters kept up a continual dance in his memory, each performing his or her own highly organized figures. He never lost sight of them, and what he sought above all was not feelings but truth.

When he came home pleased I'd say:

"Did you get a good haul, monsieur? What sort of honey are you going to make for us today?"

One night he said to me: "You know, Céleste, I want my work to be a sort of cathedral in literature. That is why it is never finished. Even when the construction is completed there is always some decoration to add, or a stained-glass window or a capital or another chapel to be opened up, with a little statue in the corner."

And so he would set out on his search.

When he was trying to find out about a dress, he had to know where the embroidery came from and what the stitch was; he stopped short of asking who manufactured the thread.

When he let Charlie, the young English friend of M. Goldsmith of "Sodom party," come to see him, it was only partly to study his very mannered behavior, and he used to imitate him to me afterward. He studied everything about him, right down to the last detail of his attire.

"His shirts and waistcoats come from Charvet's in place Vendôme," he told me.

What interested him about Charvet's was that it was the mark of a certain kind of society, a particular brand of elegance. Similarly, what interested him in Goldsmith himself, who bored him to death as a man, were Goldsmith's affectations:

"I am sure that even in his dressing gown he looks as if he were in evening dress."

He always sought to see deeper into people—into their mystery, their relationships, their encounters, the allusions between the sexes, the contacts that took place only in words. But when he talked about all this, he never dotted the i's. He left you to do that for yourself.

It's the same with the characters in his book. A great deal has been written about this, and I'm not going to play the professor. Anyway, he didn't reveal the key to me any more than to anyone else. And I don't believe this was out of mischief or mystification, out of any deliberate desire to confuse or sidetrack people—it simply corresponded to the nature of his work. None of the innumerable keys that have been tried since have been enough to open all the secret compartments. A big ring of keys is needed for each character.

I'd say that fundamentally he was as little concerned about the keys to his work as about the keys to his apartment. Some people may have taken pride and pleasure in breaking the box open and, as they thought, violating its secret like that of the Pharaohs' tombs, but I'm sure he foresaw this and was indifferent to it. When he said he saw his work as a sort of cathedral in literature, that meant he expected it to stand as long as the great churches he loved so much. And so what difference did it make if the character of the Duchess de Guermantes was based partly on Countess Greffulhe, and partly on Mme. Straus and the Countess de Chevigné, and partly on ten or a dozen others? In a hundred years, what would it matter that anyone should know this, and who would remember these ladies? But the Duchess de Guermantes and the other characters would still be alive in his books and in the eyes of new generations of readers.

During the last two years, after we'd left boulevard Haussmann and were in rue Hamelin, there was a society lady who had a house at the corner of rue La Pérouse. She had great style but a rather eccentric one for the time, because in 1920 she still dressed exactly like Queen Alexandra, the wife of King Edward VII, who had been dead ten years. And meanwhile there had been the war, with all the changes it had brought.

She had been very beautiful and was still extremely elegant, though of course very old-fashioned with her piled-up hair. M. Proust had met her at Countess Greffulhe's, I think, and had been fascinated by the way she dressed. She had no children, but a niece of hers lived with her as a daughter. M. Proust told me, laughing, that this niece admired him so much that, she said, if she couldn't marry him she knew only one other person she could marry: the famous organist Widor, who was much older than she was. As a matter of fact, she did marry Widor, and he came to share the house in rue La Pérouse. Now I noticed that from our kitchen window you could see into their dining room, where they took their meals in a very formal manner. I told M. Proust about this, and he asked me to let him know the first opportunity he could see them. He came and looked two or three times. I could tell from watching him that what interested him was the service, the way the table was set with china and candlesticks, and the relationships between the people sitting around it. His mind registered it all in a flash.

He made use of this lady in his book to describe the way Princess de Guermantes dressed, especially in the gala scene at the Opéra, where the austerity of the princess contrasted with the plumes and jewels of the duchess. And it wouldn't surprise me if he made use elsewhere of details of how the meals were served in her house.

But how are we any better off, except for a bit of society gossip, if we knew the lady was really Mme. Standish, a former friend of King Edward VII? If M. Proust borrowed some of her finery, it was because it corresponded to his own notion of the Princess de Guermantes, and the person beneath the dress that evening at the Opéra is not Mme. Standish but the princess.

The fact is, he wasn't just painting a set of portraits. There was a whole world, a whole society and way of living that he'd once known and that was crumbling gradually, in the midst of a new world coming into being. He had realized this; I'm sure he foresaw it right from the beginning. As a moralist, he tried to describe all this in its human aspects, with all its beauties and also all its follies. He was terrible in his judgments, and he foretold the fall—anyone who doesn't see that in his work hasn't understood it.

The whole point of going out to see so many people was to gather the material, in order to make as realistic a prediction as possible.

He didn't say this to me openly. As always it was indirect.

"I went to see the so-and-so's this evening, as you know, and who do you think I met there? Madame X! I was amazed. Nothing would have induced them to have her in their house in the old days."

He didn't even say in what way this was significant—but you could see his gaze looking into the past and making the comparison.

When he was working he'd sometimes ask me to bring him the

Almanach de Gotha, but very rarely, and just to look up heraldic details and marriage relationships in order to compare them and trace what became of families over the years. It had nothing to do with snobbishness or curiosity. He followed the progress or decline of families out of the same desire for accuracy that sometimes led him to say:

"Would you look in the encyclopedia, please, Céleste? I've got my provinces muddled up, and I'd like you to check out what province such-and-such a place is in."

Naturally he wanted his characters to be perfect, and that's why he dressed and combed them like so many real models. But he never grafted a real model's fault on to any of them out of malice or even as a joke. It was always the pleasure of an artist at having found what he was looking for.

He knew that going out so often was killing him, but he found the energy for it within himself. These evenings brought him a kind of exaltation, like a young man hurrying to an appointment with the girl of his choice. He was ill, but he held out in the hope of bringing home what he had been looking for. When you experience a great happiness, when something turns out as you wanted it to—a pleasant meeting or a successful journey—you come back absolutely refreshed, content, rejuvenated; you don't feel tired, you don't even need to sleep. That's how he must have felt; that's what must have kept him going. He might come home pleased either because of a person or because he'd satisfied his curiosity about a house— because he'd found out whether the person had changed or not, or whether the house still had the same roof, and who lived there, and if there were more or fewer servants than when he used to know the place.

At one time he was anxious about a hat he'd seen the Countess de Chevigné wear a long time ago.

"She was beautiful, and she always had magnificent hats. There was one, I remember, decorated with poppies and cornflowers, and a marvelous felt toque with Parma violets." And then he asked: "Do you think she might still have it? And could I ask her to let me see it?"

"Well, monsieur," I said, "the fashion's changed pretty often since the days when ladies drove around in open carriages in the Bois de Boulogne. If someone as distinguished as Mme. de Chevigné, and as elegant as you say she was, had kept all her hats, she'd have a good pile of them by now!"

Finally he couldn't rest until he'd cleared the matter up by asking Mme. de Chevigné herself.

In his youth he'd done more than admire her; he'd had the same sort of feeling for her as he had had for Mme. Greffulhe when he used to go to the Opéra just to see her go up the stairs. In the case of Mme. de Chevigné he used to stand on the corner of the Champs-Elysées and avenue de Marigny and watch her drive by in her carriage to the Bois.

"I was in ecstasy," he said.

Driven by one of his impulses, he even spoke to her once but met with a cool reception. Afterward he saw her only in society, though she was no doubt flattered by her youthful admirer.

When he went to see her to ask about the toque trimmed with Parma violets he came back crushed. For one thing, her only answer to his question had been:

"Oh Marcel, how can you expect after all this time . . .?"

And then, as he told me about his visit, he asked me to get out again a photograph he had of her when she was still in her beauty. He pointed out the details to me as usual, then put it down and said:

"She used to be a beauty, and a proud woman. This evening I found a gray-haired old lady with a cracked voice and a hooked nose, knitting on a chaise lounge with her granddaughter beside her."

His voice was infinitely sad. It was during the war. He saw her again a few times, in particular with Jean Cocteau, who lived in the same house as she on rue d'Anjou. Then it was over. He had no more need of her, except in his portraits of the past.

What he took from her for his Duchess de Guermantes were her bearing and her clothes; the graceful neck and carriage of the head he took from Countess Greffulhe. The duchess' wit was more that of

Mme. Straus. He used to draw a clear distinction in talking about the three models.

While he certainly had a deep feeling for Mme. de Chevigné and continued to admire her as in the past, as always this didn't prevent him from judging her impartially. I remember his saying with a sigh when he signed a copy of his book for her—I think it must have been *Le Côté de Guermantes:*

"And to think Céleste, that she will read these pages full of herself and not understand . . ."

Sometimes I rather forced his hand, so to speak. For example, when he quarreled with Duke d'Albuféra, the duke wrote him a long letter full of reproaches, which M. Proust read to me the day it came. The duke was furious because he'd recognized himself in the Chevalier de Saint-Loup, who has a row with an actress—it's in *Sodome et Gomorrhe,* I think. And it was true; this scene was very similar to one that occurred between the duke and Louisa de Mornand, which M. Proust knew about.

As he laid down the letter he said: "I don't know what on earth makes him think that."

"Well, monsieur," I said, "I wonder whether he really is all that mistaken. Don't you think there are certain similarities?"

He laughed and said: "Well, it is a pity, anyhow. We used to be very close friends. I shall write to him."

And so, in turn, he wrote a long letter. The duke didn't reply. When I saw Louisa de Mornand after M. Proust's death I spoke to her about this incident. She didn't know anything about it. Curiously enough, the duke didn't breathe a word to her about it. The only thing she said was:

"It doesn't really surprise me that Louis didn't reply and make up." (Louis was the duke.) "He was very kind and generous—I never had any reason to complain of him. But he wasn't very bright."

I don't think this was far from M. Proust's opinion. He never

245

saw the duke again, but he didn't miss him, as far as I know. He'd finished with him.

What always struck me—and this goes with what I've said about M. Proust's idea of friendship—was that he was never terribly upset if people recognized themselves in his characters. I don't think it was actually a matter of indifference to him, but he was sorry chiefly for their own sakes if they took it badly.

The only time I saw him really worry about it was in the case of Laure Hayman. He'd had a letter from her that was both angry and hurt, because "Coco" de Madrazo, who was a friend of both of them, had told her that Odette de Crécy, in *Swann,* was a portrait of her.

As I have said, M. Proust had a great respect for her, because of her intelligence, because of the old affection between them, and because of her love and self-sacrifice for her son. He didn't read me her letter—just told me the gist. Then he said:

"I really am very upset that she should think she recognizes herself."

"Is she really so wrong, monsieur?"

"I don't want her to think she is right, anyhow. No, I don't want her to be angry. That would make me very sad."

He thought for a long while, on his own, and then called me in again.

"I see in the paper that she has taken up sculpture. Her statuettes are supposed to be very pretty, and she recently had an exhibition. There are some photographs in the latest issue of *Vogue.* Would you buy it for me, please? As she really isn't in a very good temper, I would like to have a good look at the photographs, and then I shall ask her for an appointment to clear up the misunderstanding."

I came back with the copy of *Vogue,* and he had me stay and look at the photographs with him. As he commented on them I could tell he was deciding what he was going to say. As a matter of fact, the statuettes were very pretty.

"I am very glad," he said. "Now I shan't have to lie."

So he went to see her, and he came back relieved and triumphant. As he told me what had happened he was radiant.

"I am so glad, Céleste. I made a complete clean sweep. Everything has been put right. I convinced her she was mistaken. I showed her that one has to know how to read and that many people read words but read them incorrectly and so don't understand what the author was trying to say. Now she is sure she doesn't appear in my book at all. She was charming in the end, and we are still friends."

Then he added: "Anyway, she is much too subtle and intelligent not to understand the truth—that it would have been most painful to me to have quarreled."

I've often wondered if it still gave him pleasure to see people for themselves. In the "camellia period" he certainly was very fond of society. But during those last eight years when he shut himself up with his work, I think that was a thing of the past. When he'd finished harvesting his characters he said goodbye to his models. As long as he still needed them, I could tell, from his sudden wish to see such-and-such a person, how the chapters were going. In the same way, when he eliminated someone from the list of people he invited home, went out with, or wrote to, I could have said: "Well, another episode is finished."

I remember once when he had the opportunity of meeting the Queen of Rumania, who was an admirer of his books. The queen was staying with Princess Soutzo, who had told M. Proust her guest was very anxious to meet him. But as he told me, she said: The queen goes to bed early, so try not to come too late, Marcel dear."

That evening after he'd had his coffee and it was time to get dressed, he called me in and said:

"Dear Céleste, I am tired—I don't think I will go."

I protested that he'd promised and they'd be expecting him and that not to go wouldn't be polite either to the queen or to the princess.

"Why don't you go, monsieur? She admires you so much! But you'll have to hurry, or she'll have gone to bed."

"All the more reason not to bother," he said, laughing.

I persisted, though, and he said: "But you see, dear Céleste, even though they may not wear crowns, I have got all the queens I need."

He was certainly thinking of Countess Greffulhe, Mme. de Chevigné, Mme. Standish, and a few others.

Of course in the end he went. I remember it was one of those evenings when he almost left with his tie all covered with tooth powder and he said it didn't matter, that it wasn't his tie people wanted to see. He didn't come home madly enthusiastic, though he had been flattered by what the queen said about his books.

It was the same around 1920 or 1921, when he used to visit the Hinnisdaëls. What interested him there was that although still very formal, stiff, and traditional as they were despite the changes in postwar society, they couldn't help accepting people and things they wouldn't have tolerated in the old days. I've already mentioned his surprise and disapproval at not finding Ramon Fernandez at their house, though they allowed him to court their daughter Thérèse. Incidentally, Mlle. Hinnisdaël intrigued him, and he enjoyed studying her.

"She is the only person I know in those circles who can do these modern dances properly and still look as if she had just stepped out of a heraldic tapestry and do everything with exquisite gracefulness."

I'm not sure there wasn't something of her in the last images of Albertine in the book.

But there came a time when no more was heard of the Hinnisdaëls, just as with Mme. Greffulhe, Mme. de Chevigné, Mme. de la Béraudière, Louisa de Mornand, and so many others.

The only time he was a constant visitor with such people was in his youth. Even before the war, according to what he told me, he saw people only in installments, so to speak, according to the requirements of his work. He had already made his choice; he had chosen only the great occasions—a large dinner party, a ball, a gala at the Opéra—where his characters would glitter. He took soundings in order to complete his collection.

"Good heavens," he once said, "the number of people you have to put up with to find one who is out of the ordinary!"

But when he did find one he got all he could out of him. He would use every possible approach. First he'd think who could introduce him so that it would seem natural. Sometimes, to get access to the person he was really interested in, he'd go to great lengths to know a third person who didn't interest him at all. All his charm would be brought into play, and as everyone welcomed him with open arms for his wit and graceful manners, he had plenty of opportunity. He would bring the conversation round to the person that interested him: "Do you know him well? Do you see him often?"—until gradually the other person would himself offer to arrange a meeting. He persevered, and he always got his way. But he always made sure that people knew who he was and that he didn't appear to be asking a favor—he couldn't stand being patronized.

When I knew him, of course, all his openings were prepared. Sometimes he'd say:

"It must be at least two years since I was in touch with so-and-so, and I would like to see him again. I know what. You telephone my friend Monsieur X, who still sees him, and arrange for me and Monsieur X to meet, and I shall find a way of getting him to organize something."

But usually it was enough to telephone or to send a message to the person concerned.

Before the war, he had used Count Robert de Montesquiou, with whom he had a close relationship, to get to know the Marquis Boni de Castellane, one of the most famous dandies of the day. This was not only because the marquis provided an additional model for the Chevalier de Saint-Loup (for whom he had already drawn on his friends Gaston de Caillavet and Bertrand de Fénelon, among others) but also because M. Proust was conscious of a whole group of other characters surrounding the marquis—one of the marquis's aunts, for instance, served, like Mme. Lemaire, as a model for Mme. de Villeparisis, an eccentric aristocrat who was also a painter.

Boni de Castellane amused him a great deal at the time. To restore his fallen fortunes he had married Anna Gould, a very rich American, with whose money he'd dazzled Paris by building the famous Palais Rose, an imitation of the Grand Trianon at Versailles. M. Proust didn't rest until he had been invited there and shown around. He told me that when they got to the bedroom, Boni de Castellane threw open the door and made his celebrated remark:

"'Here's the other side of the coin.'" His wife was very ugly. But the joke was that he said it like a guide showing people around a museum.

Anna Gould eventually divorced Boni de Castellane—"He would have gone through all her money otherwise," said M. Proust. "I have never seen anyone squander money the way he did." It wasn't long before he was ruined. In 1919, M. Proust wanted to see him again—in order, I'm sure, to see how his reversals had affected him. It was in the interim period after we had left boulevard Haussmann and before we found the flat in rue Hamelin, when we were living more or less in furnished rooms in the house of the actress Réjane in rue Laurent-Pichat, that Boni de Castellane came late one afternoon and spent some time with M. Proust in his room. When he'd gone, M. Proust sent for me.

"Did you see that gentlemen, Céleste? Did you see how elegant and well dressed he was, and how eccentric his bulldog, wearing a collar studded with copper that looked like gold? Well, he hasn't got a sou—and he's not the only one! When you think of some of these people, sleeping on a bathtub cover because they haven't got a room! And yet the way they keep up appearances!"

As he said this he wore an expression almost of triumph but without malice. He'd seen what he wanted to see, and he was proud of having been right about his character of Boni de Castellane. This was the last time they met. I think he had got all the material he wanted for the Chevalier de Saint-Loup.

All the years I knew him were one long race against time, one long pursuit of chapters and characters. There had to be some reason he was always saying, "I must, I must." People have said he liked to show off. No. It was an effort for him to have to dress up in a dinner jacket or tails, and he only did it because he had to. He was never so happy as in bed with his jerseys round his shoulders and his work.

While he was resting he used to think what he still needed and how to get it, and when his plan had matured, it had to be executed immediately. I had to telephone right away or take a letter to someone. If he was inviting people out, everything had to be done at once: first telephone Olivier Dabescat at the Ritz to reserve a private room (M. Proust always left the menu to him); then, once a well-balanced list had been drawn up, invite all the guests. Getting the people together was no easy matter, because whenever he gave a dinner party it was decided on at the last minute. But it was always an enormous success.

The amazing thing was that everyone—like Louisa de Mornand who capered about the evening I brought her an unexpected invitation—would have canceled their other engagements rather than say they couldn't come. I think most of them would have come to blows to please him. It was his personality, of course. He was a sort of monarch of the mind, who attracted people like a sun.

When he invited people out it was always late, to supper rather than dinner, and he'd usually leave between nine and ten in order to be ready to welcome them. But if he was someone else's guest he never arrived early; there were always good excuses for being late— tiredness, if nothing else. But although he never actually said as much, from seeing him linger about I got the impression he wanted to be sure everyone else would be there when he arrived. I think this was because then he could be sure of feasting his eyes on everything at once.

Yes, knowing him, I'd swear he wanted to have a general view at once. He'd begin with an overall picture and then go on to the details, especially those concerning the person or persons who piqued his curiosity that particular evening.

He had fabulous powers of observation and a tenacious memory. For example, each of the two or three times he looked through the kitchen window of rue Hamelin at Mme. Standish and her family at dinner, he made only a brief appearance, as if he were just passing by. But in thirty seconds everything was recorded, and better than a camera could do it, because behind the image itself there was often a whole character analysis based on a single detail—the way someone picked up a salt cellar, an inclination of the head, a reaction he had caught on the wing.

When I expressed surprise at this he said:

"But Céleste, it isn't a gift. It is an intellectual bent that can be cultivated until it eventually becomes a habit. Lots of activities were forbidden to me, so I spent more time than most people sitting and watching, and to pass the time, if for nothing else, I used to observe what other people did. Sometimes I watched them with envy, and that made me observe all the better. It started when I was still a child. Once I began to have asthma I had to walk instead of run, both in the Champs-Elysées and in the Pré Catelan at Illiers. I spent hours watching the waters of the Loire flow by, or reading and writing in the little summer house with nature spread all around. It was the same when I went with my uncle in his gig: I saw the landscape shifting and unfolding, the village steeples revolving around the plain. Life, people, nature too, unfolds and passes, and by dint of watching and observing you become interested in the relations between things. And through thinking about relations, you come, as scientists do, to discover the laws that govern them."

He pointed to his eyes and brow and said: "It's all recorded here, Céleste. Without memory you can't compare, and it is only by comparing that you can develop your thoughts. But it is never finished. That is why I always have to go see things, or look at them again."

And another time: "The truth about life is in observation and memory. Without them, it just passes by and is gone. I have put all my memory and observation in my characters, to make them true. And to be true they have to be complete. That is why each of them is dressed in what I have noticed or remembered about people in real life."

One day he spoke about what he should write as a dedication in one of his books—I think it was *A l'ombre des jeunes filles en fleurs*, in 1919—for Jacques de Lacretelle.

"Monsieur de Lacretelle has written to ask me to explain certain things, and he shows so much penetration and understanding I would like to write something for him that I wouldn't write for anyone else. I must think."

When he'd written it he gave me the gist.

"He asked me for the keys to my books, and in the dedication I say it is impossible for me to give them to him. Not that I am afraid or want to hide them. But there are too many keys for .each character. Even if I were to give them all, people could still err and imagine, by mistake or on purpose, that there is more of this person or that than of the rest. And in any case, that is not what matters. He himself knows that what matters is the truth."

Then he said: "I wanted this inscription to be the intellectual testament of my work."

I could tell from the tone of his voice that, far from having tried to avoid the issue, he was deeply sincere.

I had proof every day that his search was for the truth—his observations about people and things, about relationships, the most subtle detail. He wasn't just recording gossip. It had all been seen, yes, but it had all been measured too, and absorbed, and assembled. And it was from the measuring and linking together, from the unremitting attention to detail, that the truth emerged.

One day after M. Proust's death his brother went back to Illiers with Dr. Le Masle, who was writing a thesis on Professor Adrien Proust. On the return journey they stopped in Chartres so that Professor Proust could revisit the cathedral his brother had loved so much. Dr. Le Masle told me what happened. The professor went into the cathedral, stood still, and looked around. He took Dr. Le Masle over to a pillar and remained a long while gazing at it. Then he turned to Dr. Le Masle and said with tears in his eyes, pointing to the column:

"That is exactly as Marcel described it. There it is."

21

MONSIEUR DE CHARLUS

Each of his characters resembled what he said about his whole work: a pillar or a little chapel in a great cathedral which he never finished adding to. The most striking example is the Baron de Charlus, who was certainly the character to whom he was most attached, who interested and amused him the most, and whom he spent the most time analyzing and refining. And there is no doubt that even though he did borrow some features from other models, his chief source was Count Robert de Montesquiou.

Of all the people he knew, Count Robert was the one he talked to me about most. One night he interrupted himself in the middle of a conversation about Montesquiou and went off on one of those inner journeys. Then, coming back, he said, as if to himself: "That's the kernel of the whole business."

He always said he was fascinated by the count's personality from the start. He met him for the first time in the spring of 1893, in the studio-salon of Mme. Lemaire. M. Proust was then twenty-two. As far as I can remember, the count must have been nearly forty. About a year before he had published a book of poems called *Les Chauves-souris* ("The Bats"), which had caused a stir, and a signed copy of which M. Proust still had in the big black bookcase in the small salon. I can still see it quite clearly, because M. Proust often took it down, like the one by Paul Bourget bound in a piece of material from Laure Hayman's dress, to show it to me or read me a poem. The count's was a luxury edition, with an unusual green silk brocade binding with motifs of bats to echo the title.

The evening at Mme. Lemaire's had been a great occasion with readings of Montesquiou's poems by Mlle. Bartet, an already well-known actress from the Comédie-Française.

"All the ladies were in ecstasy," M. Proust told me. "The Count stood proud and impressive amid the praise and the roses."

M. Proust went to congratulate him himself, and from his smile I could see he'd put all his charm into making his compliment. What is sure is that Montesquiou was immediately struck and that M. Proust didn't have much difficulty in seeing him again. He never concealed the fact that he, too, was eager to pursue the acquaintance.

This was the "camellia period," when his curiosity led him to extend the field of his acquaintance and when, though he frequented the salons of Mme. de Caillavet, Mme. Straus, Mme. Daudet, and Mme. Lemaire, he had not yet really entered the world of the Faubourg Saint-Germain and the aristocracy, which attracted him. Knowing his impatience, one can well imagine how he used all the means at his disposal. Count de Montesquiou, because of his ancient family and his marriage, was received everywhere. It was said that his family dated as far back as the kings of France and the Crusades; among his forebears was the Marechal de Montluc, who, according to history books, was very cruel toward the Protestants. The Château d'Artagnan was one of the family properties. Through his aunt he was related to the princess of Caraman-Chimay; Countess Greffulhe, whose beauty M. Proust so admired, was his cousin. He was also well known in literary circles and in particular enjoyed the friendship of the poet Stéphane Mallarmé.

I learned all this through M. Proust. Even though he never said so openly, I could tell that in the old days Montesquiou had been one of the people he sought after most. Apart from anything else, it was through him that M. Proust finally met Countess Greffulhe. Until the count brought them together at a party at his house, M. Proust had been introduced to Mme. Greffulhe and encountered her at various receptions but always formally. After the meeting at Montesquiou's house he was invited to the Greffulhes'. He didn't go there often or become a very intimate friend, but he was able to get a closer look at what he wanted to study.

But it wasn't only that the count was useful to him. That soon became a secondary consideration. In any case, the count's chief concern was that people should admire him and his poetry; when it came to introductions he usually had to be coaxed. And for M. Proust, the fascination of the count's personality soon came to matter as much as the rest, and long before the war came, it was the only thing that mattered at all.

It was a difficult and complicated relationship. In my time the two men practically never saw each other, but they still wrote often. I gathered from M. Proust's comments, and from the stories he told me about the count that there was a sort of mutual exchange of ideas, respect, and even admiration between them. But that respect was diluted with a fair amount of distrust, especially on the part of M. Proust.

Montesquiou was highly cultured, and this was the kind of thing M. Proust always admired. He was also very intelligent—"even if the glare of his vanity and pride often prevented one from seeing it," M. Proust said. He also said he had "breeding, class, and a ready answer."

He also told me about the elegance of his clothes, which once had been rather showy—sometimes he used to dress all in white, with a flower instead of a tie—but he had sobered considerably with age, and now the count wore only black or gray, excellently cut.

Montesquiou had also singled out M. Proust right away, though he still put on his condescending airs. Almost immediately after their first meeting they started to see each other often, and as the years went by it was the count who kept up the contact rather than M. Proust. I even suspect M. Proust took some pleasure in playing hard to get. And, as in all the other cases, once he had stored up all he needed for his Charlus, he severed relations. While he still needed to study the character, he observed his every step.

I think the count must gradually have become uneasy at M. Proust's enigmatic attitude. He must have felt he was being judged, and at the same time his pride was wounded. At first he'd seen only a charming young man, intelligent, attentive, and polite. Then he realized this youth was also a writer. And when people started to talk about his books, the count soon became jealous.

But there can be no doubt that at the beginning he fell under the spell—he used to call M. Proust "the bluebird." In the early days he wrote a little note in verse, on a sheet of pink paper, a little crazy but pleasant, which M. Proust laughed at as he recited it to me. In the same way when he took down a book of Montesquiou's poems from the bookcase in the little salon, he read them aloud with a touch of irony. And as I've said, the count's letters used to make him laugh aloud.

They looked like paintings. The writing was large, upright, and bold, on very handsome paper. M. Proust used to write his answers on any paper that came to hand. I remember one day he made a blot, and said:

"Never mind, we will send it just the same. I am too tired to copy it out. But he will say I have no breeding, you will see."

As usual he was right. The letter was found after the count's death in 1920, and against the blot he'd written in his large handwriting: "Crap." That was the sort of word he must have been obsessed with. In *Sodome et Gomorrhe* there's a whole passage where Charlus talks like a cesspool, and M. Proust certainly didn't invent it.

What fascinated M. Proust most in Montesquiou, at the same time as it filled him with a sort of astonishment and horror, were his insolence and malice. He had innumerable stories on the subject.

"What he liked best was to ruin some hostess's party. He could be downright vulgar or deliberately insulting."

Among the many examples he cited I remember that of a large dinner party where Montesquiou found himself sitting next to a lady who didn't happen to be to his taste.

"And do you know what, Céleste? In the little silence at the beginning of the meal, as people were picking up their knives and forks, suddenly Monsieur de Montesquiou's voice was heard blaring out to his hostess: 'Madame, why in the world have you put me next to such an awful old cow?' I need hardly describe the effect. The hostess nearly passed out and couldn't think of anything to say. The count's neighbor wished the floor would open and swallow her up or that the chandelier would crash down into the middle of the table.

"The worst of it was, the whole thing was gratuitous. The count's unfortunate neighbor was one of his own circle and had never been anything but pleasant to him. The strange thing is that even when he was being coarse he still had such lordly manners that everyone overlooked his whims. There was an embarrassed silence, people stared at their plates, it was as if the whole table had furled itself up like a flower—and then conversation started up again, all the more lively because everyone was trying to make up for having been secretly amused. I never knew anyone who could be so insulting and get away with it."

Another time Montesquiou got on a tram with a lady he had some grudge against and suddenly opened a little wicker basket he had on his lap and revealed a poisonous snake. The poor lady almost fainted, while the count laughed stridently.

His voice tended to be shrill. When he recited his own poems he used to stamp his foot; he'd do this even in conversation in a salon or in the street. He always stood pompously erect, with his head thrown back. This was all the more striking as he was tall and thin, with a very high-bridged nose and a thin, curled, waxed moustache.

"Just like a cobra about to strike," said M. Proust, who did an excellent imitation of him.

He imitated him so well, in fact, that at the beginning of their relationship stories got back to the count, who was very angry. It took all M. Proust's diplomacy to convince him that he wasn't making fun of him but imitating him out of sheer admiration.

But the count's outlandish behavior in public was nothing in comparison to his attitude over his brother's early death.

When the brother died, M. Proust wrote to his mother, Countess Paule de Montesquiou, to tell her he shared her sorrow. The countess was so touched that she replied, pouring out her grief and asking him to go to see her. He did so, and years afterward he was still horrified by what happened.

"I found Count Thierry de Montesquiou, the father, in the garden, stricken with grief. I tried to comfort him, but he was inconsolable. And yet he was a proud man, well known for his harsh and rather cynical wit. Count Robert was with us, and suddenly, as I was speaking, seeing there were tears in his father's eyes, he said, 'Cheer up, Father! You will soon be frolicking about in paradise yourself!' No one else could have carried cruelty to such an extreme.

"And that was not all. As I was offering my condolences to his mother again before I left, he interrupted me again and said, 'Do you know what Japanese gardeners do, Marcel? To get the best possible blooms they pinch off every bud but one.' In front of his mother he was outrageous enough to turn his brother's death into his own triumph. What cruelty, and what pride! He thought he was superior to everyone. He called his house at Neuilly 'the Palace of the Muses' and when he moved to Le Vésinet, he called his residence 'the Palais Rose,' like Boni de Castellane. He would have ruined himself to overshadow him."

I've said M. Proust and Count Robert mistrusted each other but that the mistrust was chiefly on M. Proust's side. Even when he talked to me about him I could feel he was being cautious: he'd state the facts without venturing an opinion. He was ironic but didn't actually say anything against him. You could tell he didn't really like him but that he wanted to keep on the right side of him, partly out of fear of his spitefulness and partly because he didn't want to lose him as a model.

"Heaven knows what he will say about me in his memoirs. And I am sure that one day he will publish all my letters."

The surprising thing was that when the memoirs were published they contained nothing malicious about M. Proust—a fact that does honor to the count's admiration, which turned out to be greater than his spite. As for the letters, they were put up for sale after both

Montesquiou and M. Proust were dead. Professor Robert Proust bought them, but I don't think he attached any special importance to them. M. Proust's anxiety on their account was certainly not about their content; it was just part of his general anxiety about the publication of his correspondence.

Of course one of the things that fascinated M. Proust most about the count was the special nature of his love affairs. He followed closely Montesquiou's deep feeling for Yturri, his secretary, a South American fellow who lisped and called his employer *Moussou lé comté*. The affair was the talk of Paris society, and I'm sure it provided M. Proust with inexhaustible material for his Baron de Charlus. He often said he was very fond of Yturri and couldn't understand why the count's friends made fun of him—he was a nice young man and extremely devoted to the count. He smoothed out all his employer's troubles, including his money difficulties, which he had frequently.

"His devotion killed him," M. Proust said. "When he died, not long after my mother, in 1905, I wrote a long letter to the count to tell him I understood and shared his grief—in a way, he had lost a sort of mother too, and I said, 'Your sorrow is the same as mine.'"

But when Montesquiou found a successor to Yturri in Henri Pinard, M. Proust wasn't interested—he had obtained all the material he wanted. Gradually his relationship with the count cooled off. The pursuit went on by correspondence, but it was chiefly the count who did the pursuing.

The main reason was of course that Montesquiou recognized himself in the Baron de Charlus.

"The first time he thought he recognized himself," said M. Proust, laughing, "he was like a caged lion."

Naturally, M. Proust bemused him with explanations, and the count allowed himself to be convinced.

"At least, so he pretended," said M. Proust. "Anyway, he is used to it now."

And he told me how Huysmans had used the count as a model for Duke des Esseintes in his novel *A rebours*. You couldn't help wondering, in the end, whether Montesquiou wasn't really flattered.

Among the arguments M. Proust employed to win him around was the fact that Baron de Charlus was a big man, whereas Count Robert was as thin as a Gascon rooster. But I don't think M. Proust went so far as to tell him he'd got Charlus' ample figure from the Baron Doasan, who also belonged to the "accursed race of men-women, descendants of those inhabitants of Sodom who were spared by the fire from heaven," as it says in the book.

Certain it is, though, that Montesquiou's last visit to M. Proust was still linked to Baron de Charlus.

It was in 1919, at boulevard Haussmann. It was the only time I ever saw the count, and the event was unforgettable.

It had been years since M. Proust had last seen him. For one thing, he'd got as much as he wanted for the character, and for another, he didn't hide that he was somewhat afraid of Montesquiou. He was capable of anything, as he told me after the count had left.

Montesquiou had written a letter asking to be allowed to come, but M. Proust didn't want to see him. Then came a telegram: "Marcel, I am leaving for the South of France. I shall come by to see you this evening." As the telegram was sent from Le Vésinet, the count must already have been in Paris.

"He is staying at the Hôtel Garnier, near the Saint-Lazare train station," said M. Proust. "I know his habits."

Then he said: "I don't want to see him, Céleste. Absolutely not. We must manage to prevent it. I know he goes to bed early now. So you telephone him at the Hôtel Garnier and say you haven't seen me yet and you don't know when you will. Say that when you left me this morning I said I wanted to rest. . . . Oh no, that won't work—if you telephone he will know I have seen the telegram. . . . No, tell him I am in the middle of a bad attack and I don't know how long it will last. Say I could not possibly see him before two or three in the morning."

I phoned. The count came to the telephone. He listened to my tale, and then he said:

"Two o'clock in the morning. I shall be there."

There was nothing I could say. M. Proust was trapped.

At two o'clock in the morning there was a ring at the door, and I let in a man of about sixty who looked like a country gentleman, with wrinkled cheeks that looked made up. He was wearing a big gray overcoat, very elegant, with a white silk scarf. I looked at him, and he gazed loftily down on me. He came in, and I could see self-importance at once in his face and whole attitude. He'd hardly got inside when he stopped with his head thrown back in front of a picture hanging in the hall.

It was a painting by Helleu, whom he, like M. Proust, had known in the "camellia" days, when the painter went to Mme. Lemaire's studio and was famous for his portraits and his scenes of the Paris at the time of carriages. There was a story attached to this particular painting. One autumn day M. Proust had asked my husband to drive him to the Bois de Boulogne, along the river, and to Versailles. "I'd like to see the red of the leaves again," he said. When they'd got as far as Versailles he asked Odilon to stop near a man accompanied by a girl and painting the landscape. It was Helleu and his daughter. And M. Proust was caught at a disadvantage, for as so often happened, he'd decided on the excursion at the last minute and hadn't dressed or shaved. He was wearing just a shirt, striped trousers, and a fur coat with a silk acarf round his neck. "I can't get out of it!" he said to Odilon. "They have recognized me, and here I am practically in my nightshirt!" He got out of the car and talked for some time with the painter and Mlle. Helleu. Not long afterward the painting in question arrived at boulevard Haussmann, finished and mounted in a magnificent old carved frame. M. Proust returned it with a letter, saying it was much too fine for him to accept, but it came back again, now signed, "To my friend Marcel Proust," so this time he couldn't refuse it.

As I said, Count de Montesquiou planted himself in front of this picture, and after a moment turned, gave me another piercing look, and asked me to announce him. M. Proust had said: "When he comes, show him into the small salon and come and tell me." I went through the big salon with the count, thinking of the rude remarks M. Proust told me he'd made once when he came to a reception given by Professor Adrien Proust at boulevard Malesherbes, criticizing aloud the furniture and decorations.

After letting him wait in the little salon for a minute, I showed him into the bedroom. I know there have been exaggerated accounts of this last visit. It's been said Montesquiou stayed six or seven hours. In fact he didn't stay more than two. I can remember quite clearly that it was four o'clock in the morning when he left. Then M. Proust called me in and gave me a summary of what had happened.

The first thing the count said, M. Proust told me laughing, was:

"Marcel, where on earth did you find that person?"

He said it looking down his nose, though M. Proust took it as a compliment to me.

Of course, after they'd been talking for a while, Montesquiou brought the conversation around to his poetry and began to recite some of it. I could hear him from my own room—not the voice, because of the cork walls, but the stamping on the floor which he used to underline the importance of a line. He went on doing it even during the rest of the conversation. M. Proust was still quite upset when I saw him.

"I was worried about the noise. All the other tenants are so kind about keeping quiet in the morning so as not to wake or disturb me."

"But why does he do it, monsieur?"

"He needs to convince himself, Céleste. You might not think it, but he is very unhappy at not being famous. He would have liked his work to be celebrated and immortal. I am afraid it will not be, and he is even more afraid than I."

At the end of the conversation the count had shown his perverse side. "Do you know what he asked before he left, Céleste? 'Marcel, do tell me how your Baron de Charlus is getting on.'"

M. Proust didn't tell me what he answered, but from the way he smiled I could tell he'd managed once again to throw dust in the count's eyes.

Finally, Montesquiou said: "I would like to go on a long journey and come back with white hair. But I am only going to the

South of France. I shall send you some gold-wrapped chocolates from Nice."

I can still see M. Proust telling me that. Once before he'd said, "You know, Céleste, I don't exaggerate—the count is quite capable of sending me poisoned flowers." This time he said:

"If he does send any chocolates, throw them straight into the dustbin without opening them. It wouldn't surprise me in the least if they were poisoned."

There weren't any chocolates, and there weren't any more letters. The count died in the South of France the following year.

The strange thing is, and it shows the real fear he could inspire, that after his death M. Proust said one night when we were talking about him:

"There are moments when I don't really believe he is dead. I know him; he is perfectly capable of pretending to be dead and adopting another name just to see whether he is famous and people still remember him."

And he went on speaking of him in the present tense, as if he had no doubt that the count's death was only a pretense.

"You can't imagine what an idea he has of himself!"

I've always thought that at that moment the two had become one, and Montesquiou still lived on for him in Charlus. Anyway, I think the count himself had long since ceased to exist for M. Proust. He'd become one of the "dream people" mentioned in *Le Temps retrouvé*, "for whom life itself had become more and more a dream." The true reality was Charlus.

22

"I'VE WORKED WELL, CELESTE."

You'd need to have seen him elated night after night during those eight years to get a real idea of the passion for his characters and his work that filled him and finally consumed him. You'd wonder when it all stopped going around in his head. It was only afterward, in the course of the years, that I realized he never faltered from the pursuit of his book. If I frequently say "his book" in the singular it's because, even though at any given moment he might have a particular chapter in mind, the whole of his work was always present in his thoughts.

When I went to live at boulevard Haussmann he was working on what was to become *A l'ombre des jeunes filles en fleurs,* which is now books three, four, and five of *A la Recherche du temps perdu.* But the way everything is linked in the work is enough to show he bore every sequence and development in mind simultaneously.

I'm certain that when he went out at night it was the same as when he was talking to me in the small salon or in his bedroom: he never abandoned whatever problem he'd formulated in his mind and tried to solve it. If at the time I hadn't been so caught up in what was happening at the moment, and if I'd been older, I'd have been able to sense the activity of his mind behind the smile he gave me as he came in and put down his opera hat, saying, "Come into my room, Céleste," or, "Come, let's go into the small salon for a little while."

Sometimes, after two, three, or four hours of conversation, he would interrupt himself for longer than usual, and I'd pluck up my courage and ask:

"Why don't you go further, monsieur? Why don't you tell me more?"

Then he'd look at me with his warm smile and say, with a kind of gravity and sadness in his voice:

"I must work, Céleste. We will go on again later."

I've told how when he went out he used to leave his bed strewn with newspapers, reviews, and scraps of paper covered with notes. The first thing I did was tidy it all up so that he'd find everything where he wanted it when he got back. A little incident will show his constant preoccupation.

One evening he came home earlier than I'd expected, with a searching look in his eye and his hat at an anxious angle. Before he even took his street clothes off he said:

"Céleste, my whole evening has been spoiled thinking about the notes I left lying on the bed. I know you never lose anything, but I couldn't help worrying. If this particular one got lost it would be awful. It was so much on my mind I couldn't enjoy myself at all, and I came away as soon as I could."

We went straight into his room, and he looked hastily through the papers I'd arranged on his little table. He found the note and was beside himself with relief.

"Here it is! I knew it would be! Dear Céleste, you really are celestial! I can never thank you enough."

It's as difficult to say when and for how long he worked and when he slept. I've always wondered if he actually slept at all. He rested, yes. He dozed, of course. But whether he ever completely abandoned his vigil . . . During the hours the apartment was silent—I didn't know whether he was working or resting—you were absolutely forbidden to go near any of the doors, you weren't really supposed to move, for he heard everything. When I saw him later, after he had rung for me, he might say:

"At such-and-such a time you were in such-and-such a place. I know."

And it was true.

Anyway, as he lived only for his work, you could say he worked without respite.

There were evenings and nights—especially when he neither went out nor received guests—when he scarcely spoke to me at all except to call me and ask me to fetch him something. And even after he'd been out, or had a visitor, and he called me in to tell me about it, the moment always came when he interrupted the conversation.

"Dear Céleste, I have not much time. I must do some work. Go and get some rest."

I'm sure there were days when he worked on for a long time after I left him, no matter what the hour. On the evenings he didn't go out he would often start working as soon as he had had his coffee, looked through the papers, and read his mail. Then three or four hours might go by before he rang for something, or in order to talk to me. When he went out I could tell if he was going to work by the time at which, after his account of the evening and before his withdrawal into silence, he asked me to bring in his breakfast that afternoon. If he said "about" four or five o'clock, or sometimes six, that meant he'd decided what he was going to write about and would be making progress with a particular chapter.

When you think of the state I saw him in when he woke up and had his fumigation, you wonder where he got the strength. He not only didn't eat, but he piled one effort on another. So where and how did he "recharge" himself? It's a mystery. The only possible answer is that he drew constantly on the substance of his own being and his own life. And it had been like that since he was a child: when he wasn't observing he was writing. In Illiers it was in the little pavilion in the Pré Catelan. In Paris, when friends came to see his parents during the day, they found him sitting with his books and notebooks at the dining-room table. And very early on he began to write in his bedroom at night, recording when he came home what he had stored up during his evening out. He used to say to his mother, "Don't forget to keep that article for me, will you, Mother? It will be useful."

In those days he worked sitting down. Now he worked in bed. I never saw him write even the shortest note standing up. Every time I found him working he was always in the same position, and it's inconceivable he could have got up to work when I wasn't there. He was always more than half lying down. He didn't even prop himself up on the pillow. At the most, all the sweaters that had accumulated around his shoulders made a sort of chairback, as I've said. All he had for a desk was his knees. How he didn't get stiff in that position is another mystery. Anyone else would at least have got numb. But I never saw the slightest trace with him. After hours like this, every gesture of wrist or hand, every movement of the head, would be elegant, supple and lively. There he would recline in the light from the little green shade of the lamp, always quite flat—I never saw him turn to one side.

His friend Horace Finaly once sent him a beautiful writing-box as a present. It was antique and very valuable. The day it was delivered he showed it to me and said:

"Look how splendid and beautifully made it is, Céleste." Then: "Put it away. I shall never use it."

I imagine it was the same as with everything else; it would have meant breaking an old habit and creating a new one, and he didn't think it worthwhile. Changing his ways would have disturbed him inside the cocoon of his work.

It was astonishing how fast he could write in a position no one but he could have found comfortable. The pen flew along, line after line of his fine cursive writing. He always used Sergeant-Major nibs, which were plain and pointed, with a little hollow underneath to hold the ink. I never saw him use a fountain pen, though they were becoming popular at the time. I used to buy stocks of nibs, several boxes at a time. He always had fifteen or so pen holders within reach, because if he dropped the one he was using it could only be picked up when he wasn't there, because of the dust. They were just little bits of wood with a metal holder for the nib—the ordinary kind used in schools, like the inkwell, which was a glass square with four grooves to rest the pen and a little round opening with a stopper.

"Some people need a beautiful pen to write with, but all I need is ink and paper. If I didn't have a pen holder I would manage with a stick."

He had everything he required beside him: next to the screen, the pretty little bamboo table laden with books and, on the left, a pile of handkerchiefs; then the night table with the doors open, holding the manuscripts he was working on, and in front of them a bunch of pen holders, one or two inkwells, and his watch. They were always ordinary little watches—I used to buy them for five francs each, I remember. He wouldn't have any others.

"If I break these," he used to say, "they can just be thrown away without a pang. It costs more to have one mended than to buy a new one."

That was part of his practical attitude to things.

Spectacles were added to his writing equipment when his sight began to fail—which was hardly surprising, after all those nights of hard work, and the glare of the light projected straight onto the white paper. I read somewhere that he was already wearing glasses in 1915, but that's incorrect. I remember we were still living at boulevard Haussmann when he started to use them, but toward the end of our sojourn there, and so it must have been around 1918 or 1919. I can still see him in his room at boulevard Haussmann about that time, asking me to look up a word in the dictionary because the print was to small for him. I wasn't as quick as he was at alphabetical order, and he used to get impatient and say—I can still hear him:

"No, dear Céleste, not there! Further on, further on! No, now you have gone too far. . . ."

So one day he sent me to the optician's. I was to bring back a selection of spectacles with the lenses already in, for him to try.

"But monsieur," I said, "don't you think it might be better if you had your eyes examined first?"

"Oh no, Céleste," he answered. "It would be such a rigma-

271

role—it would take hours. You know I haven't the time." Then: "Just bring me the most ordinary kind there is—steel rims will do."

He gave me a few vague indications about the sort of lens. I managed as best I could with the optician and came back with an assortment of lenses all in steel frames. He tried them, found some which more or less suited him, and as usual kept the whole lot. There must have been ten or twelve pairs in all, and he kept the ones that suited him best on his table.

Apart from the writing equipment, there were the pullovers, the hot-water bottles, and, when it was cold, the fire. He'd ring and say:

"Dear Céleste, would you be kind enough to bring me another hot-water bottle?" Or: "Céleste, I am very sorry to bother you, but could you hand me another pullover?" Or: "Céleste, would you mind putting another log on the fire?"

Lastly there was the pad of little squares of paper which he used to light the fumigation powder. He also used it to write down what he needed when he decided not to speak—when he was tired or had difficulty in breathing or didn't want to interrupt his work or the thread of a thought, and also when it would have been too complicated to convey his wants by a gesture.

I was with him during the period of his life when he must certainly have written the most. I'm not bragging; this just was so by chance. And here again I can only say what I actually saw. I don't think he ever really told anyone, any more than he told me, either the way he conceived his work in his mind or the exact method he followed in writing. All that has been said about it has been deduced from the state of his manuscripts. My only advantage is that I saw him at work and helped him with it physically within my humble limits.

He trained me to help him in this just as he did the other tasks, and I for my part cooperated with the same willingness, because I loved and admired everything about him.

When I first came, *Du côté de chez Swann* had just been published, and he was writing *A l'ombre des jeunes filles en fleurs,* which was later to win him the Prix Goncourt.

The main aspect of his methods of organization was that he always kept all his work within reach as it grew, just as he kept all his working equipment ready at hand. I soon learned to distinguish between the five main categories of his work: the old exercise books, which dated from long before; the new exercise books, in which he was currently working; the exercise books with notes; the little notebooks; and what have been called (though he himself never used the word) his "paperoles," which were odd notes written down on scraps of paper or the backs of envelopes or even the covers of magazines.

About these "paperoles" there's a detail which has a certain importance that I'd like to point out. When people write about M. Proust, they almost always confuse the "paperoles" with the additions glued into the exercise books when there was no more room left on a page for further corrections. These additions were the "paste-ons," as printers call them. But the "paperoles" were never pasted into the exercise books containing the manuscripts. They were just notes —a passing phrase or idea—like the one he was so anxious about that he came home early one night to see if I'd lost it. Either he just left them where they were, or he rewrote them and incorporated them into his text.

A subject in itself was the old exercise books, which were the nucleus of the *Recherche* and of all his work. They contained his first drafts of the book, long fragments and even whole chapters written in the course of earlier years, even of his youth. These books stood in a neat pile on a corner of the chest in his bedroom. They were the only part of his work he didn't take with him when we went to Cabourg in 1914. In the big case we kept with us on the train, I had only packed the exercise books he was working on, the exercise books with notes, and the little notebooks.

He called the old exercise books the "black books" because they had black imitation-leather covers. There were thirty-two of them, numbered with big white figures that looked as if they'd been written with a finger dipped in paint or white ink. They were big school exercise books. When he needed to consult them he used to say:

"Would you hand me that black book, please, Céleste?" and he'd specify—the third, or the twentieth.

He didn't usually consult these books for long; he'd look for a

273

passage, read it, and then ask me to put the book back. I've seen them open in front of him. The white pages were covered with perfectly even writing without any smudges or crossings-out. I don't think they had been written in bed for they dated from the time when he still wrote sitting down, a period I never knew. From the way he made use of them it was clear they already contained the essence of his work. Starting from them he reworked, developed, expanded, embellished.

About these "black books," too, there has been some confusion which I am able to clear up. Some people, I'm afraid, have got them mixed up with the exercise books with notes. In fact no trace remains of the "black books" themselves, because at a certain point he made me destroy them, and all thirty-two of them were burned to ashes in the big kitchen stove.

It was at boulevard Haussmann during the war, between 1916 and 1917, after he'd finished *A l'ombre des jeunes filles en fleurs* and had all the rest in his head. He gave them to me to destroy one or sometimes two or three at a time, as he came to have no further need of them. I remember talking to my sister about this once when she came up from Auxillac to see me in Paris, and also to André Maurois, after M. Proust's death. André Maurois was inconsolable. He kept saying: "What a pity, what a pity!" I seem to remember that on the last occasion I burned three or four of them at one go. I just did as he said; I did not ask any questions.

The fact that he really wanted them destroyed is proved by his sending for me one day and saying with an innocent air but a searching look:

"You really are burning those books, aren't you, Céleste?"

I was vexed. "If you don't trust me, monsieur," I said, "why do you ask me to do it? If you ask me to do a thing, I do it. If you don't believe me, why don't you do it yourself?"

"Come now, Céleste," he said, "don't be angry. I was only joking. I know you burn them."

It was obvious that, as often happened, he'd had a sudden fit of mistrust and wanted to test me to make sure I wasn't keeping them for myself.

The exercise books that survive today are those with notes and those I've called the "new exercise books," that is, those containing the manuscripts.

These weren't black. They had cardboard covers reinforced with canvas and were very thick, much thicker than the "black books." Some of them became very much thicker still with all the additions that were stuck in.

I used to buy them in an exclusive stationer's on boulevard Haussmann. I was served by a very distinguished young lady who, like everyone in all the shops I went to, couldn't do enough for me once she knew I came for M. Proust. I chose the exercise books, and the shop sent the bill. For the books that were to be used for the manuscripts, I would stick a little rectangle of paper on the cover—the paper he used to light the Legras powder—and M. Proust himself would write the number on in Roman numerals.

There were only three exercise books with notes, but the books containing the manuscript accumulated gradually right up to the end—the fact that the Bibliothèque Nationale has seventy-five of them gives you an idea.

The little notebooks had also accumulated over the years, and they were all tall and narrow, with rather dandyish figures on the covers. Mme. Straus had given them to him. Toward the end, M. Proust gave me one that hadn't been used. I still have it.

The "black books" stood on the chest of drawers, but the three other kinds were always kept within reach, carefully arranged on the night table beside his bed. The order never changed: in the middle of the table, beside the lamp, were the little notebooks; behind the lamp were the exercise books with notes and the exercise books containing the manuscript.

With these, and the little squares of paper for lighting the fumigation powder, but which he also used for odd notes and written orders, M. Proust had within arm's reach everything he needed for his work.

He rarely consulted books when he was working—he never kept them near the bed. Sometimes, as I've said, he would look up a place or a person in the encyclopedia or the *Almanach de Gotha*.

Every so often he'd ask me to bring him a book; he'd leaf through, shut it, and give it back:

"Thank you, Céleste. You can take it away. I have seen what I wanted."

"You are strange, monsieur," I'd say. "You ask for a book, but you hardly glance at it before you ask me to put it away again."

He'd smile. "I have done a lot of reading, you know, Céleste. I know what is there already."

Nevertheless, his room was full, probably just in case, of books, though he never touched them any more.

One of the things I'm proud of in connection with the modest assistance I was able to give him is having helped him solve the problem of the additions. For the main part of his work consisted in adding, ceaselessly adding, and correcting.

One day he rang for me, and when I got into the room I saw he was tired and anxious.

"Dear Céleste, I am at my wits' end with worry!"

"What's wrong, monsieur?"

"All the margins are full, and I still have corrections to make and lots of things to add. I don't know what to do. I could just insert extra pages, but the printer will get them all mixed up and it won't make sense. What on earth am I to do?"

Almost without thinking I said: "If that's all, monsieur, there's no problem."

"No problem, Céleste? I would like to see you solve it!"

"It's as simple as anything, monsieur," I said. "Just write your extra pages, making sure you leave a bit of blank space at the top and at the bottom. And when you've finished I'll stick them in as carefully as I can at the right place. In that way you can add as much as you like—all we have to do is fold the paper. Then the printer will have to unfold the strip that's stuck in, and he cannot but take it all in the right order."

His face lit up. He was beside himself with relief.

"Do you think you can? Oh Céleste, how marvelous! You have saved my life!"

He was so pleased he told everyone about it and wrote to several people, saying I was an extraordinary woman and had solved his problem and that I pasted in his extra pages so that no one would ever be able to detect where the addition had been made.

And that's how the exercise books containing the manuscript expanded. There was a famous one, which has been shown in exhibitions, which has a strip about four and a half feet long when it's unfolded!

And that's the story of the "paste-ons."

As for saying exactly what I saw him working on apart from *A l'ombre des jeunes filles en fleurs,* it would be telling a lie to say I knew. But from the way he set about it, I can say without fear of error that the whole work was already complete in his mind and that while he might sometimes work continually at one book, he often worked also at the others, depending on some new idea, or on corrections and additions he had thought of, or after receiving some new information. Events and details were so closely linked in his mind by the presence of his characters that his books formed a single work.

About his work and his method of writing I was struck one day by a remark he made concerning Vermeer's scene of Delft and the famous little patch of yellow wall. He talked about it often. It was toward the end, after he'd see the picture again at an exhibition at the Jeu de Paume. He came back exhausted. During the night he said—and his look was full of ecstasy, as if he were still looking at the painting:

"Céleste, you can't imagine the detail, the subtlety! The tiniest grain of sand! The minutest touch of pink here and of green there! The work he must have put into it! *I* must go on correcting and correcting, adding grains of sand. . . ."

Meticulousness and subtlety were an essential part of him. He couldn't be happy until he was sure he had everything down to the last detail. I remember, for example, how he cross-questioned Odilon when he wanted to reproduce street vendors' cries in his book.

"Odilon, you are out all the time—you must know all about these cries. You hear them, whereas I only catch them vaguely through the windows. Will you try to find out about them for me?"

"Yes, monsieur, of course. I'll tell you what they say."

And when Odilon came back with what the hawkers really said, you should have seen M. Proust's smile, his warmth, his gratitude!

"My dear Odilon, thank you! How kind you are!"

The cries my husband told him about are almost all there in *La Prisonnière*. "Winkles, a penny a pint! Fresh snails, six cents a dozen! Green tender artichokes, fine artichokes! Any old pots and pans to mend?"

It was marvelous to hear M. Proust repeating them all. A kind of joy emanated from him, as if he were offering us all the sweetness and fragrance of his heart.

Because of moments like this, there was no sacrifice in pleasing or helping him. For me it was an amusement and pleasure to be completely drawn into his work. It wasn't difficult for me to smile like la Gioconda, because I was as happy as a buttercup.

If I was able to be of some service with his writing, it was probably because I was so familiar with his work habits and his peculiarities. He had only to call me and I often knew at once by his attitude, by the mere beginning of a gesture or look, what he wanted. Before he'd finished speaking or scribbling something down, I would say:

"Of course, monsieur. Here you are."

And I'd hand him the volume or exercise book he wanted.

He never got over his astonishment.

"Thank you, dear Céleste," he'd say, smiling. "But how did you guess?"

I'd have been hard put to explain it. It was a kind of reflex, a second nature. And yet at the same time it was easy, and as I said before, I didn't deserve any credit. Being with him, listening and talking to him, watching him work, and helping him to the best of my ability, these were like walking through a landscape where new springs are always welling forth.

I didn't realize at the time that I'd become indispensable to him. I only saw this from an incident that occurred toward the end, in 1921, when I suddenly became very tired and felt I wasn't up to doing all he needed me to do. He was very anxious then to get on with his work. Everything had to be done very quickly, and everything was an effort for him. So I said:

"Monsieur, you need someone more educated than I am. You could dictate to them, and you'd do much more much faster. I'm tired myself, and I really need a bit of rest. It would be better for me to leave when you've found someone to help you. All I ask is that if I go you'll let me come and see you sometimes."

His face was in shadow, against the pillow. He didn't move. He just said:

"Dear Céleste, you *are* silly! I know you are tired. I am tired too. We will talk about it."

A little while later he rang for me.

"Céleste, when Odilon comes home, will you kindly send him in to see me?"

I sent Odilon in. I thought he was never coming out again. When he did, I said:

"You were in there a very long time. What were you talking about?"

"Oh, nothing. The stock market, you know—various things." But then he added—he was incapable of dissembling:

"I might as well tell you. I gather you said you want to leave him, and he asked me to persuade you not to go."

I explained. M. Proust must feel I wasn't quick enough when, say, he dictated a short passage to me or asked me to look something up. And as both he and I were tired it would be in his own interest to find someone better qualified.

"Perhaps," said Odilon. "But he doesn't see it like that. He said he understood your point of view, but he also said, 'Odilon, you must get her to stay. She's the only person who can guess what I want before I put it into words. She's used to my ways and my papers. If she needs anyone to help her she can have them—two or

279

three if she likes. But whatever you do, try to get her to stay. Be sure to tell her that if she ever left, I wouldn't be able to go on working.'"

The strange thing is I didn't really believe it at the time. I thought the main reason he wanted me to stay was so as not to have to change his habits. But I stayed, and I don't regret it.

The only other helper he had apart from my sister Marie, who was already with us then, was my niece Yvonne, who came to stay for about a month at rue Hamelin to type his business letters and the manuscript of *La Prisonnière*.

Apart from the pleasure and amusement of the work itself, the great reward for my labors was to go into his room certain evenings after he had finished working and rung the bell, and find him pleased with his work. When I came in he'd be exhausted, but his face in the shadow was radiant, and he'd smile at me affectionately.

"Oh, Céleste, I am so tired. . . . But look—one, two, three . . ."

And he'd hold up the pages he'd written, running his other hand through his hair.

"It went very well this evening. I worked well. Yes, it is not bad at all, what I have written. I am quite pleased with myself."

And then I was pleased too, and proud to see him happy.

Of course there were days when it didn't go well, and he only rang for me because he'd had enough of it.

"My poor Céleste, I am exhausted. I have worked, but what I have done is not good. I am not at all pleased with myself."

The pages would be there, covered with crossings-out, and this time he wouldn't hold them out to me. I'd say:

"Ah well, monsieur, it will go better tomorrow."

And his look would be so affectionate and grateful that on those days too it was a reward just to be there, with him, respecting his work and his fatigue, sharing his disappointment, and admiring everything about him.

23

THE REJECTION

If you add his passion for his work to the iron will with which he set about anything he'd decided on and to that impatience that turned into patience in order to achieve its own ends, you can imagine what it must have been like when he decided his book was to be published. For the striking thing was that when he knew it would take some time to arrive at a particular object, his impatience was all projected onto other people and from his bed he manipulated them like an admiral controlling his fleet.

It was only through what he told me that I knew how his dealings with publishers had started. *Du côte de chez Swann* had just come out when I started to go to boulevard Haussmann as the "courier." He had signed a contract with Bernard Grasset in the spring of 1913, in March, about the time I married Odilon, when I didn't even know of his existence. As for knowing how a book was put together, I didn't have the slightest idea in those days—I was twenty-one and had just arrived from the country.

I learned later, from him, how he set all the necessary machinery in motion to get *Swann* published. He made use of his connections—on the one hand, his friends and salon acquaintances, and on the other, the people he knew on *Le Figaro,* for which he sometimes wrote articles, and in particular Calmette, later to be murdered by Mme. Caillaux.

As always, he didn't like to present himself out of the blue. The preliminary work had to be performed by others. But he didn't just want their recommendation—they had to be aware of the value of his book and of what he himself stood for. And I don't think I'm wrong in saying that if he hadn't been aware of this himself he wouldn't have made the advances.

Getting *Du côté de chez Swann* published was no easy matter. To begin with, it was a very long manuscript—between a thousand and twelve hundred handwritten pages, I think, and about seven hundred when typed. Moreover, the book was quite different from anything else that was current then.

The first steps were taken in 1912. M. Proust concentrated on two publishing houses: Fasquelle, which was then solidly established and where he had introductions, and the Nouvelle Revue Française, which was still young as a publishing house, but which he really preferred. This was because their literary review, the *NRF*, and their authors, who backed one another up and were much talked of as representing a new generation of writers: they included André Gide, Paul Claudel, Francis Jammes, Jean Schlumberger, and Jacques Copeau—the latter, with his Vieux-Colombier theater, concerned himself mainly with drama. The business side was managed by Gaston Gallimard, who had married a daughter of the powerful Lazare banking family—a very pretty woman, slim, elegant, urbane, and witty.

It was Prince Antoine Bibesco, always mad about the latest thing, who urged M. Proust toward the Nouvelle Revue Française, first getting him to take out a subscription to the *NRF*. M. Proust had, as it happened, met Gaston Gallimard at a friend's estate during one of his summers at Cabourg. I think he also mentioned giving a dinner party once at the Grand Hôtel at Cabourg at which Gaston Gallimard, who wasn't yet a publisher then, was one of the guests.

André Gide was not a stranger to him either; he'd been a salon acquaintance fifteen or twenty years earlier.

In short, M. Proust could perfectly well have introduced himself if he had wanted to. But that wasn't the way he would set about it. Both at Fasquelle's and at the Nouvelle Revue Française, friends of his undertook to deliver the lengthy manuscript. Calmette of *Le*

Figaro gave Fasquelle's a revised and corrected copy at the beginning of 1912, and though, through Prince Antoine Bibesco, M. Proust saw Jacques Copeau, and though he did write once to Gaston Gallimard, in the end it was Prince Antoine who took the second copy, not entirely corrected, and gave it to André Gide at a dinner he and his brother gave for this purpose in the autumn of 1912.

Both brothers were warm defenders of M. Proust and his work. They'd read the manuscript of *Swann* and liked it very much.

"Because I knew they were so kind and intelligent," M. Proust told me later, "I gave it to them to read, at least the beginning. And both of them, with the rather Latin enthusiasm of Rumanians, and rolling their r's said, 'Marrrcel, it's marrrrvelous! Nobody else wrrrrites like you!'"

And so there was the manuscript, submitted twice. Then silence from both quarters. No answer from Fasquelle for months. And two, three, four weeks, went by, and nothing from the Nouvelle Revue Française either. Prince Antoine came to see M. Proust.

"Well, Marcel, what news? What do they say?"

"Nothing. They still haven't answered."

"What? They have not written to you?"

In the end Prince Antoine went to see Gide at the Nouvelle Revue Française, which was then in rue Madame near Saint-Sulpice. Gide came down from his office to meet him and told him the manuscript had been rejected.

"We publish serious books. There can be no question of our bringing out something like this, the work of a fashionable dandy."

He gave the manuscript back to Antoine Bibesco. It was two days before Christmas, I think. There was a letter later from Jacques Copeau, less blunt but to the same effect, confirming the rejection.

All this is connected with the famous story, or quarrel almost, of whether Gide, who was the only one who had the manuscript in his possession, read it or not, or whether he even opened the parcel. There's a complicated and rather comical tale about the string it was tied up with, and of course there's the inevitable accompaniment of fairy tales.

Although Gide later confessed to his error of judgment, he always swore adamantly that he'd read the manuscript, and in support of his rejection of it he quotes a phrase which is supposed to have shocked him very much in *Du côté de chez Swann*. It's somewhere in the first hundred pages, and it's where M. Proust, talking about "Tante Léonie" (more or less his own Aunt Elisabeth) and "her sad brow, pale and lifeless," to give an image of her thinness describes how the "vertebrae" showed through "like the points of a crown of thorns or the beads of a rosary." [*Translator's note:* Scott Moncrieff tactfully renders *vertèbres* as "bones."] It was these vertebrae which are supposed to have stuck in André Gide's throat and taken his appetite away for the rest of the book.

That's all very well, but this explanation came long afterward, and my evidence, which is the same as M. Proust's version, is completely different. It's a little historical point he often talked about, and every time he said quite categorically:

"Céleste, I assure you they never opened my parcel at the Nouvelle Revue Française."

The proof he gave me always seemed conclusive to me. But here I have to go back a little, to Nicolas Cottin, in fact, for it was he who wrapped the parcel for Prince Bibesco to give to André Gide.

But to return to Nicolas. I've already said how at the beginning, when I was the "courier," it was he who wrapped the signed copies I delivered. He was, as I said, extremely meticulous, and the parcels were beautifully done. He took special care in tying the string and in fact was something of an artist in knots, with a particular and more or less inimitable style. For M. Proust this was always incontrovertible proof that his manuscript had never been opened, either by André Gide or by anyone else at the Nouvelle Revue Française.

"I saw the parcel before and after, Céleste," he said. "And I am absolutely certain it came back intact, exactly as I sent it. However clever anyone was, to untie Nicolas' peculiar knot and then tie it again, and in exactly *the same place,* would be very difficult, not to say impossible."

Nicolas, too, was sure the knot hadn't been undone.

But the whole story gave M. Proust a good deal of amusement. He always laughed when he told me about it, reliving the whole tale with great amusement. He said:

"As the manuscript was so thick and heavy, Nicolas went out and bought some very strong paper at the stationer's downstairs. And when I think of all the trouble he went to with the string!"

Anyway, he remained convinced to the end that André Gide's rejection was caused by prejudice; precisely because he'd known M. Proust in the salons and still heard of his frequenting them, he'd dismissed him in advance and by hearsay as a "fashionable dandy" without taking the trouble to read the book itself.

"He judged me by the opinion he'd formed about my life and my mixing in society. My camellia boutonnière had probably made him and his friends imagine I was good for nothing," said M. Proust, his eyes sparkling with irony.

But never, even when I first went to work for him and he started to confide in me, and when the memory of the incident was still comparatively recent, did he show the slightest trace of acrimony, rancor, or resentment—even when he said that, after all, if Gide heard about him in society circles, it must have been because he frequented them too and was perhaps as much of a "dandy" as M. Proust.

When I told him that he must have been angry or hurt at the unfairness, he shook his head and smiled. It was clear he knew too much about human nature not to take the matter magnanimously, as a simple inconvenience.

Even his comments, though amused and satirical, were full of kindness and indulgence.

Yet the end of 1912 doubled his disappointment: two or three days after the Nouvelle Revue Française sent the manuscript back, he received, the day after Christmas, a letter from Fasquelle, who also rejected *Du côté de chez Swann*—though this time, it must be said, with more courtesy, and at least after the manuscript had been carefully read.

It should also be said that M. Proust got his own back for this disappointment, and that, if I knew him, he certainly never had any doubt that his vengeance was near at hand.

I'm not going to give a recital of his publications and his various publishers. It is of no interest. I'll just say that after the double failure with Fasquelle and the others, he made contact with the young publisher Bernard Grasset through his old friend René Blum, the brother of Léon, the Socialist, to whom M. Proust's mother said: "My dear Léon, I don't see how you can profess such advanced ideas and not give all your money away."

According to the contract signed at the beginning of 1913, M. Proust was to pay for the publication of his book. He had foreseen this from the beginning; the novelty of his work was bound to make it difficult to publish. Anyway, money was of no consequence to him, and he never wrote with the idea of earning money.

Almost immediately after it was published, *Du côté de chez Swann* made so much of a stir in literary circles that there was an uproar at the Nouvelle Revue Française. Jacques Rivière, editor of the *NRF* review, was furious that Gide had rejected the book, and from the beginning of 1914, Gallimard and the others started to make efforts to mend matters.

And then it was M. Proust's turn to laugh, and I can speak about that from experience. It was almost two years to the day between February 1914, when Gallimard's committee sent a letter of repentance, and February 1916, when Gide himself went to his Canossa at boulevard Haussmann, as we shall see later.

I think it was one of the most entertaining times of his life for M. Proust. He kept me up to date with developments as they occurred. Once again he maneuvered the whole thing from his bed. On the one hand, he really wanted to be published by Gallimard.

"I would like my book to have a really good publisher. Not that I have anything against Grasset—far from it. But he has been called up into the army, his business is paralyzed, and the publication of my second volume is put off indefinitely. And at the Nouvelle Revue Française there are people like Jacques Rivière who are really devoted to encouraging what is new and good."

But partly out of scruples toward Bernard Grasset, partly to pay back Gide, Copeau, and Gallimard for being so irresponsible and prejudiced, M. Proust, usually so impatient, wasn't at all in a hurry now. The situation made him laugh like a schoolboy.

"So they are interested in the fashionable dandy now. Well, Céleste, we will just let things take their course. I have them where I want them. I am the master now, and we will just wait and see."

Sometime during the first two years of the war, I remember, Gaston Gallimard and Jacques Copeau went on an official propaganda mission, I believe, to the United States, and they continued to pursue M. Proust even from there. There was a secretary at the Nouvelle Revue Française called Mme. Lemarié, who passed on the messages. Heavens, the number of times she rang at our door to ask me to deliver the message and press M. Proust for an answer! He never saw her, it was always me. Poor Mme. Lemarié, I can hear her now—he must do this, he must do that.

"Monsieur Gallimard has written to me saying Monsieur Proust must make up his mind. There are so many difficulties because of the war. And Monsieur Gallimard is so anxious for it to be published. But for that to happen Monsieur Proust must decide soon. . . ."

They actually entreated. When I recounted these visits to M. Proust he said:

"We will wait and see, Céleste, we have plenty of time. This Monsieur Gallimard is a bit of a butterfly. Now he has seen the flower he wants to settle on it. But we will let him flutter about a bit more."

But I'm sure he'd already decided in his own mind. Despite his affection for Grasset, he'd give his second book, *A l'ombre des jeunes filles en fleurs,* to Gallimard and his friends. He thought them more suitable for his work.

But his conscience still bothered him about Grasset. When, after numerous letters and other approaches from Gallimard and the others, he finally said yes to them in 1916, he talked to me several times, and at length, about Grasset.

"Of course I am pleased at the thought of being published by the Nouvelle Revue Française. But I am very sorry to have to break my contract with Bernard Grasset. I know I am free to do as I like; he published *Du côté de chez Swann* at the author's expense, so I paid for it and don't owe him anything. I can back out whenever I like. But it pains me to leave him, because he is not only a gentleman but very intelligent and capable, and he is bound to become an important publisher someday. Besides, he is a man of sensibilities. He has been magnificent with me, Céleste. But his being away at the war means his business is at a standstill and will not be able to publish my other books for a long time. And I am ill, I haven't much time, I cannot wait. My only hope, my dearest wish, is that he will understand: I shall have to write to him, much as it pains me.''

They exchanged letters, and Bernard Grasset released him with kindness, regret, and dignity.

''He has been wonderful,'' M. Proust said. ''He has made it possible for me to leave him without any unpleasantness. I am so relieved. I told you how magnanimous he was, didn't I?''

And he always felt great respect and gratitude toward Bernard Grasset.

His feelings for Gaston Gallimard were very different. I vowed to M. Proust's memory that I wouldn't write anything here but the truth, and I'm bound to say he never really felt in sympathy with M. Gallimard. M. Proust was too polite, too suave and courteous to show anything, but, for example, he let Gaston Gallimard come to see him only once, and even then he made a certain amount of difficulty. It was three years after he'd become his publisher, and in special circumstances which I'll describe in due course, after we'd moved and were living at rue Hamelin. He never saw him at boulevard Haussmann, and I don't remember his mentioning that they'd met outside, even in the company of other people. I seem to recall that a few weeks before M. Proust died, Gaston Gallimard wrote to ask for an interview. But I don't remember letting him in, and I'm sure the last person M. Proust saw from the Nouvelle Revue Française was Jacques Rivière, who visited with him for a long while.

Apart from that, there were no social relationships between the two men. Nor, in fact, did M. Proust have any such relationships with any but two people at the Nouvelle Revue Française. One of these was Jacques Rivière. The other I shall come back to.

The only relationship with Gallimard concerned the printing of the work. M. Proust would send me with messages, or ask me to telephone to check details and make sure they were incorporating changes and corrections. I remember he was angry once—with all the politeness and mildness, as well as all the firmness, that anger created in him—because, presumably for reasons of economy, *A l'ombre des jeunes filles en fleurs* was printed in very small type so that it would go into one volume.

"Look at that, Céleste—it is unreadable! How can people be expected to buy it? It will just put them off. They will have to print it again, and make it into several volumes if necessary."

I often, late at night, brought such messages to Mme. Lemarié in her flat on rue de Liège.

As for the financial picture: Between the year he was taken on by the Nouvelle Revue Française and the year of his death, I can only remember their sending money twice: once, at the beginning, ten thousand francs, and the second time, much later, almost at the end, thirty thousand francs. I'd have known if there had been any other times.

But this only amused M. Proust. What mattered to him was that his book should be printed, and he was quite ready to sacrifice the rest. I'd say, from the ironic way he talked about it, that if he sometimes inquired about the money, it was more to tease than out of self-interest. He once said:

"Whenever I ask Gaston Gallimard if he has anything for me, he always makes some excuse: there is this or that, would I mind waiting a little, it is not the right date yet, the accounts have not been made up."

Once, in my innocence, I asked: "It's all very well for Monsieur Gallimard to say he hasn't any money, but what about the Lazare bank?"

That really tickled him, and he answered: "All the more reason, Céleste! All the more reason!"

He gave me another mischievous look when they sent the thirty thousand francs, toward the end.

"Thirty thousand francs. Well, dear Céleste, things are beginning to move. You will see, they will come round!"

There were two exceptions—two very different men from the Nouvelle Revue Française whom M. Proust was always pleased to see. One was Jacques Rivière, the famous editor who built the reputation and prestige of the *NRF*, and the other was M. Tronche, who, I believe, was the business manager.

M. Proust had great confidence in Jacques Rivière. He found him intelligent and extremely kind—I hope it's clear, from the people he applied this word to, what he meant by it and how much he valued it.

"He is a child," he used to say. "He deserves to be loved. He has an immense purity."

He respected him too and had a kindred feeling because Rivière also had poor health, though like himself he was an indefatigable worker.

Rivière, for his part, admired M. Proust's work so much he was quite overwhelmed by his presence.

"He dares not speak to me, Céleste. And yet I like being with him—he talks so sensitively."

Tronche was quite different.

"He is a good fellow and an honest man," M. Proust said. "But I am afraid he is not too popular with his colleagues."

M. Proust had as much confidence in him as in Rivière. He even listened to his opinion on his books. I think it was he who suggested the title *La Prisonnière,* which originally was just to be called *Sodome et Gomorrhe III et IV.* Tronche, as a good business manager, pointed out that people who already had *Sodome et Gomorrhe I et II* might think they already had the new book.

Though very respectful, Tronche was outspoken, and M. Proust liked that. I remember how pleased he was one night after Tronche had been to see him—it must have been in 1920, when M. Proust was beginning to be well known and his books were selling.

"Apparently Gallimard and his company are proud to have me now. I can understand Rivière's being pleased. He was the first one to say to Gide, when he rejected the manuscript: 'How could you do such a thing? You can't have read it!' But the others! However, it seems they have good reason to congratulate themselves. Do you know what Tronche told me? He said: 'It was you who saved the publishing side of the Nouvelle Revue Franąise. We were in an awful situation before.'"

I think Jacques Rivière confirmed this.

Tronche and Rivière confirmed this.

Tronche and Rivière were also inseparable friends and shared the same views. This was another thing M. Proust liked about them.

"They're hand in hand in integrity," he said.

M. Proust was gone when Jacques Rivière died, otherwise I'm sure he would have grieved. Tronche was inconsolable. He'd given his own blood for Rivière, who was dying of leukemia. I saw him, and he told me about the transfusion in the simple words he always used: "I lay down beside him and they fixed the syringe. But it wasn't any good."

I always understood M. Proust's affection for these two. I was very fond of them myself. They put their heart into their work, but they had a heart for other things as well. That's what M. Proust meant by "kind," and that's why he singled them out from the others.

I can't say I knew Gaston Gallimard myself, so it's not for me to judge. In 1971, at the celebration of the centenary of M. Proust's birth at the Hôtel de Ville in Paris, Jacques de Lacretelle made a fine speech, and afterward I was introduced to a gentleman they said was Claude Gallimard, the son. He didn't make a very strong impression on me. All I remember about his father is his taste for "butterfly" ties—but perhaps that's through association with the joke M. Proust had made.

24

THE FAKE MONK

Though perfectly polite on the surface, M. Proust's relations with the man who became his sole publisher were restricted to matters concerning the publication of his books. In the same manner, M. Proust hardly cultivated literary society or looked to it for friendship. Not many literary names cropped up in our nocturnal conversations. I think he was too conscious both of the futility of that ambience and of the solitary nature of his work to bother about making such contacts there. Not to mention the waste of time.

The reason he liked the author Daniel Halévy, his contemporary, was that they had both fought on the same side in the Dreyfus affair, they were both fond of Mme. Straus, who was Halévy's cousin, and Halévy himself was a historian of immense culture who in his own way studied the decline of the same society as M. Proust. And from the way M. Proust praised his erudition, I'm sure their conversations provided a rich source of material for M. Proust's work.

One name that was mentioned sometimes was that of the poet Fernand Gregh; he and M. Proust had been friends since their youth, when a group of them started a small literary review.

"Oh, it didn't last long," M. Proust would say. "It stopped after eight issues. We called it *Le banquet*. It didn't expire from any

293

shortage of ideas. We probably had too many. Most likely it died of indigestion.''

He sometimes mentioned René Boyslève, whom he once admired but had lost sight of. Sometimes he spoke of Paul Bourget's novels but with a certain amount of scorn.

"He too is interested in more or less the same society, but I don't care for his analysis. He explains too much."

He exchanged some correspondence with Paul Claudel while I was with him—I remember my sister Marie delivering the letters. M. Proust wasn't very drawn to him.

"I am not devout enough for that sort of person," he said.

His feelings toward François Mauriac were rather similar, though much warmer. He always said he'd admired his work from the beginning.

"But he is a bit too pious for my taste, and he says I am not pious enough. I think he restrains himself from trying to convert me," he said, but with a friendly smile.

They wrote to each other more often than they met, and there was a real affection between them. I remember how moved François Mauriac was when his son Claude married M. Proust's great-niece, long after M. Proust's death. I went to the wedding and was introduced to him. He put his arms around me and said, in the famous "wounded" voice: "Céleste! How glad I am to meet you at last!"

M. Proust was more attracted by writers younger than himself, those who, though contemporaneous, were ten or fifteen years his junior: they had much more understanding of his work than his real contemporaries. Everything, for him, was related to his work, and even someone else's reaction to it was a kind of intellectual enrichment.

That is why his close friends, those who had most access to him during the last eight years, were men like Jacques de Lacretelle, Paul Morand, Jean-Louis Vaudoyer, and even, for a time, Jean Cocteau, who, as I've said, also amused him by his eccentricities and his efforts to be original at all costs.

I remember Jean Giraudoux too. They didn't see each other much; there wasn't time. But M. Proust was very fond of him, and he had enormous admiration for M. Proust. I think M. Proust brought him home one night after an evening at the house of Jeanne Hugo, then divorced from Léon Daudet. I can still see him—tall, thin, with a slight stoop, charming, with a look full of sweetness, kindness, and intelligence. It was at rue Hamelin, in the last years. I made M. Proust laugh because when he told me Giraudoux was from the Limousin I exclaimed, "The same part of the world as Madame Chevalier!"—Mme. Chevalier being Dr. Gagey's cook, my only friend at boulevard Haussmann. "I shall put that in my book," M. Proust said. And he did.

But among the people that gravitated around him much more than he gravitated around them, I must pay special attention to André Gide, firstly because it was he who was responsible for the rejection of *Swann* at Gallimard's and also because after M. Proust's death a misunderstanding arose about a supposed intellectual and personal intimacy. This misunderstanding was deliberately fostered by Gide himself in what he said and wrote, perhaps with the idea of making people forget his former error.

Anyway, I can vouch that M. Proust neither liked nor admired Gide. Not that he bore a grudge about the rejection of *Swann*—he was too generous, high-minded, and tolerant of human weakness for that. What he didn't like was the personality of Gide and his work, though he had a certain admiration for his style and for his talent as a writer: "Not bad," he said of *Les Caves du Vatican,* for example. But as to the rest:

"He would like to draw me into his set now" he said. "But as he can't see anything but his own ideas, he gets me all wrong. I am *not* 'The Immoralist.'"

In fact they had nothing in common. From what M. Proust said, it was clear he thought the only reason Gide came around to him was to try to repair the blunder that had màde him look so silly before.

After *Du côté de chez Swann* was published by Grasset in 1913 and the first favorable reviews appeared, the people at the Nouvelle Revue Française vied with one another in writing to M. Proust: Rivière, Copeau, Gide. M. Proust never doubted Rivière's sincerity.

Antoine Bibesco, who always knew the latest gossip, had told him at once of Rivière's outburst at the *NRF* committee, and how, though he knew nothing about the story of Nicolas' knots, he'd openly accused Gide of giving back the manuscript without having read it. But the letters from Copeau and Gide—from the latter especially—were probably less sincere.

Years later M. Proust was still laughing at Gide's sudden discovery of his merits: "I have not been able to tear myself away from your book for days. I'm steeping myself in it. . . ."

One must admit it was funny. Fasquelle woke up at the same time as the Gallimard people and offered to publish future books.

Anyway, in 1916, after having kept them on tenterhooks for two years, M. Proust decided the time had come to make peace on his own terms with the Nouvelle Revue Française. He wrote a letter to Gide, since Gide represented the committee, and Gide replied as fast as he could with a visit of remorse and repentance.

I remember it all, including the date, because I was directly involved. It was February 25, two years after Gide's first letter in which he'd said he was "largely responsible"—it was the least he could say—for the rejection of *Swann* but that he was now reading the book with delight.

So on February 25, 1916, M. Proust called me in and gave me an envelope obviously containing a long epistle.

"Céleste," he said, "I have written to Monsieur André Gide to make peace, since he seems to think we are at war. I would like you to take a taxi and deliver this letter to him personally. There is the address: Villa Montmorency. It is somewhere in Auteuil, in the sixteenth arrondisement. It is not easy to find, but the taxi driver will know."

So off I went, found myself in front of a little narrow door, and rang. After a moment the door was opened by a woman carrying a lamp. It was wartime, of course, and there must have been a power cut. Beyond the woman, I could see a kind of large balcony in the shadows, with a staircase with wooden banisters. The woman was dressed in a long dark robe. I recall being struck by the somberness of her dress and the expression of great sadness on her face, and I remember thinking: "How strange, she looks like a peasant."

"What do you want?" she asked, raising the flame of the lamp to see me.

"Could I deliver this letter to Monsieur Gide personally, please?"

"Who is it from?"

I gave the name, and she said at once: "Wait a moment and I'll tell him."

She didn't say who she was; she might have been the maid. I watched her go up the dark staircase and disappear.

Gide came down immediately. He took the big envelope and asked if there was to be an answer. I said yes. He asked me to sit down while he read the letter. I had a good look at him while he did so. He was enveloped in a homespun cape, his hands alone emerging. There was something indefinable I didn't like about him, both in his face and in his way of looking at you—something not genuine, a false sincerity or rather a sort of forced sincerity. But apart from that, very affable.

I went back to boulevard Haussmann with the message that he would be glad to accept the invitation and come immediately. I got the impression he would have come running.

As a matter of fact, I just had time to deliver my report before he arrived—for whenever I delivered a message, especially at someone's house, I always had to give M. Proust not only the answer and an account of what had been said to me, but also as detailed a description as possible of what I'd seen, both of the people and of their surroundings.

That day, I remember, he was particularly eager to know. As soon as I'd given him the reply, he said:

"Right. Now tell me what Villa Montmorency is like."

I described the little door, the staircase, the balcony, the darkness.

"And who let you in?"

I described my "peasant," and he shook his head slowly.

"Céleste, that was poor Madame Gide." He looked very sad. Then: "And what did you think of Monsieur Gide himself?"

"Oh, very pleasant, monsieur. But I don't know . . . there's something about him I don't like. No, I don't like him."

"But why, Céleste? You must know why?"

"Now I've seen him I'm not surprised he gave that answer about your manuscript without having read it. Just the sort of thing he would do."

I could tell he was examining me with amusement, and it suddenly came into my head to say:

"He looks like a fake monk, monsieur. You know, the ones that look at you all the more piously to hide the fact that they're not sincere."

He roared with laughter. He was obviously delighted.

At that point the bell rang. Gide had arrived. It was very early in the evening—early, that is, for M. Proust: about six or seven. I went to the door. He was bareheaded and wearing his homespun cape, which he didn't take off. I showed him into the small drawing room, then went and told M. Proust.

"The fake monk's here."

I showed Gide and his cape into the bedroom. M. Proust was of course in bed. Gide went right over to him, one hand holding the cape in front; this was his favorite attitude when moving about. He halted near the fireplace, and I silently withdrew as usual. A little while later M. Proust sent for me to ask for something, and I can still see Gide as I came in. His cape now fell straight down, his head was tilted to one side, and he was saying, in a solemn voice with deep vibrations—a voice of bronze, as they say:

"Yes, Monsieur Proust, I confess . . . it was the greatest mistake I ever made in my life. . . ."

He was obviously referring to the rejection of the manuscript.

He stayed for some time after I came out again, but it wasn't a very long interview.

After he went M. Proust of course sent for me to tell me about it. He was smiling and triumphant. Earlier, when I had come in in the middle of the conversation, I'd seen the familiar movement of the eyelids, first lowered, then suddenly raised with a piercing glance, an indication that he was evaluating the sincerity of the person he was talking to, followed by a sign that he was inwardly satisfied with his conclusions. This time it clearly meant: "Whoever you are, I've got you where I want you."

He told me Gide had made amends and that he himself did not hide what he thought of the frivolous excuse about the "fashionable dandy."

But I insisted: "It is all very well to say it was the greatest mistake of his life, monsieur. But did he say whether or not he opened the parcel?"

"Of course he didn't open it! But that is of no importance now. To err is human, you know, Céleste." Then he said, laughing: "But I agree he does look rather fake."

We always referred to him between ourselves as the "fake monk," and I remember we sometimes imitated him with his cape in our nocturnal conversations, or talked like his *Nourritures Terrestres:* "Nathanaël, I am going to speak to you of this and that. . . ."

I think André Gide's basic mistake was that despite his pretended modesty he was so engrossed in himself and his own ideas and inclinations that he tried to see M. Proust's work as a confession of the same ideas and inclinations, on the basis of passages and characters in *La Recherche du Temps perdu* where particular vices and manners are examined. And it's probably largely because of him that so many people have focused their attention on this aspect of the work and on characters like Charlus and concluded that they represent the essence of his work.

I know Gide talks somewhere of notes he was supposed to have taken after two other visits to M. Proust, which he said took place in May 1921 and therefore at rue Hamelin. It's strange, but I don't remember any further visits, especially because I remember such visitors all the more clearly because they were so few and it was always I who showed them in. What surprises me even more is that Gide says M. Proust sent Odilon to fetch him—I would remember that too—and that he found M. Proust "so fat he looked like Jean

Lorrain, and shivering in an overheated room.'' M. Proust did suffer from some edema toward the end, but Gide is certainly the only person who ever thought he looked ''fat.'' And the room couldn't have been overheated, because at rue Hamelin there wasn't any heating at all. The truth was it was freezing cold there, as I shall explain later.

If Gide didn't come, at least he isn't the only one to claim he did. If he came, I'm afraid he exaggerated again about his supposed agreement with M. Proust about homosexuality. If, as he also asserts, M. Proust really did remark that Gide could ''say anything as long as you don't say 'I,''' it does sound like a shaft of M. Proust's wit, especially as Gide was always itching to talk about himself.

But there is one thing I remember perfectly and which I offer for consideration by sceptics and sectarians.

Late one afternoon M. Proust was opening his letters as usual after his coffee. There was a letter from Gide introducing a young man and asking M. Proust to help him. M. Proust read it and told me the drift. Then he put it aside and said:

''I'll have nothing to do with that.''

There was a long silence, as when he traveled faraway into his thoughts. When he came back he said with a grave look, stressing his words:

''One day, Céleste, they will see no one has done more serious moral harm than Gide to the younger generation.''

He shut his eyes to retreat again into his thoughts, and then said, more quietly, to himself:

''Sad. Very sad.''

37 A memorandum of mine, which I consulted whenever Monsieur Proust asked me to call up one of his friends. There were just as many names on the other side. The heading "Groceries" makes me laugh now, when I think about how, when he'd come back from some meeting I'd arranged, I would ask, "Well, Monsieur, did you pick up anything for your book?"

38 Marie de Benardaky, his first great love.

39 The great actress Réjane playing the part of the Prince de Sagan.

40 Louisa de Mornand.

41 The Comtesse de Chevigné, with whom he was in love.

42 Madame Lemaire in her studio/salon.

43 The poet Anna
des Noailles.

44 Madame Straus, perhaps his only friend.

45 Laure Hayman.

46 The Comtesse Greffulhe. He thought she was so beautiful and regal that he went to the Opera to observe her carriage and posture as she ascended the staircase. She was the main model for the Duchesse de Guermantes in his books.

47 Comte Robert de Montesquiou, who fascinated him and at the same time filled him with mistrust. He was the cousin of the Comtesse Greffulhe. The character of Charlus is almost entirely based on him. "That's it in a nutshell," Monsieur Proust said to me.

48 Left: Prince Emmanuel Bibesco.
49 Right: Prince Antoine Bibesco. It was Prince Antoine who gave
André Gide the manuscript of *Swann*, which Gide turned down.

50 Below: Reynaldo Hahn, Proust's closest friend until his death. In
this drawing by Sem, he's at the piano. Behind him, Madame Lemaire
and Montesquiou. In front, "Coco" de Madrazo.

51 The Duc de Guiche.

52 Charles Haas,
the model for Swann.

53 The Comte de
Salignac-Fénelon, who
was killed at the start of
the war and whom Proust
greatly admired for his
elegance and bravery (he
was one model for Saint
Loup in the books).

54 Alfred Agostinelli, about whom there were plenty of stories.

55 Agostinelli in his airplane. He was passionate about flying and disappeared with one of his planes in the middle of the ocean.

56 His companion Anna with my husband Odilon, who called her the flying flea.

57 Monsieur Proust with Robert de Flers and Lucien Daudet, one of his closest friends.

25

FAME

There's a question I've often asked myself. If his lucidity about others derived from his lucidity about himself, wasn't the ease with which he classified and then dismissed them the result of his certainty of his own value, and the comparison he made between himself and other people? This sense of himself emerged very clearly when he began to receive honors and success.

He won the Prix Goncourt for *A l'ombre des jeunes filles en fleurs* in December 1919.

The prize hadn't been awarded during the war, and there were two competitors for this first postwar Goncourt. There was much praise for Roland Dorgelès' war novel, *Les croix de bois (The Wooden Crosses),* and some people, not realizing how ill M. Proust was and why he hadn't been in the army, regarded him as a "home front" writer.

It has been said he got the prize through intrigue and because his friend Léon Daudet was on the jury. There was no intrigue on his part. His friends wanted him to have the prize, and he let them do as they pleased. The most he did was to reply in the affirmative and to say he was very honored when the writer J. H. Rosny (the elder) wrote to ask if he would accept the prize if it was awarded to him. I think Rosny wrote twice, and came twice to rue Hamelin, before M. Proust said yes.

Léon Daudet certainly campaigned for him. But although as usual he was the one who made the most noise about it, he wasn't the only one. Rosny made no secret that he would vote for M. Proust, and their friendship was only a coincidence in this case; Léon Daudet sincerely admired M. Proust's book, and he was a fighter and would not beat around the bush.

Of course, after the award, M. Proust heard all the gossip about the voting from Antoine Bibesco and others. He told me Léon Daudet lost his temper with the supporters of Dorgelès because they said the Goncourts' will specified that the prize should go to a young writer, whereas M. Proust was forty-eight. Some members of the jury, either prejudiced or misinformed, said he was over fifty.

Apparently Léon Daudet flew into a furious rage and said, "That shows you don't know anything about the will. I do, and I'll get it and read it to you. The clause in question doesn't say a young man—it says a young *talent*. And that applies exactly to M. Proust; he's a writer more than a century ahead of his time."

M. Proust told me Reynaldo Hahn was one of the first and most enthusiastic in urging him to let his name go forward as a candidate.

In the end *A l'ombre des jeunes filles en fleurs* won by six votes to three.

It was December 11—the award must have been announced about four or five hours earlier—when there was a ring at the door. That is, it must have been about five or six in the evening and our daily routine had just begun. I went to the door and opened it, and there was someone who introduced himself as Gaston Gallimard, accompanied by Jacques Rivière and Tronche. Gallimard was in a state of high excitement.

"I expect you know M. Proust has won the Prix Goncourt?" he said.

How could we have known? We hadn't been on the telephone for ages. We were quite cut off from the world. And even M. Proust's closest friends respected his habits too much to disturb him outside the usual hours even for such news as this.

Gallimard was bursting with impatience. He'd hardly set foot in the hall when he said, "I must see Monsieur Proust at once."

I could sense Jacques Rivière and Tronche there behind him, much more reticent. They'd hardly uttered a word.

"Very well, monsieur," I said. "I'll go and tell Monsieur Proust."

He was awake and had finished his fumigation and had his coffee, and in such circumstances it was agreed I could go in without being sent for if something exceptional had happened. So in I went. He was lying quietly on the pillows, gradually getting into the rhythm of his day.

"Monsieur," I said, "I have some important news, which I'm sure you'll be glad to hear. You've won the Prix Goncourt!"

He looked at me. All he said was: "Oh?"

Just as if it were a matter of sheer indifference—though I knew that deep down he was really delighted. But he was always like that—calm, master of himself in all circumstances, never disturbing his own harmony.

"Yes, monsieur. And Monsieur Gallimard is here, with Monsieur Jacques Rivière and Monsieur Tronche. He's terribly worked up and wants to see you at once."

"Well, you must tell him he can't, Céleste. I don't want to see him. Later on perhaps . . . yes, about ten this evening . . . perhaps."

"But monsieur, it looks as if he's got urgent things to say."

"No, Céleste. Tell Monsieur Gallimard I am extremely grateful to him for coming but I'm not able to see him. Ask him to come back at ten o'clock this evening . . . or tomorrow."

I gave Gallimard the message. He started to paw the ground.

"But I *must* see him, I tell you. It's of the utmost importance! He doesn't realize! I must catch the nine o'clock train tonight for Deauville and go to see the printer in Abbeville. If I don't, we shan't have enough copies and it'll be a disaster. Please, I must see him, it's urgent. Tell him it's against his own interests . . ."

Back I went to M. Proust.

"He insists, monsieur. As far as I can make out he has to catch a train today to go and arrange about printing and the paper. He really does seem to have difficulties. I think you ought to see him."

As he didn't answer I went on: "Come, monsieur, please—make a little effort."

He sighed and smiled. "All right. Tell him to come in. But only for a minute. And alone."

So I showed Gaston Gallimard in for the one and only time. Jacques Rivière and Tronche didn't have to wait long in the hall; it was a short interview.

After I closed the door behind the three visitors M. Proust rang. When I went in he was looking pleased and amused.

"Right. And now, my dear Céleste, now that I have sent Monsieur Gallimard about his business, let me tell you this. They'll ferret out where I am, and from now on there'll probably be a lot of people ringing our bell. I don't want to see anyone. Especially not journalists and photographers—they're dangerous, and they're never satisfied. Turn everybody away."

And he added with mock severity: "As for you, if anyone asks you questions, don't say anything."

His instructions were scrupulously obeyed. Not one journalist or photographer ever entered the apartment of rue Hamelin.

Even though he didn't show it, there's no doubt he was delighted to have won the Goncourt. That evening, or soon after, he told me about it in a way that showed how pleased he was.

"There are lots of literary prizes, Céleste, to reward authors and confer distinction on them—so many, in fact, that one loses count. But there aren't many important ones that are worth it. There's the Prix Fémina, then the Grand Prix for Literature of the French Academy—but even they are nothing compared with the Goncourt. That is the only one that really counts, because it is awarded by men who know what the novel is and what a particular novel is worth."

He was really very proud, then, of this distinction and of the congratulations he received—including eventually those of the three members of the jury who had held out for Dorgelès. So in the end it was as if it had been unanimous.

One of the gestures that touched him most was that of the actress Réjane, whom he'd admired ever since, at the age of ten or eleven, he saw her on the stage for the first time. She persuaded her son, Jacques Porel, who knew M. Proust and was very fond of him, to ask what she could give him as a present to show her pleasure about the Goncourt. He said the best present he could have would be a photograph of herself if she had one, dressed as the Prince de Sagan in a famous show of which she had been the star at the Epatant theater. The evening Jacques Porel brought the photograph, signed by Réjane, M. Proust showed it to me, pointing out the details as usual.

"Look, Céleste. No other woman could have had the audacity to dress as a man, with a top hat and monocle, and carry it off with such delicacy and elegance. Look at the gardenia in her buttonhole. It is a pity though, that she has kept on her pearl earrings."

He was as delighted as a boy.

But the Prix Goncourt didn't bring about any change in his daily life. Some people say he spent the five thousand francs of the prize on dinners and receptions to show his gratitude. I don't remember that he altered his usual way of life. If he had given any such parties, the first people he would have asked would have been those who'd voted for him on the Goncourt jury, especially Léon Daudet and Rosny. But he didn't invite them, I'm sure.

On the other hand, I think it was after the prize that he saw a few critics, particularly Paul Souday of *Le Temps,* a great literary pundit. Souday had written a rather qualified article about him, and that was why M. Proust wanted to meet him. For him, anything to do with his work was of primary interest. He was extremely sensitive to critical opinion, not out of susceptibility but out of curiosity about how other people's views differed from his, and also, admittedly, with the hope and desire of bringing others around to his own views.

I forget the exact circumstances, but probably he went through all the maneuvers necessary to make the meeting seem as natural as possible. There were two dinners or suppers with Paul Souday—both in a private room at the Ritz. The first was not entirely successful. The two men were still more or less at odds—politely, of course, because it was a social occasion with others present. I remember M. Proust saying:

"He is rather obstinate, this Monsieur Souday. It is hard for him to extend his understanding to others. He would like everyone to think as he does. But I believe he is honest and sincere in his prejudices, and that is something." And he added, as if to himself: "I shall manage it."

The second dinner set everything right. I remember inviting, on M. Proust's behalf, Comtesse de Noailles, her son, and Walter Berry, a very civilized and cultured American who was president of the American Chamber of Commerce in Paris and a fervent admirer of M. Proust's books. This time M. Proust returned home in triumph.

"Everything is all right, Céleste. It went splendidly."

And I believe that, after that, Paul Souday's articles acknowledged the value of M. Proust's work. M. Proust certainly always respected him, and I don't know who had the absurd idea of telling the story of a New Year's gift of a box of chocolates, which M. Proust supposedly asked me to throw into the fire in case they were poisoned, saying, "That man is capable of anything." The person concerned in the real story of the chocolates was of course Count de Montesquiou, though as I said earlier he never actually sent any chocolates, poisoned or otherwise.

Another fairy tale comes to mind among the hundreds hawked about, amplified and distorted and, what's worse, written down in books that are supposed to be serious and "definitive." It shouldn't be for an old woman like me to have to tell these gentlemen that it is not enough to make a card index—you have to check what's on the cards. They would do better to follow the example of M. Proust, who never wrote anything without having verified it. However, their method serves their small purposes. The purpose he served was a great one.

The only official honors he received came toward the end, and there were only two of them, the Goncourt and the Legion of Honor. He had to solicit the latter because that is the rule, and if he did so, it must have been because he wanted it. But most of his friends urged him, too, and I wouldn't be surprised if he was really thinking of his mother and father and the pleasure it would have given them. Professor Adrien Proust had an impressive collection of medals himself, from all over the world. Every time he went on a tour of inspection or was invited as a consultant abroad he came home with another decoration from some potentate; and M. Proust treasured these decorations.

He was awarded the Legion of Honor exactly a year after the Goncourt, in December 1920, at the same time as Countess de Noailles and a little while after Colette—two months after, I seem to remember. There was no ceremony. His brother, Robert, handed it over to him. As soon as Professor Robert Proust heard the news of the award he said, "I shall come to present you with it and a kiss, my little brother." He came one evening and dined at M. Proust's bedside, and they stayed chatting gaily about their childhood until very late.

His cross is the only real present I saw him get in all the years; he had a horror of receiving presents, though he loved to give them. It's been said the cross was given him by an art dealer, but in fact it was from Jean Béraud, a painter who had been a close friend since they met in the studio salon of Mme. Lemaire and who had been his second in the famous duel with Jean Lorrain. Béraud wrote and asked him to accept the cross as a token of friendship. He had bought it at Cartier's, and he asked M. Proust if he'd kindly have someone pick it up at the shop as he didn't want to send it through the post. My sister Marie went. It was a very pretty, very fine little cross set with small diamonds. When he woke up, M. Proust asked:

"Is Marie back?"

"Yes, monsieur."

"Did she get the cross?"

"Yes, monsieur."

"What's it like?"

"Very elegant, monsieur."

"I shall ring in a little while to see it."

I took it in when he rang, and he held it in his hand and looked at it, smiling, his expression one of childlike pleasure.

"How kind of him! It is not the gift itself I am delighted with, Céleste; it is the delicacy of the gesture and the thought."

He didn't say whether he was pleased about the distinction itself, but I could see he was brimming over with inward joy, and I think his pleasure with the decoration and his pleasure with the friendly gesture were intermingled.

I suppose that if he had lived he would have been elected a member of the French Academy, and I'm sure he would have been proud of that because it would have fulfilled his father's prophecy. I've seen a letter to the writer Maurice Barrès, in which M. Proust refers to this possibility (Barrès was himself a member of the Academy). M. Proust never actually spoke about it to me, but there can be no doubt he would have liked this honor. Small things didn't interest him; he preferred to save himself for significant ones, those which put the right values in their proper place in society and in which, therefore, he himself would be in his proper place.

For one of the most extraordinary things about him was his profound awareness of his own value. He had a high idea of his own superiority, though he was careful not to show it and could disguise it at will behind an elegant politeness. He could make himself small—but he didn't think himself small.

I can still see him the evening he showed me the photo of himself as a fair-haired little boy—the "little prince," as I called him, with his little cane. After looking at it with me he held it out in an impulse of affection:

"It was Grandmother Weil's favorite photograph. I would like you to have it, dear Céleste."

The photo is framed in leather stamped with gold. I kept it for some time, then presented it to the museum at Illiers. But that evening I said:

"Your grandmother foresaw you'd be famous, monsieur, when she had the lilies of royalty and the future embossed on the frame."

This made him laugh, but you could tell he was also proud.

Like his sensitivity about the critics, this had nothing to do with vanity. He only valued praise insofar as it was true, and what he was most sensitive to was the value of the critic himself. When Curtius, the famous German critic, wrote that he considered M. Proust the greatest classic writer of the twentieth century, he showed me the letter:

"I am very proud. 'Classic.' That is wonderful! Especially coming from a man of his integrity and intellectual distinction."

Similarly, when I delivered a letter or message to anyone, they always asked me, "How is he? How is his work?," and almost every time they talked to me about his books. When I returned home I had to give an account, and he would listen carefully and ask me to repeat what interested him to make sure his first understanding was accurate. I remember once going to the house of Gans, the banker. He wasn't married and lived with his mother and aunt. While I waited in the salon to give him the letter, his mother said:

"And how is Monsieur Proust these days? How is his health? Is his writing going well? Our lives are all wrapped up in him, you know. When shall we have his next book? We can't wait. His work is so rich, so dense! It has everything in it. One is always discovering new things. . . ."

When I got back I recounted this conversation to M. Proust, who listened with a pleased little smile.

"'Dense'—is that what she said? I like that, Céleste."

On such occasions he would put on an air of naïve modesty, but he was really transfigured with pride.

This pride did not impair his lucidity. He used to tell me how, when he went out in the evenings, people frequently came up to congratulate him.

"I thank them, Céleste, and they think I'm taken in. If they knew! They have not read a word of what I have written. I see through them immediately!"

He had no illusions even about some of the people he sent signed copies to. About the Countess Greffulhe and Mme. de Chevigné he said:

"They don't read them. And if they did, they wouldn't understand them."

Many persons have thought that he resented being underestimated by anyone. Nothing could be further from the truth. He didn't bother about such little things. If anyone hurt him, he scornfully withdrew, but that was all. But he didn't forget. Credit and debit were both set down in his memory, although he didn't make people pay for their pettiness. I'd say he even got satisfaction out of analyzing them, and he usually tried to rationalize their motives.

At the time of the Goncourt, Albin Michel, Dorgelès' publisher, was quicker than Gallimard and brought out copies of *Les Croix de bois* wrapped in a band which read "GONCOURT" in large print and "three votes" in small letters underneath. The Nouvelle Revue Française and several of M. Proust's friends wanted to prosecute the publisher. M. Proust wrote to Gaston Gallimard, saying he thought that such a lawsuit wasn't in very good taste; and if my memory serves me well, there the matter was left.

In all the time I knew him he only once took a little revenge (and not a very nasty revenge at that). It was in the last months of his life, at a large reception given by Countess de Mun. He insisted on going although he was terribly tired and already had influenza, which later grew worse. He was so ill he was afraid he might faint, and when I said it wasn't wise to go in his condition he answered:

"I shall get Paul Morand to come with me. There is a big curved staircase without any banisters, and if I became dizzy, and slipped and fell, I would kill myself. But with Paul I am all right. I would not mind taking his arm if necessary."

When he came in, late, he looked amused and pleased despite his exhaustion.

"All things come to him who waits, Céleste. I did something that made me laugh this evening. There were many people there—too many, in fact. It was rather mixed. Among them was Marcel Prévost, the novelist I've often mentioned to you. He kept hovering around me. I was with some people who were congratulating me about my books, and he came up and said: 'Good evening, Monsieur

310

Proust.' I tried to get out of it by pretending not to have seen or heard. A moment later he returned with: 'My dear colleague.' Again I didn't see him or hear him, but he didn't get the message. He came up behind me a third time and said, 'Dear Monsieur Proust, would you believe it, the other day we were taken for each other.' Then I turned around and said in a loud voice so that everyone nearby would hear: 'Only the initials could be confused!' After that he didn't want to come up to me again, I can tell you. Which is just what I wanted."

Then, laughing: "*I* don't write novels for people to read on the train."

"But what had he done to you, this Monsieur Prévost?" I asked.

He made a vague gesture. "Oh, it was a long time ago. . . ."

Afterward I gathered that Marcel Prévost had written a hostile article about him. But paradoxical as it may sound, what struck me at the time was the absence of unpleasantness in his way of telling the story. He laughed but without gloating, without bitterness or malice. He'd simply enjoyed it, that was all. I never heard him boast of his success. He talked about his work with modesty. But there was almost always something that showed how certain he was about it.

One evening he came in from a soirée and said: "Come here, Céleste, I want to tell you something."

I remember he started talking in the hall, as he was taking off his coat.

"Do you know what someone said to me this evening? 'Marcel, watch out or you will get yourself banned, with your Monsieur de Charlus.' Well, what do you think of that, Céleste? I thought I was safe after Monsieur Gide reproached me for being severe on 'uranism.'"

I was putting away his coat and hat, and I turned round and said without thinking: "Supposing you were banned, monsieur? You couldn't have a better piece of publicity. But I'm certain it will never happen."

He burst out laughing. "You have something there, Céleste! It *would* be good publicity. But I agree—I don't think they will ban me."

Then he stopped laughing and added with a force and succinctness I shall never forget:

"And do you know why, Céleste? Because if you know how to say things, you can say anything. And Marcel Proust does know how to say things."

The way his eyes flashed showed that the cry came from the heart, from the deepest conviction.

For many of the people who knew him he had long been "little Proust" or "little Marcel," always very polite and charming, almost too ardent and sensitive. And then, because of his work, he suddenly seemed to soar above them. But he had always seen himself there; it was only for others that it was any surprise. I remember how delighted he was the first time he had a letter from Count de Montesquiou in which the count addressed him as "my little Marcel." It wasn't that he was pleased and flattered by the familiarity. His was an inner laughter. The letter, on the contrary, showed that he'd cast a spell over Montesquiou and got the upper hand and that one day Montesquiou would see that "little Marcel" was his superior. And so it turned out, to the mortification of Count Robert.

His certainty about his future fame would sometimes betray itself. His first book, *Les plaisirs et les jours,* which was first brought out in 1896 with a preface by Anatole France, was not selling, and one day the publisher wrote to say he was going to dispose of the remaining copies. M. Proust read me the letter and said:

"What a pity I haven't anywhere to store them. They will sell one day, I can tell you."

Sometimes his assurance emerged with such magnetism and conviction I was quite bowled over.

I shall never forget the evening when we were in the small drawing room and he was telling me about an article on Stendhal someone had recommended to him. He was sitting in his chair with the review in his hand, and suddenly he said with his beautiful, bright, grave look:

"Listen, Céleste. I shall die soon. . . ."

He often used to say it, and I always protested:

"No, monsieur! Why do you say that? Why are you always talking to me about dying? I don't like it. Anyway, I'm going to die before you do."

I meant it. It's strange but true that throughout all those years I was sure I'd die before he did, though I had no idea of what or why I thought so.

"No, Céleste, you will live. And when I am dead, you will see. People will read me; yes, the whole world will read me. You will see my work grow in the public's esteem. And remember, Céleste, this article says it took a hundred years for Stendahl to become famous. It will take Marcel Proust less than fifty."

26

UPROOTED

Death began for him with our leaving boulevard Haussmann. It was an emotional uprooting. I don't mean that even without it work and illness wouldn't still have got the better of his constitution, but I've often thought since, that if M. Proust had stayed on at boulevard Haussmann, the end would have been delayed.

To understand this one has to bear in mind how much he was attached to family roots and the memory of his parents on one hand, and on the other, to his habits.

He had already been affected a great deal by moving away from his parents' flat on rue de Courcelles in 1905, after the death of his mother. Once Mme. Proust was gone he almost fled from the huge apartment, partly shut up since the death of Professor Adrien Proust. In theory he was supposed to have continued there as tenant after his parents.

"A vast place like that was difficult to rent in those days," he told me one day. "It belonged to the Phoenix Company, and when I asked them to terminate the lease because it was too big for me alone and much too sad, they said at first they couldn't because it was against company rules. Then, because of my dear father's position and the services he'd rendered not only to Paris but to the whole world, they agreed to make an exception."

But he didn't look after any of the arrangements himself. It was his brother, Robert, who saw to the moving and who had to divide up what their parents had left them, while M. Proust took refuge in the Hôtel des Réservoirs at Versailles with Félicie, his mother's faithful old servant.

Before he went to Versailles he'd already thought it necessary to spend a few weeks in a nursing home in Billancourt—Dr. Sollier's clinic, which had often been mentioned to him by Léon Daudet, who had been a medical student with Sollier. What really made him go there? Did he truly think he needed and would benefit from psychological treatment? Or was it just out of curiosity? With him it was always difficult to tell which was the true motive. Perhaps it was a bit of both. He never told me. But mistrustful as always, he had taken his precautions.

"I only half-trusted Sollier," he told me. "Supposing I had gone there and he wouldn't let me out again! That wasn't what I wanted at all. So I explained to him before I went in that I was prepared to be treated on condition I could leave whenever I wanted to."

I don't think he took it all very seriously. He recalled with amusement: "There was no lack of distraction. There was a rather beautiful garden, and one day I went out and sat on a bench. A moment later a very handsome and elegant young man came and sat next to me and began almost at once to tell me his life history. He said he'd been shut up there to prevent him from inheriting his parents' money. I felt quite sorry for him, though I did have some doubt. The next day, or perhaps a bit later, he came and sat beside me again and began on the same story. Then suddenly he pointed in front of him and said: 'Look, monsieur, can you see her?' 'Who?' 'The Virgin Mary, of course! Can't you see her coming across the lawn?' So then I realized . . ."

I don't think this incident increased his confidence in Sollier.

As for his stay at the Hôtel des Réservoirs in Versailles, I don't think his memories of it were very happy. All he said to me about it was:

"I don't know if it was the hotel itself or just the time I went there, but the memory I have of it is of gloomy boredom, as I said in my letters to Reynaldo Hahn."

He didn't really begin to feel well until Félicie helped him settle at boulevard Haussmann in 1906. There, he was at home. It was the apartment where his Great-Uncle Louis had ended his days after leaving his villa in Auteuil. Uncle Louis had had no children and left everything to his niece, Mme. Proust, and her brother Georges Weil. But as Georges Weil had died, it was his widow, M. Proust's aunt, who now owned the building, and he became her tenant. Much of the furniture which he'd inherited from his parents and, through his mother, from Uncle Louis, had been sold—there had been far too much of it. But even after the rest had been divided up between him and his brother, M. Proust still found himself with more furniture than he knew what to do with. So the dining room became the repository crammed to the ceiling.

But he felt comfortable among the pieces he'd chosen, those with most memories attached to them. And at boulevard Haussmann he established his habits. The apartment was really a desert surrounding his room. The big salon was only a thoroughfare; he never entertained there. For such few visitors as there were, and there was rarely more than one at a time, the small salon was just a brief halt on the way to the bedroom. M. Proust and I sometimes spent hours there, but we were the only ones.

The whole building was practically at his command. The other tenants couldn't do enough for him. He too, though his only contact with them was a chance encounter or a letter of thanks for some favor, was fond of them. Dr. Gagey, on the ground floor, had a daughter whom M. Proust found charming. She used to organize charity bazaars, and whenever she announced one to M. Proust he used to send her a bank note. Once she left a little handmade lace-trimmed cushion for him, with a letter. M. Proust didn't want the cushion, but he found the letter "delightful" and full of feeling. After M. Proust's death, when he had become famous, Mlle. Gagey told me she couldn't forgive herself for having burned the letters to her.

Above us was the extraordinary Dr. Williams, the American dentist. During the day he had technicians working for him in a laboratory overlooking the courtyard, but there was no noise. He was fond of sport and every Saturday drove off with his chauffeur to play golf. He'd married a musician, very distinguished, very perfumed, who was a great admirer of M. Proust and had written him so. I remember she played the harp. Her flat was on the third floor, above her husband's office. M. Proust said they were an "odd" couple. I don't think he ever met Mme. Williams, but they corresponded, and I know he liked the elegant style of her letters.

All this explains why it was a real uprooting for him to leave boulevard Haussmann.

The tragedy, for that's what it was, was aggravated emotionally by the circumstances in which it took place. M. Proust's aunt sold the building without letting him know, so that at the end of December 1918 he found himself faced with a *fait accompli*. The Varin-Barnier Bank had bought all the lower part of the house and intended to open a branch on the courtyard. The work began at the beginning of 1919, and M. Proust, who had been desperately hoping to be able to stay on in spite of everything, realized there would be no more peace and quiet and that his life, like the house he was so attached to, would be completely changed.

From the way he spoke of it both at the time and, often afterward, I could tell how deeply he was hurt: "I was always so nice to my aunt. To think she sold it without saying a word to me!" Although he never said anything directly about it, I'm sure that if his aunt had told him she wanted to sell, he would have bought the building himself without hesitation. For despite what has been said—and some have gone so far as to suggest that he owed his aunt money, three years' rent, I think they have said—he could have afforded that amount without affecting his life-style. If he had had money troubles as people have said, I'd have known.

Anyway, because he was a writer, the law afforded him a certain amount of protection, and he could have stayed on for another eighteen months, but he didn't want to.

"I would rather give up my rights than put up with all their noise," he said.

Then there was the problem of what to do with the furniture. And that was another drama, another liquidation of a past which was all his life and almost all his soul. The dining-room suite and all his parents' furniture that had been piled up there for thirteen years was sent to be auctioned. Some of the furnishings in the main salon, including a large crystal chandelier, went too. I even remember the man from the agency; his name was Dubois. Everything was sold in defiance of common sense. M. Proust refused to take care of it; he was far too upset. He only asked me to go to the sale.

"Go and see how they conduct their trade, Céleste."

M. Dubois had had his eye on M. Proust's desk, and it was sold to him. The crystal chandelier was about to go for five francs, and thinking how sorry he'd be if that should happen, I took it upon myself to buy it for M. Proust. He said I'd done right. All the rest was sold in the same way. People have said he sold the furniture to raise money. If he did, you could hardly call the operation a success!

There is another lie I ought to correct. It's been said that "for economy's sake" he asked his friend the Duke de Guiche to sell the sheets of cork in his room to a firm that made corks for bottles. There is no truth in this. He had the sheets taken down very carefully and stored in a garage so that they could be put up again when he found a suitable new flat. It's possible that the Duke de Guiche offered to see to the matter or that M. Proust asked him to do so, but the duke was no further involved than that.

When, after several months of searching, he finally found the apartment on rue Hamelin, M. Proust had no thought of staying there permanently. He always regarded it as merely temporary.

Meanwhile there was another transition. We had to live somewhere, but finding an apartment to suit him was no easy matter. Everyone joined in the search. I remember Odilon coming back one day with the address of a nice building on boulevard Péreire. But down below, in a clearing among the trees, passed the railway.

"Trains going by! Oh no, Odilon, never!"

Mme. Gagey, the doctor's wife, was also obliged to look for new accommodations, and she offered to share the fruit of her researches with M. Proust. She gave us some addresses, but none of them would do.

Sometimes he didn't like the neighborhood; sometimes there was no lift and so his asthma ruled it out. Or else the place wasn't on the top floor, and there'd be the problem of people walking about overhead and the ceiling would have to be soundproofed and that would never be really satisfactory. There was one address at the beginning of boulevard Malesherbes, near Robert Dreyfus, one of his childhood friends; but that fell through. A fifth-floor flat on rue de Rivoli, a stone's throw from the Ritz, was tempting. But:

"It would be noisy, and I couldn't stand the mists from the river."

Everyone was on the lookout, and as a temporary measure there came an offer from the actress Réjane, who had a house on rue Laurent-Pichat, a little street between avenue Foch and rue Pergolèse. Réjane lived on the second floor, and her son Jacques Porel, who knew M. Proust well, on the third. Her daughter, who had the fourth, was in America. So we moved in there temporarily, taking with us, as well as we could (the flat was furnished), the things from M. Proust's bedroom, except of course the cork.

Réjane was already an old lady suffering from a serious heart disease, but M. Proust admired her as much as ever. La Berma, the great actress in his book, is largely based on her. The idea of going to live near an idol of his boyhood and youth intrigued him very much, and he talked about her a great deal at the time.

"Sarah Bernhardt is of course a great actress, but she can only play certain roles. But Réjane can play them all, from tragedy to a variety show. She's more than an actress, she's a great artist. There's the same distance between the two women as between a good novelist and a great writer. Do you know, when she used to come out of the theater hundreds of people would be waiting for her? She would have to sneak out through a side door. She once had such a triumphant success in Spain that the king sent her a present of a mule-drawn carriage. And when she came back to Paris I saw her drive up the Champs-Elysées in it. It was magnificent!''

He was also very fond of Jacques Porel. I remember one very amusing evening we spent doing imitations with him at rue Laurent-Pichat. Afterward M. Proust asked me what I thought of him.

''Very good-looking and nice,'' I said, ''but a bit frivolous.''

''That is true, Céleste. But he is as charming and pleasant as a breeze on a summer night.''

Réjane was worried about her son's frivolity, and after we'd moved to rue Hamelin she wrote a long letter to M. Proust asking him, when she was no longer there—for she knew death wasn't far off—to be her son's mentor. M. Proust was very touched, and this entreaty, for such it was, upset him.

''It is awful, Céleste. I know Monsieur Porel is a weak fellow. But I am ill. I cannot take on the responsibility.''

He wrote back a long letter saying this and asked me to take it to Réjane. She was in bed, and she talked to me for a long time of her admiration and affection for M. Proust. She said how impatient it made her that she had to rest because of her heart. But she still had amazing strength and gaiety and said jokingly of her salt-free diet: ''Who would have thought that Réjane, at her age, would still be so salty?''

She died soon afterward. She'd insisted on returning to the stage to play in *La vierge folle (The Foolish Virgin)* by Henry Bataille, in which she met with an acclaim equal to that of her earlier triumphs. I remember M. Proust being very worried about it.

''You will see, Céleste, she will die in the theater. I do wish she hadn't accepted that role!''

One evening when he had booked a box at the Opéra to see Gide's *Antoine et Cléopâtre,* in which the star was Ida Rubinstein, whom everyone was mad about then, he received a message during the performance that Réjane had just rendered up her beautiful soul. He left the Opéra and his guests and hurried to rue Laurent-Pichat.

He came in early that night. He was very sad and upset. It's been said he wept and meditated on Réjane's death for many hours that night. I wonder who could have seen him. He was moved, yes, when he summoned up memories of Réjane with me. But memories were never dead things for him; on the contrary, they were a source of happiness, almost of exaltation.

To go back to our brief stay at rue Laurent-Pichat, the accommodations were certainly not ideal. There wasn't the isolation he needed, and he thought that the trees on avenue Foch nearby caused a certain amount of dampness, and this made him fear new attacks of asthma. It has been said it was noisy, but people have greatly exaggerated, including probably M. Proust himself. On the other side of the courtyard we could see the actor Le Bargy, of the Comédie-Française, coming and going in his bathroom, occasionally letting out great howls, either declaiming his lines or quarreling with his wife—it was sometimes hard to tell. M. Proust was very amused by this.

But the worst was that he didn't feel at home. So the search for a new place went on, and finally we found rue Hamelin. We'd applied to a real estate agent in place Victor-Hugo. They told me the address. He quite liked the district. He inquired who lived there. Then he said: "Go and see, and let me know."

It was on the fourth floor with a lift. The woman who owned the building had just bought it and wanted to rent furnished apartments. The house was number 44. I came back with all the details, and he made his decision.

"Ask her to let us have the flat on the fifth floor. I shall pay for it as if it were furnished, but ask her to move the furniture downstairs."

So the lease was signed—I found it some time ago, among other papers, with M. Proust's signature. We went to rue Laurent-Pichat toward the end of May 1919 and moved into rue Hamelin at the beginning of October, after having some preliminary work done. M. Proust wanted carpets everywhere against the noise, and I saw to it they were fitted as he wished. An outlet for electricity was put in above his bed, with the same arrangements as at boulevard Haussmann: the three switches, one for the bell, one for the bedside lamp, and one for the kettle. On the floor above there was a small flat consisting of one room and a kitchen and several bedrooms. These were empty, but the flat was occupied by Mme. Pelé, who did the cleaning for Aristide Briand, who lived on the corner of avenue Kléber and rue Lauriston, just opposite us. There were never any children in the building to whom M. Proust gave felt slippers to muffle their running-about, as has been alleged. There was only this kind lady, and M. Proust asked me to give her some money in exchange for a promise not to make any noise.

On the day we moved in, he went out while the finishing touches were being put to his room.

Gradually life returned to normal. It was a quiet middle-class street with nice people. On the ground floor there was a baker's shop kept by a very decent man from the Puy-de-Dôme, who didn't have a tooth in his head but always had a pleasant word. His name was Montagnon, I remember. I arranged to do my *téléphonage* from his place, for of course he was open almost all night to make bread. I used to go straight into his dining room without asking. I don't know where some people got the information that he was also the owner and concierge of the building. The owner was a lady, as I have said—Mme. Boulet. And the concierge was an old woman whose husband had been killed when the boiler for the central heating exploded in the cellar. There's another legend, too, according to which the baker-concierge had a little girl who used to bring M. Proust his mail. This child only existed in someone's imagination. Once M. Proust, wanting to write something about bread, asked me to ask Montagnon if he'd mind sending up his assistant one evening to explain how bread is made. The boy came up, M. Proust asked him some questions, then sent him away with a tip.

I mention these silly little tales in passing because when supposedly intelligent people give credit to such nonsense concerning small concrete details, they can't help wondering how much truth there can be in major theories about M. Proust and his work. When I think that even a writer like Edmond Jaloux, who was considered a serious enough man, wrote that "great shreds of paper and tattered tapestry were hanging from the walls," it depresses me.

I know M. Proust said in a letter—to Montesquiou, I think—

that there was just enough space in his room for his "cot." But that was just a picturesque joke.

Of course rue Hamelin was not boulevard Haussmann—and the proof is that, as I have said, M. Proust always considered it just a temporary refuge. Nevertheless, to a certain extent the magic circle was re-created. Although the rooms were smaller and there was less furniture, the layout was much the same as before. On a smaller scale there was the same sequence of salon, small salon (or rather boudoir), and bedroom. That was the route for visitors. I usually went by the corridor and the boudoir, and entered the bedroom through a double door as at boulevard Haussmann. Here, too, there was a second door, opening into the room near his bed; he could go through this door to the bathroom, just across the hall. After the bathroom came a bedroom full of books and silver not in use. Then of course there was may room, which was off the hall to the right.

Many things were no longer in M. Proust's room; the grand piano, the big chest, the huge mirrored wardrobe, and a number of other pieces were in storage. But there was still the bed, tarnished by the fumigations and in the same position as at boulevard Haussmann—near the fireplace, with the screen behind it. But now there was only just room at the foot of the bed to open the door on to the corridor and squeeze through. The little Chinese cabinet he was so fond of was still there, in roughly the same position as before. And there was a large armchair for visitors. And he still had the three little tables with all he needed for his work: the exercise books of manuscript and notes, the pile of handkerchiefs, the box of paper for lighting the Legras powder, the glasses, the watch. There were books on the mantelpiece. The black imitation-leather notebooks had gone—burned, as I have said. (Someone has written that, before leaving boulevard Haussmann, M. Proust got me to destroy lots of papers and photographs and so on. This is not true.) And there were long, very handsome window curtains of blue satin.

The boudoir now contained the black bookcase that used to be in the small salon, with his favorite authors: Mme. de Sévigné,

Ruskin, Saint-Simon in a beautiful binding stamped with the initials
"M.P." Instead of the armchairs, there were now low fireside
chairs.

We had also brought with us from boulevard Haussmann a very
pretty portrait of a little princess which now hung in the salon at rue
Hamelin, as well as the portraits of Mme. Proust and Professor
Adrien Proust, the painting by Helleu, and of course the portrait of
M. Proust by Jacques-Emile Blanche.

So once again life and the machinery of his habits resumed: the
rings at the bell, the coffee in the afternoon, the long talks at night,
the work on the books, the silence. The only difference was that
M. Proust went out less and less as he plunged deeper and deeper
into his work, and more and more often he said:

"I haven't much time, Céleste . . ."

When I think about it now it seems to me he "smoked" much
less at rue Hamelin, although everything was always kept ready for
the fumigation rites. The candle was always kept lighted in the
corridor, as at boulevard Haussmann.

But when I recall the apartment and then see people write about
it as his "last home," the words take on a tragic quality. For those
last two years of his life were spent there in an atmosphere which
already resembled the grave. Indeed, there was a sort of bareness in
comparison with boulevard Haussmann, and there was also the deep
pang of being separated from many of the things that were dear to
him. But he never once complained to me.

After the big fireplaces at boulevard Haussmann, those at rue
Hamelin were very small, or seemed so. As he couldn't stand
central heating because of the dust, I tried to light a fire, as much for
cheerfulness as for the warmth of the old days. But the draft wasn't
good, and the smoke seeped back into the room.

"The smoke makes me ill, Céleste," he said. "I can taste it in
my mouth and chest. I can't breathe. We will have to give it up."

So I didn't light a fire any more.

I can see him as he lay there in bed, with the little green light falling on the pages he was writing or correcting, and the sweaters slipping down one after the other behind him as he asked me for another to put around his shoulders. And never a complaint.

"You'll catch cold, monsieur," I would say.

And there would be just a smile, sometimes without a word, or a look as if to say: "We are only passing through. When I have finished we will be more comfortable." Or else: "You will see, dear Céleste. When I have written 'The End,' we will go away to the south and rest. We will have a holiday. We both need one badly. You are tired too."

But first he must finish. That was the one thing that mattered. Anything else was superficial, unimportant.

Rue Hamelin was his last home. There he worked and worked without respite, often in icy cold. And there he was to die.

27

THE POULET QUARTET

It was in the reduced setting of rue Hamelin that M. Proust treated himself, or rather his work, to a last luxury. To conceive of such a thing at all you'd have to have the spirit of a *grand seigneur*, as well as that extraordinary certainty he had of being able to get what he wanted whenever he wanted it.

It was a wish he had nursed for a long time. It was linked both to a piece of music he had heard and been much struck by, and to the performers he considered best able to give an almost ideal performance. The work was César Franck's Quartet, and the musicians were the Poulet quartet.

M. Proust took after his mother in his great love of music. He'd kept all her scores. Throughout the "camellia period" he frequently attended concerts. He was interested in all the arts. So just as he would talk to me about cathedrals, Vermeer, Renoir, and Degas, and just as he might tell me about Diaghilev's Russian Ballet, so he often mentioned the names of Debussy, Fauré, and even Ravel. Those who know his work know the importance in it of the character of the composer Vinteuil, for whom M. Proust mixed what he knew about dead composers like Beethoven, Mozart, and Franck, what he knew about living composers like Debussy, and those he had met, like Fauré and Vincent d'Indy.

I've described earlier how the young members of the Poulet quartet had impressed him at a Fauré concert and how he had wanted to meet them, especially the violinist, Massis.

After the letter I delivered to Massis, in the middle of the war and the middle of the night, Massis came to see him at boulevard Haussmann, to talk about music several times—three times, if I remember rightly. M. Proust no doubt wanted to check about the music he attributed to Vinteuil. I can still see the young violinist quite clearly, ringing at the bell one evening in army uniform, probably toward the end of the war. And I can hear M. Proust saying:

"Aren't you hungry?"

Then, turning to me: "Céleste, would you fix him some fried potatoes?"

I fixed some, and he ate them with cider or champagne, I don't remember which, talking with M. Proust. But at that time he always came alone. Apart from one of his colleagues and Reynaldo Hahn, he's the only musician I ever saw at M. Proust's except for the evening I am about to tell about. And in my time that evening was unique in every respect. It has been said that at the beginning of 1914 M. Proust "summoned" the Capet quartet to boulevard Haussmann. I can vouch that such a thing didn't happen then, and it would surprise me very much if it had happened before. If it had, M. Proust would certainly have mentioned it, even if only by allusion, at the time of the Poulet quartet.

Anyway, at rue Hamelin he began to feel he'd like to hear César Franck's Quartet again. He had heard it first in the 1890's.

It is possible that when he began to feel this desire he was working on the manuscript of *La Prisonnière,* where Vinteuil's music reappears in full splendor. I can't guarantee it, because he went to and fro in his work all the time. But the coincidence is striking.

The desire took some time to ripen. He thought about it, and he talked to me about it, saying the simplest thing would probably be to have the Poulet quartet come to the flat. I think he even confided in Massis, either he invited him to call or he just wrote.

He kept going over it in his mind until one day he said:

"Céleste, I think I must make up my mind and ask M. Poulet if he can bring his ensemble here. I shall prepare a letter, and Odilon can deliver it."

The letter was delivered, and Gaston Poulet accepted in principle. But it didn't happen at once. Everything had to be done to make sure it was perfect. At M. Proust's request Louis Ruyssen, the violoncellist of the group, came around one evening for a conference. Then, another evening, M. Proust asked Odilon to take him to Gaston Poulet's. He went without warning but came back delighted.

"Monsieur Poulet was in bed. He opened the door in his pajamas, and we both apologized. He was very kind, and we have fixed a date. I'm letting myself in for a great deal of expense, Céleste, but it can't be helped. There are people who would give a lot of money to be present at such an occasion—to hear that great work and those great musicians, in private. I did think of inviting a few people. But if I did I'd have to look after them, and then I wouldn't be able to listen, or not properly. And since it's for myself I need it, it's best not to have anyone else."

Then came the instruction and the preparations.

But before I go on, there is one thing I must make clear. It has been suggested that M. Proust might have had the Poulet quartet to play for him several times. That is quite untrue. There was only that one occasion. Also it has been said the quartet was played at boulevard Haussmann, and in M. Proust's bedroom. That's wrong too, together with other details I'll correct. I don't know who could have given rise to this mistake. If it was Massis, who used to come to boulevard Haussmann before, perhaps he confused the two settings and saw cork walls where there weren't any. I can state categorically that the concert took place at rue Hamelin in 1920. Just once, and not in M. Proust's room.

Not only can I clearly remember the setting, but it was I who made all the preparations. And M. Proust's instructions were far too precise for me to remember wrongly. I can still hear him saying:

"Dear Céleste, make sure you arrange the salon properly. Whatever you do, don't forget to cover the chimney—M. Poulet was very insistent about that. He said the sounds must be concentrated so that there's as little dispersion as possible.''

I can see myself arranging the chairs and bringing in from the boudoir a long reclining chair of green velvet with a strip of tapestry in the middle, so that M. Proust could lie down while he was listening. The musicians were to be in a group in the middle of the room. No, I cannot have remembered incorrectly.

There is also a story that M. Proust had Odilon drive him to collect the musicians at their own homes without notice, at midnight, waking them up to bring them, some of them protesting, back to the flat. Knowing M. Proust, the least he would have done was to send Odilon to fetch them. But no one forced them.

The legend goes on to say that M. Proust, in the taxi, was almost invisible beneath an eiderdown and that on the floor of the taxi beside him he had a tureen of steaming potato purée! I don't know how such nonsense can be printed without being checked. In the first place, the only eiderdown in the place was still in a cupboard and was never taken out until M. Proust was dying. When he went out in the car he never wore more than his fur-lined coat; he never even took a rug or a blanket. As for the steaming tureen, that's ridiculous. M. Proust never ate purée. I used to make it for Odilon's diet, but to say the poor man took it with him and ate it in his taxi . . . !

The truth is that the musicians were called for, and they must have arrived at about one in the morning. M. Proust lay on the reclining chair while they prepared their instruments and their music and I carefully drew the curtains. Then I went out, all the doors were closed too; and I waited in the hall for M. Proust to send for me if he needed anything.

They played Franck's Quartet, and he listened to it lying down with his eyes closed—I saw him. There was a pause at one point, during which, according to one story, I served fried potatoes and champagne, as I did to Massis at boulevard Haussmann. I didn't cook anything or serve anything.

After the interval, M. Proust asked the musicians, if they weren't too tired, to play again, not the whole quartet but a certain part of it. I don't know enough about music to say exactly which part.

When it was all over he thanked them warmly and went out with them. I don't remember there being four taxis waiting, as has been said. I doubt it very much, because M. Proust went with them and Odilon was on duty. And I'm almost sure he accompanied them in order to ask further questions. It wouldn't surprise me if he took them to supper at the Brasserie Lipp on boulevard Saint-Germain.

Before they all left he gave them money. Various figures have been bandied about, ranging from a hundred and fifty to five hundred francs each. I'm sure it was more than five hundred. He wasn't stingy over such things; on the contrary, he was always more than generous. All the money was given to Gaston Poulet, and M. Proust didn't conceal that it was a large sum. He repeated the thought he had had before:

"It has been a great expense, Céleste. And all the trouble and fatigue! But I had to. It was necessary."

He didn't say "for my work." There was no need.

It's been said he asked the musicians to repeat the entire quartet because he had fallen asleep the first time. That's too silly. I said his eyes were closed. I've often seen him like that with a visitor—but what attention there was behind the lowered eyelids! It often happened when he was talking to me, and he would either go on talking with his eyes shut or listen without missing a word.

I mention these misrepresentations because, in the first place, of course, there is my duty to the truth. But also because it is terrible to think that in order to bring attention to themselves by adding a touch of the picturesque, people haven't hesitated to distort the passion of a man who devoted himself so entirely to his work that he gave his life for it, a man whose great and sole preoccupation was the truth.

Anyone who'd seen him, as I did, radiant and intense after an experience like the evening I have just described, would see all that the experience meant to him and know it wasn't just the whim of a dilettante.

He was transfigured and lit up from within, much as he was

when he talked to me about the little patch of yellow wall in Vermeer's painting. It was with experiences such as this that he managed to keep the flame of life alight within himself. He kept it alight only for his work, which was consuming him.

28

"THE END"

What consumed him in his work was time. He ran after it in his books; yet in life he felt himself being overtaken. During the years I spent with him, in that sort of upside-down and almost completely closed world where we seemed to have our own special calendar consisting either of all Sundays or all ordinary days, and our own clock whose hours were dictated by M. Proust and had nothing to do with other people's hours—during all those years, there couldn't have been one day when at some moment or other there wasn't some sign of his fear that he might not be able to finish what he had started. This was never expressed in the form of complaint or impatience; it was always said with his typical gentleness and his typical smile. It was like a sigh of the will escaping from the depths of his immense fatigue after an evening which had not brought him what he was looking for, or at the end of one of our long nocturnal conversations.

"Céleste, I went out for nothing. How awful! All those hours wasted, a whole evening lost . . . and I have so little time!"

"Still, monsieur, you must have a break now and again."

"No, Céleste, I must hurry. I still have so much work to do. I would have done better to stay at home quietly and work."

Or suddenly, at about nine in the morning:

"Good heavens, Céleste, how long we have been talking! I had no idea it was so late. The time we have wasted!"

And though he didn't say so, I was sure that instead of resting he was going to work.

If I dared to ask: "But tell me, monsieur, when do you sleep?"

"I don't know, Céleste," he would say. "I don't know."

I think that even when he was drowsing the work must have gone on. It was like a fever in him.

Once when he was talking about wasted time I told him a saying of my mother's: "He who made it didn't sell it."

He made me repeat it.

"That is lovely, Céleste! I shall put it in my book."

And it is there.

But the leitmotiv of his life was the dread of not finishing what he wanted to do.

"Dear Céleste, I am exhausted, I can't go on, and yet I must. If I don't finish I shall have given my whole life, sacrificed everything, for nothing."

How many times he said that to me. How many times did I hear: "I have so little time."?

And one day: "Céleste, I shall never finish, and death is pursuing me. It is at my heels."

In my innocence I tried to answer with a joke: "Well then, monsieur, instead of making it longer and longer, why don't you just bring it to an end?"

He looked at me with his patient, indulgent smile, which managed never to be hurtful.

"Dear Céleste, do you think it can be done just like that? I can't. It is not as easy as you think to write 'The End.'"

"Anyway, monsieur, that's no reason for always talking about dying."

"Of course it is, Céleste. I worry about it just because I am going to die."

"Oh no you're not, monsieur. I always tell you, 'You'll live longer than I will.'"

334

"And I tell you I won't, Céleste. You will close my eyes. And listen carefully. . . . You must learn to listen carefully when people talk to you about their death. We each carry our own death within us, and we feel when it is there. I more than anyone because I don't lead the same kind of life as everyone else. My life is not normal— no air, no food. Ever since I was a child my health has been ruined by asthma. I don't know how many times I have told you my bronchial tubes are like old elastic, my heart scarcely breathes any more—it is worn out by years of gasping for air. I am a very old man, Céleste—as old as my old tubes and my old heart. I shan't live long."

"Don't talk like that, monsieur. It's not true."

"It is true, Céleste. And that is why I am so anxious to finish."

When he died the critic Paul Souday wrote: "He had been telling us for so long he was dying, we can't really believe he is dead." And that's really what I couldn't help thinking while he was still alive. Not that I thought for a single instant that he was seeking sympathy or pity—he would never have done that. But because I always saw him finding the strength to go on and to keep that extraordinarily youthful look, not to mention the frequent moods of cheerfulness and laughter, I interpreted his references to dying soon as expressions of fatigue, which was bound to be greater some days than others—as when someone says, "I'm tired to death." Whenever he had worked well or come in from a successful evening, all his tiredness was gone.

But there was one extraordinary morning—that is, morning for us, but in fact it was afternoon.

Because I never kept a diary, to my great regret I can't say exactly what date it was. But I do remember clearly that it was at the beginning of the spring of 1922.

We had stayed up talking late, and I had left him just before nine in the morning. I got up at about one or two in the afternoon to start preparing his coffee. For a long time he hadn't had a crois-sant—nothing except the milk in the coffee.

It was about four o'clock when he rang. I went in through the small salon. He'd rung only once, so I went in empty-handed (he would ring twice for the tray). He was resting in bed, his head and shoulders slightly raised on the pillow as usual, with the light of the little lamp leaving his face in the shadow except for the eyes, the look that was always so strong that you felt it watching or following you. I noticed straightaway that he hadn't had his fumigation. It always struck me when he hadn't "smoked."

Usually, as I've said, there was no speaking when he first saw me after waking up—just a slight gesture of thanks, or another movement, or even a mere glance, to indicate that he needed something. Speaking wasn't necessary. I understood the smallest signal.

He looked very tired, but he smiled at me as I came in. Suddenly I was struck by the radiance of his expression.

As I came up to the bed he turned his head slightly toward me, opened his lips, and spoke. It was the first time he'd ever spoken to me immediately on waking up and before having had his first cup of coffee. And it never happened again. I couldn't help looking surprised.

"Good morning, Céleste," he said.

For a moment his smile seemed to savor my surprise. Then: "A great thing happened during the night."

"What, monsieur?"

"Guess."

He was enjoying himself. I rapidly went over in my mind the things that could have happened. It couldn't have been an unexpected visit—I'd have seen and heard, and he would never have gone to open the door himself. That he could have gone out was equally inconceivable. He would never get his own hat and coat out of the cloakroom—everything always had to be ready and waiting. Still trying to think, I looked around the room. "No one has been here," I thought. "He didn't ask for his clothes. He hasn't been out. He hasn't boiled the electric kettle dry. He hasn't broken anything. Everything is in its proper place. . . ."

So I said: "I don't see what it can be, monsieur, I can't guess. It must be a miracle. You'll have to tell me."

He laughed like a boy who has played a trick on someone.

"Well, my dear Céleste, I shall tell you. It is great news. Last night I wrote 'The End.'"

And then he added smiling, and with that light in his eyes: "Now I can die."

I can still hear him saying it; it was like an explosion of happiness and relief.

"Don't let's speak of such things, monsieur," I said. "I can see you're very happy, and I'm very pleased too that you've finished what you wanted to do. But if I know you I'm afraid we still haven't finished sticking in little bits of paper and making corrections."

He laughed.

"That is another matter. The important thing is now I am not anxious any more. Now my work can be published. I shan't have given my life in vain."

What he said that day was proof of the ceaseless labor of all those years. I've said I don't know when he slept. In order to write "The End," he must often have had to work after I left him, during all those hours which were daylight outside but night for him. And I'm sure that must have happened almost every time I left him after our nightly conversation was over.

Especially because since we had moved to rue Hamelin he practically never went out and had fewer and fewer visitors. During 1921 his only memorable outing was with the writer Jean-Louis Vaudoyer, whom he was fond of, to see the exhibition of Dutch painting that spring at the Jeu de Paume. He went chiefly to look again at the paintings of his beloved Vermeer, especially the little patch of yellow wall. Jean-Louis Vaudoyer came for him at eleven in the morning. As far as I remember, M. Proust returned home toward the beginning of the evening, exhausted. He had felt dizzy at the exhibition. I don't think he actually fainted, as has been alleged—he would have told me if he had. But certainly his tiredness didn't prevent him from keeping me very late that night to tell me how happy he had been to see the Vermeers. And it was a young man I saw and listened to.

I only remember his going out a few times in 1922—the last year. There was the party at Countess de Mun's when he brushed off Marcel Prévost in a couple of words, even though Prévost was a member of the Academy. And there were two large dinner parties. One was at the Ritz at the end of May, given by his English friends the Schiffs. If I remember rightly, the other guests included Diaghilev of the Russian Ballet and the then little-known Irish writer James Joyce. The second dinner party was at Mme. Hennessy's, at the beginning of June. I've already mentioned it because it was there he met Gaston de Caillavet's widow, now remarried—Jeanne Pouquet of the flying fair tresses on the tennis court, the great unrequited love of his youth, now the white-haired Princess Radziwill. When he offered to see her home and she said, "Another evening, perhaps," he said in that case he would never see her again. And so it turned out.

I don't remember many visitors either, apart from a few close friends like Reynaldo Hahn and Paul Morand. It was at this time that the two Princesses Bibesco, Marthe and her cousin Elisabeth, Prince Antoine's wife, called one evening after the theater and didn't get beyond the hall.

The last notable visits, Paul Morand's and Lucien Daudet's, which was sometime in June 1922, had something in common: each was a sort of farewell. Like Paul Morand, Lucien Daudet couldn't bring himself to go. It had been a long time since he and M. Proust had met. I know that in the course of the interview, which was a long one, M. Proust gave his old friend some object as a souvenir, but I've forgotten what it was.

When the visitor had gone M. Proust called me in as usual. He looked moved, but he spoke of the visit gaily.

"He was strange this evening, Céleste. Yes, very funny. He hardly spoke a word—he seemed shy and sad. When it was time to go he asked if he could embrace me. I said, 'No, no, my little Lucien, look—you can see I haven't shaved or washed—I smell!' It is true, isn't it?"

I was far from suspecting the tragedy behind that gaiety. I think

I was simply blind to the idea of his death. And I saw him laboring as hard as ever in spite of having written "The End," just as I had predicted. He went on correcting and correcting, sometimes on the manuscript of *Albertine Disparue*, or of what became after his death *Le Temps Retrouvé*, and sometimes on the proofs of *La Prisonnière*, about which he sometimes saw Jacques de Lacretelle. And of course we continued gluing in paste-ons.

But I remember one night, late, that ought to have opened my eyes. I struggle with my memory to try to recall exactly when it was. I know one thing: The incident has been told as an anecdote and attributed to the evening after his visit to the exhibition at the Jeu de Paume with Jean-Louis Vaudoyer. But I'm certain that's not correct. The exhibition was in 1921, and I remember that after the evening I'm speaking of now he never set foot outside again. Apart from the parties I mentioned there were a few minor evenings out that year, and the scene I'm talking about probably took place after one of those.

He was in a state of extreme fatigue when he came in about six or seven in the evening. He'd asked Odilon to come up with him. My sister, Marie, was still there, which means it was evening but not very late, or else she would already have gone home to sleep.

When he came in he often went through the big salon, then the boudoir, to his room. But he never stopped, much less sat down in the salon.

But this time he didn't even pause for me to take his overcoat; it was the fur-lined one, so it must have been winter, or midseason.

He went on into the salon, and there, with his coat still on, sank into a chair. The picture is engraved in my mind; it will go with me into my own grave.

He was leaning to one side in the chair, and his coat hung open. He seemed absolutely exhausted, and I'd never seen such sadness on his face.

I can still see the four of us, fixed as in a picture. Marie was still in the hall, Odilon was in the doorway, and I was standing just by M. Proust's chair.

In the hall he had said: "I asked Odilon to come up with me because I want to go out again. But I am so tired I decided I would think it over first. I don't know if I have the heart . . ."

We were all silent as he thought, his eyes closed. Then Odilon plucked up his courage and said:

"Monsieur, it's not surprising you're so tired—you don't eat anything. Suppose I were to go and get a nice tender chicken for Céleste to cook for you? You could have just a little piece, and that would give you the strength to go out again."

When he heard my husband's voice he opened his eyes and looked at the three of us—Marie had come up behind Odilon. The look was so full of sadness, and at the same time such sweet affection, that we were all overcome.

"That's right, Odilon," he said. "Go and buy a chicken. But I don't want any. You three eat it. I want you to take care of yourselves."

His look embraced us, and he added, smiling, with heartrending tenderness: "I love you all so much."

Then, more gently still: "You are my children."

And he turned to me. "I don't think I shall go out. My room is ready; I had better go to bed. . . . My dear Odilon, would you mind staying, in case I need you for anything?"

But he didn't need anything, and I don't remember his calling me in to talk to him that night.

All sorts of tales have been told about the last three months before he died. He is supposed to have had such bad and frequent attacks of dizziness that he fell on the floor as soon as he set foot out of bed. He is supposed to have had lapses of speech and thought and memory. His sight is supposed to have got much worse. He is supposed to have thought that gas leaks in the chimney were partly responsible for making him ill. And I don't know what else! All exaggerations or inventions.

I know he himself referred in his letters to lapses of this kind. I've already explained about them. And more than ever during the last months he tried to protect himself from the outside world in order to save his strength for his work. I think when he said such things in his letters it was mainly to evade requests to visit him or to explain a delay in answering someone's letter.

If he had fallen down in his room I would have heard or he would have told me. And if he had had trouble in speaking, or lapses of thought and memory, would he have kept for me the moments when his voice was clear and precise and his mind perfectly lucid? And if I had seen the slightest sign, what reason would I have for hiding it? Where would be the dishonor for M. Proust if I admitted it? The most remarkable thing about him in this connection is that he had absolute control over himself right up to the end.

As for gas fumes, nonsense. As I've said, there was no heating of any kind at rue Hamelin after we noticed that the chimneys were too narrow and the smoke came back into the room.

It was probably because of that icebox of a room, where he lay working for hours motionless, with no other heat but that of the hot-water bottles and his woolens to defend his weakened constitution against the cold, that he caught influenza at the beginning of autumn 1922.

It has been said that his asthma got worse again about this time, but that too, I fear, is pure invention. He was certainly aware that he was getting progressively weaker. His phobia about germs was worse than ever, and it was in these last months that he got me to buy the long metal box and put formol in it to disinfect the letters before he opened them.

At the beginning of October he went out to his last big party, where all Paris society, as it was then, was gathered at the house of Count and Countess de Beaumont. For him it was a supreme gala of the society he had wanted to know and observe in his youth, and of which he alone probably foresaw the death, at the same time as his own, which would precede it.

I very much regret not having remembered his account of that evening. It seemed then just one evening among many others. I don't know if he himself felt it as a kind of farewell. He didn't say or show anything. Nor did he mention that he had caught cold again on top of his influenza on the way home.

But it was coming away from that reception that he set foot in the anteroom of death.

29

TIME STOPS

He knew he was going to die, and I still thought he'd live to a fine old age. He had been an invalid for so many years that no one, not even his close friends, could believe that for him time would stop so soon. I most of all, living with him day after day, could not believe it. He and I had this in common perhaps: I have to bump right into something before I realize that there are times when there's no use continuing.

From the day when the illness in the poor worn-out body got worse, I didn't close my eyes. When I was told afterward that I didn't go to bed at all for seven weeks, I said I hadn't realized it, and it was true: I simply hadn't noticed. For me it was quite natural. He was suffering, so my one idea was to do all he wanted and anything I could to relieve his suffering.

He didn't sleep any more either. When he wasn't shaken with coughing or struggling for breath he was working, dreading he might not finish correcting the proofs of *La Prisonnière* in time for the Nouvelle Revue Française. He was always ringing the bell, either for a hot-water bottle, or a woolen, a book, an exercise book, a bit of paper to be stuck in. I came and went. Later on there were telephone calls to be made to Dr. Bize and to Professor Robert Proust (as his brother, not as a doctor). I went back and forth. I made hot

343

milk and coffee. He wanted some stewed fruit, right away. He wanted some iced beer; I sent Odilon. But what did it matter? What was my fatigue beside his suffering? I'd have worn my fingers to the bone rather than not do what he wanted.

Those last weeks are a sort of long tunnel, more than ever without days or nights—a long darkness with no light but the gleam of the little green lamp, but in which the details of the end stand out so clearly I shall never forget it.

People have said and written much foolishness about these last weeks and have distorted my words and even made me say things I never did say. I've never corrected these stories till now. It was enough to say to myself that M. Proust was still watching me and knew my real thoughts, as he always had the art and power to do. He knew I couldn't betray him.

But now, before it's my turn to go, the thought that there can be any doubt about what I saw and know to be the truth has become so unbearable that I want it to be said once and for all that the pages that follow, even more than all the others, are the exact records of my memory, and I've turned over, re-examined, and checked the facts in my mind enough to be certain that I'm faithfully adhering to what really happened. What I write here is a testament, not just a testimony.

As I've said, it started with a touch of influenza, and then he caught cold again coming out of the party at the Count and Countess de Beaumont's. But even before that, the extraordinary resistance of his constitution had shown signs of weakening. I had to insist that he go to his niece Suzy's birthday party, saying his brother and even more so his niece would be upset if he didn't. Later, when the illness declared itself and I'd sent for Professor Robert Proust, he told me he'd thought his brother looked "a bit swollen" that evening and suspected it was edema.

In fact, I see now he'd begun to decline over the past year, and a turning point in that decline was his visit to the exhibition of Dutch paintings in 1921 and his dizziness when he was looking at the

Vermeers—not going up the steps of the museum, as some have said.

When he had influenza he said: "I think I ought to see Dr. Bize. What do you think, Céleste?"

As the influenza seemed to be getting a hold, I said I thought he was right, that he really must look after himself and not work quite so hard. He didn't answer that, but we did call in Dr. Bize.

He came several times. At first he prescribed some medicines, which M. Proust didn't take. As the combination of influenza and asthma made breathing difficult and brought on fits of coughing and sneezing, Dr. Bize then recommended injections of camphorated oil to relieve the congestion of the lungs and bronchial tubes. But M. Proust wouldn't have them.

When I think of it now, one of the most awful things about those last weeks was his obstinate refusal to let himself be looked after. Dr. Bize told me it really was just the beginning of a slight attack of influenza and if he had agreed to have the injections of camphorated oil, the congestion of the bronchial tubes and lungs would have passed. If he had been willing not to work for a little while and to rest, there's no doubt he would have got over it. But no one could tell M. Proust what to do. I think that from the day he told me his work could now be published, the will that had enabled him to overcome his physical weakness and carry his task through to the end began to flag. I'm sure he still hoped to go on living, but the impetus relaxed once he'd written "The End."

I remember Dr. Bize saying, the day he prescribed the camphorated oil: "Maître, this flu is nothing, I assure you. If you will agree to look after yourself as I suggest it is only a matter of a week."

And the gentle, gasping voice of M. Proust: "My dear doctor, I must and shall go on correcting the proofs. Gallimard is waiting for them."

"Look after yourself first, maître. You can correct the proofs afterward."

When he went Dr. Bize left a prescription, and as usual M.

Proust asked me to go and get all the things prescribed. That was the rule. We bought it all whether we used it or not, and in the end we often threw it away. But I didn't buy the phials of camphorated oil. M. Proust refused to have injections, on principle.

Faced with his patient's obstinacy and the worsening of the bronchitis and the cough, and the resulting difficulty in breathing, Dr. Bize finally made up his mind one evening, as he left, to go to see Professor Proust, his friend and former fellow-student.

"Your brother won't look after himself," he told him. "He will keep on working in an icy room, which is impossible to heat because of his asthma. You are the only one who has enough influence over him to persuade him. But something must be done at all costs, or I am afraid the illness will get to a stage beyond remedy. I haven't the necessary authority myself."

Professor Proust came round to rue Hamelin that evening, and there was a painful scene between the two brothers. I was surprised to see the professor; Dr. Bize hadn't said a word to me about his decision. Later he told me: "It was my duty. I was afraid of pneumonia."

The professor began by trying to make his brother see reason. M. Proust told me about the interview afterward. Here is the gist of it as he recounted it to me.

"My dear little Marcel," his brother said, "you absolutely must look after yourself. I am a doctor and your brother. What I am telling you is for your own good and the good of your work."

As he was not getting anywhere, he finally said: "Well, we will have to look after you in spite of yourself."

This offended M. Proust deeply, and he retorted: "What! You mean to force me?"

"I don't want to force you, my little Marcel. As you know very well, I just want to get you out of this ice-cold room. Just around the corner in rue Puccini there is a marvelous clinic, very well run, very well heated, with excellent doctors. You'd have a nurse to do all that was necessary. You'd be better before you could blink an eye."

"I don't want your nurses," said M. Proust. "Céleste is the

346

only person who understands me, and I don't want anybody but Céleste."

"But you can keep Céleste, dear brother. She will have the room next to yours and not leave you for a moment."

Then M. Proust got angry, though he didn't "shout," as has been alleged. He said to his brother:

"Go away, I don't want to see you any more. And don't come back if it is only to try to force me."

Professor Robert Proust went. He didn't show any emotion to me, but I think he must have been shattered. He asked me to let him know if his brother got worse.

M. Proust called me in immediately after his brother left. Even before he told me what had happened he said:

"Dear Céleste, don't ever let my brother or Dr. Bize or anyone else in again. I don't want anyone but you here."

Then he told me what had happened. I protested:

"But monsieur, your brother doesn't want to force you. What he says is for your own good."

"And I tell you, Céleste, I mean to do as I like right to the end."

"Just the same, monsieur, do you really mean what you say? If your brother comes, I can't turn him away."

"Do as I tell you, Céleste." And he said again: "I don't want anyone here but you. And I forbid you to call Dr. Bize."

He was obviously shattered too. When I came in I'd found him sitting up in bed.

It was that day, a little later, when he had calmed down—not, as has been said, in the last days before his death—that he repeated what he'd told me long before about his horror of injections.

"Céleste, it is awful to think doctors can torture a sick person by injecting serums. And for what? To give his patient ten more minutes, twelve more hours perhaps, of a wretched life?"

And as when he talked to me about it before, he asked me: "Céleste, promise me you won't ever let them give me an injection."

I remember answering: "Monsieur, who am I? Nobody. You

347

know very well that if the doctor comes it's because you've sent for him. You decide about everything you do, and if the doctor wants to give you an injection and you don't want him to, who can force you? But still, I promise."

People have said that I have nothing to reproach myself for, that I did all I could for him through all those years. But I can't help feeling remorse at having failed two of his wishes that last day: I called in Dr. Bize without his knowing it, and I let the doctor give him an injection in spite of my promise.

The end is still a nightmare for me. I know that Paul Morand wrote to Mme. de Chambrun, Pierre Laval's daughter, saying about me: "You wonder how she possibly kept going." But what about his poor body under the sheets, martyred with coughing and choking and tortured by the longing to finish his work?

He had been suffering from this illness for more than a month. He coughed constantly but never coughed anything up.

"I can't, Céleste," he said. "I haven't the strength. And it is choking me."

And the coughing and shortness of breath were getting worse. Sometimes he would pause in his correcting and turn to me with that profound and beautiful look:

"If you knew how ill I feel, Céleste . . ."

It wasn't a complaint. It was just a gentle, resigned statement.

I would beg him to rest.

"No. I have not finished." And with a radiant smile: "But you will see, dear Céleste—I am a better doctor than the doctors."

For a long time he hadn't been eating anything, and now sometimes he didn't even have coffee. I tried to persuade him at least to have some hot milk to give him some strength and help fend against the cold of the room. But most of the time he just left it untouched. He wasn't interested now in anything but his work; nothing else had any allure for him. If he asked me for some lime tea, he would just have one tiny sip and then put the bowl aside or hand it back to me. The same with the stewed fruit he sometimes asked for: he hardly tasted it. Probably because of the fever, all he fancied was cold beer, which in his state and in that icy room was madness. But anything was better than opposing him. He wouldn't have allowed it anyway: just one reproachful look and you were ready to cut yourself into pieces. I don't know how many times Odilon went to the deserted kitchens of the Ritz for beer.

As M. Proust was approaching the extreme of exhaustion he spoke as little as possible. I was there, and I watched for a sign or look to anticipate what he wanted. Sometimes he communicated with me on the little squares of paper. I was so used to them that he didn't even need to hand them to me; his writing wasn't easy to decipher, but I knew it so well I could read it upside down as he wrote.

I threw almost all those little bits of paper away—over all the years they'd have made up a book! Sometimes they expressed impatience that something wasn't being done fast enough. Then he might put at the end of the note: "If you don't, I shall get very cross." But as he wrote the word "cross" he'd smile and look up at me to show it was like when he used to mispronounce the word for fun—it was part of a joke between him and Reynaldo Hahn when they were young.

It is terrifying to think he was completely lucid up to the last minute. He was not only seeing himself; he was watching himself die. And yet he still found the strength to smile.

I suppose it is for literature's sake that people have said he took notes on his own death in order to complete the account of the death of Bergotte in his book. It isn't true, but he would have been quite capable of it.

Dr. Bize used to come by to see him, but there was nothing he could do. It was just a struggle now between the illness and the patient's will.

Professor Robert Proust came again. Immediately after the scene between them, it was all forgotten. A few days later M. Proust asked me to telephone his brother. The professor saw there was nothing he could do, and as long as he didn't try to force anything on his brother he could come as often as he liked, just as did close friends, such as Reynaldo Hahn. These visits were simply visits between brothers who were very fond of each other, the doctor compelled to be silent and watch the illness extend its ravages.

October gave way to November. I don't know who it was who said M. Proust reminded me that November was the fateful month in which his father had died. This sort of heavy allusion wasn't at all his style. He did not mention his father's death to me at this time, any more than he spoke about his mother, except once, as far as I remember, to say that she'd been a marvelous nurse when he was ill as a child.

On November 17, the day before M. Proust died, Professor Robert Proust came at about eight or nine in the evening. A little while before, M. Proust had said:

"Céleste, I don't feel too bad this evening. You want me to eat and look after myself. Well, cook me a sole, and I shall have that."

I was getting it ready when his brother came.

"Can I go in to him?"

"Yes, monsieur, he's awake."

"How is he today?"

"He seems a little better. He asked for a sole, and I was just going to take it in."

"Don't take it in yet. I'd like to see him first."

They were a long time together, and during the visit M. Proust called me in and said: "I don't think I shall have the sole after all, Céleste."

Then the professor came out. He said to me in the hall before he went: "I advised him against having the sole because when I examined him I found his heart rather tired. But I am pleased because he said he would keep you with him all night."

And he went without giving me any other instructions.

It was a Friday.

That same day, November 17, there was a very moving incident. I can't remember exactly whether it was before or after his brother came. But at one point in the evening M. Proust rang to ask me for something. While I was in the room he asked me to turn around and not look at him.

"I want to try to sit up on the edge of the bed," he said.

350

Then a few moments later he said: "You can turn around, Céleste. I have finished."

I turned round. He was lying back in bed again, covered up, with his head on the pillow. He looked at me and said in a weary voice, with great sadness:

"My poor Céleste, what is going to happen if I cannot manage by myself any more?"

"It's nothing, monsieur," I said. "Just a passing weakness."

He didn't answer––just closed his eyes.

Perhaps he had called me in so that I should be there in case he became dizzy. When you know how modest and dignified and elegant he was in everything, it's terrible to think what that must have cost him.

It's certain that by then he must have been suffering from pneumonia and an abscess on the lung, which Dr. Bize and Professor Robert Proust had feared, though it declared itself later than has been said—in the very last days, not in the first week of November.

I was probably the only one still under the illusion that he would recover. It wasn't that I rejected the idea of his dying—it simply didn't enter my head. It worried me terribly to see him getting weaker and refusing all treatment and food, but I was sure he would get over it.

Yet there were signs that should have warned me. In the week before his death he asked me to have a bunch of flowers sent to Dr. Bize. "Out of remorse," people have said. Remorse for what? For not having followed his advice? No, I'm sure it was out of gratitude for the doctor's care and kindness over the years. He also asked me to take a bunch of flowers to Léon Daudet, who had just published a long article on him. It was a Sunday, I remember. When I got back he was waiting for me to give an account of what had happened. I told him I'd seen Léon Daudet himself. He had talked to me for a long time and had seen me out to the stairs. He had said: "I would do anything for M. Proust. I know no other friend, no other man, I can compare with him for intelligence, sensibility, and feeling. And I know what you have been to him, madame. If you need me, please don't hesitate. I shall come at any hour of the day or night." He had wept as he said it. M. Proust listened and made no comment. He looked pleased and moved. All he said was:

"Well, that is one more thing settled."

But I still didn't pay any attention, in spite of Léon Daudet's tears. I was so used to people showing signs of affection for him when I delivered messages, and I had sent or delivered so many beautiful flowers for him.

On the night of November 17 he sent for me at midnight to stay with him, as he had told his brother he would. He welcomed me almost gaily.

"Well, dear Céleste, you sit there in the chair, and we will do some work together."

Then: "If I get through tonight I shall have proved to the doctors that I know better than they do. But first I have to get through it. Do you think I shall?"

Of course I protested quite sincerely that I was sure he would. I was anxious at the thought that he was tiring himself, but that was all.

So I sat down and didn't leave him for hours, and then only for a few moments. At first we talked a bit; then he started adding material to and correcting his proofs. He started by dictating to me—until about two in the morning. But I couldn't have gone very fast, because I myself was reaching the end of my tether, and the room was terribly cold.

At one point he said: "I think it is more tiring for me to dictate than to write, because of the breathing."

So he took up his pen and went on on his own for over an hour.

The hands of his watch, when he stopped moving the pen across the paper and put it down, are engraved in my memory. It was exactly half-past three in the morning.

"I am too tired, Céleste," he said. "Let's stop. I can't do any more. But don't go."

Professor Robert Proust explained to me later that it was probably then the abscess burst and septicemia set in.

"You won't forget to paste the strips in the proper place, will you, Céleste?" he said. "Don't forget—it is very important."

He told me exactly the right places. Then he said again: "You will do it, won't you, Céleste? You won't forget?"

"Of course, monsieur," I said. "Don't you worry. Now try to rest. How about a warm drink?"

He said no, and then added with that look of affection I've never seen in anyone else:

"Thank you, dear Céleste. I knew you were kind, but not that much. . . ."

He said that over and over again before the night was over.

He asked me to put away his notebooks and papers carefully; then he went on talking, telling me about the things he would like to do for me. I learned afterward he'd found the time and the strength, during his influenza, to consult the banker Horace Finaly on my behalf. During that Sunday night, after I'd taken the flowers to Léon Daudet, M. Proust had said to me:

"Céleste, if I write a letter addressed to you and put it in the little Chinese cabinet, will you promise not to open it until after I am dead? I would like to leave this letter."

I never opened a cupboard or drawer unless he asked me, and as a joke I answered:

"Women are inquisitive, monsieur.. How could I resist? Of course I would open it!"

"You would! All right then, I shan't write it!"

And I went on in the same vein: "I should think not, monsieur—you've better things to do than write to me. You've only got to tell me anything you want."

In the small hours of the eighteenth he mentioned the shares he had sold—in sugar, I think they were—and a check he wanted to give me. "Suppose they contest it? But they ought to be able to recognize the signature of someone who's dying, oughtn't they?"

"Please, monsieur, don't talk about it," I said. "You make me cross."

He went on looking at me and said: "My God, Céleste—what a pity. What a pity . . ."

"Please, monsieur," I said, "don't talk, don't tire yourself. Don't think about anything but getting better."

I could feel he was troubled. And sitting there beside him I could see he looked different—more ill. His eyelids would sometimes flutter rapidly, and his breathing was very difficult.

After a moment, although he didn't say anything, he opened his eyes. I thought he might be a little rested, so I said:

"Do you feel better, monsieur?"

He looked at me, and answered: "If you think so, so much the better, dear Céleste."

At about seven in the morning he said he would like some coffee: " . . . to please you and my brother I shall have it hot, if it is ready and you bring it right away."

I remember getting up out of the chair like a sleepwalker and going into the kitchen. I could hardly walk. I said to my sister Marie: "I have managed to hold out till now, but I think I'm finished. I can hardly stand."

And actually I don't think I could have held out much longer.

I went in again with the coffee and milk on the tray. He was so weak I suggested: "Would you like me to help you, monsieur— hold the saucer?"

"No, thank you, Céleste."

He picked up the bowl and held it to his lips, looking up and saying again: "Just to please you and my brother . . ."

He drank a little and then gave it back to me. I put the bowl down on the tray. He told me to leave it there. Then: "I think I'll just stay quiet a moment." And he signaled that he wanted to be left alone.

I went out. But I was so struck by the change in him that I began to be terribly worried.

Instead of going back into the kitchen or to my room, I did as I'd done that time at boulevard Haussmann when he went two days without ringing for me. I went back as quietly as I could to the corridor between his room and the bathroom and stood holding my breath just behind the door beside his bed—not inside, behind a door curtain, as has been said. I would never have done such a thing.

That must have been at about eight in the morning. The situation repeated itself with almost incredible exactness. I'd been there for some time, without moving, frozen, when M. Proust rang. As before, I went around silently the other way so as not to arouse suspicion and entered his room through the door from the boudoir. I saw his searching look as soon as I entered.

"What were you doing behind my door, Céleste?"

"I wasn't behind the door, monsieur."

"Céleste, Céleste, don't lie."

"You're right, monsieur, I was there. I was afraid you might need something. I just wanted to be near to be sure I could come in straightaway."

He didn't answer. Then he asked: "You won't switch off my light, will you?"

"Monsieur, you know I'd never take it upon myself to do a thing like that. It's you who give the orders."

"Don't switch it off, Céleste. There's a big fat woman in the room . . . a horrible big fat woman in black. I want to be able to see . . ."

"Don't you worry, monsieur. Just wait—I'll chase her away. Is she frightening you?"

"Yes, a bit," he answered. "But you must not touch her . . ."

He had often talked to me about death, through the years, but never in the form of the hideous woman in black who some people have said used to haunt him, especially on the anniversary of his mother's death. What nonsense! Up until then he'd mentioned death only to say he wasn't afraid of it.

So when he talked now about the horrible fat woman I thought he was having a nightmare or that he was delirious. But a little while after, when I saw he was calmer and seemed to be resting again, I left the room. And it was then I disobeyed M. Proust, who had forbidden me to send for anyone, and I told Odilon to fetch Dr. Bize. And I went down to the baker's to telephone Professor Robert Proust.

There was another thing about M. Proust that made me uneasy: while he was talking to me about the woman in black he was pulling up the sheet and picking up the papers strewn over the bed (I wasn't allowed to move them while he was there, because of the dust). I'd never been at a deathbed before, but in our village I'd heard people say that dying men gather things. And those movements of M. Proust's fingers had frightened me.

The strange thing is that many years later my dear Odilon said the same thing as M. Proust before he died. One day in his hospital room I noticed he was gazing into the corner, and I asked him why. "I'm looking at death," he said. "But you're not going to die!" I cried. "Yes, I am." "And looking at death frightens you?" I asked. And like M. Proust, Odilon said: "Yes, a bit."

It must have been ten in the morning on Saturday, November 18, when Dr. Bize came. Meanwhile M. Proust had asked for some cold beer, and Odilon had gone to fetch it.

I was still sure that M. Proust's condition was due chiefly to extreme weakness, and I'd told my husband to ask Dr. Bize to bring something to strengthen him. But at the same time I was rather perturbed because I had the feeling someone from the family ought to be there, and when I'd telephoned from the baker's, M. Proust's sister-in-law had said: "Oh dear, this is what we were afraid of."

Then she told me that her husband was out, that was the day he taught at the hospital, the Tenon hospital. But she said she would get a message to him at once.

When I opened the door to Dr. Bize I said—and this was the second time I disobeyed: "Please, Doctor, save him. He's weaker still now. Give him an injection."

"But you know he doesn't want it."

"Doctor . . . he hasn't any resistance left. You absolutely must do something to give him some strength."

We went into the bedroom, and I told a lie. I told M. Proust that Dr. Bize had been just passing by and had stopped to see how he was getting on.

"I thought you'd like to see him, so I took it upon myself to bring him in."

M. Proust didn't answer. All he did was just look at me—so that I should see, once again, that one couldn't lie to him.

At that moment.Odilon came back. A few minutes before, M. Proust had asked if he was back from the Ritz with the beer, and when I'd said not yet, he'd answered: "Well, Céleste, the beer will be like the rest—it will come too late."

Dr. Bize, who had gone over to the bed, just said: "Good morning, maître."

M. Proust looked past him to my husband, who had brought the beer. And his voice seemed to go through the doctor without answering him, and he said:

"Good morning, my dear Odilon. I am so glad to see you."

But he didn't drink the beer.

Dr. Bize prepared the injection, but I could see he was ill at ease. I heard him mutter, "How am I going to manage?" I asked him where he was going to make the injection, and he said in the thigh.

"I'll lift up the sheet, Doctor," I said.

We both went over to the bed, and I lifted up the sheet carefully, doing everything not to offend M. Proust's modesty.

He was lying on the edge of the bed with one arm hanging down over the side. It was slightly swollen, probably because the circulation had almost stopped. I put his arm back under the clothes and held the sheet. The doctor bent over.

What happened then is impressed on me forever. M. Proust reached out his other arm and pinched the skin on my wrist. At the same time—and even if I wanted to I could never drive that cry out of my ears—he said:

"Oh, Céleste . . . oh, Céleste!"

It was worse than if he had actually accused me of breaking my promise never to let anyone give him an injection when he was incapable of defending himself.

And my remorse is all the greater because by then the injection was useless: it didn't even circulate through his veins.

Dr. Bize went away. Almost immediately after, M. Proust's brother arrived. I was so overcome that before I showed him in I told him what I had done and how full of remorse I was. He tried to comfort me:

"You've nothing to regret, Céleste. You did quite right."

And then he said: "I came as soon as I got the message. I was outside in my car when Dr. Bize arrived, but I wanted to let him come up first, so I waited in the car until he had finished. I didn't want my brother to think I'd come to do something to him that he didn't want."

He only stayed a moment with M. Proust; then he left me with him. It must have been about eleven or twelve o'clock by then, and he came back in less than an hour. He must have known it was all over and that there was nothing to be done, although he didn't say anything to me. He asked my husband to fetch some cupping glasses and asked me to bring an eiderdown. I went to the cupboard for the famous Liberty eiderdown that M. Proust never used because of the feathers and his asthma. Odilon came back with the cupping glasses, and at the professor's request I got more pillows. He raised M. Proust as gently as possible while I arranged the pillows.

"I'm tiring you, my little Marcel," he said.

"Yes . . . yes, Robert dear."

It was about one in the afternoon.

The cupping glasses didn't hold and were useless. Then the professor asked Odilon to fetch some oxygen cylinders. The breathing was getting more and more difficult.

Professor Proust gave him a little oxygen, then leaned over him and asked: "Is that a bit better, my little Marcel?"

"Yes, Robert."

A little while later the professor asked us to send for Dr. Bize again. He came at about half-past two. They had a consultation and decided to call in Professor Babinski, one of the greatest physicians at that time. Earlier during his illness M. Proust himself had said to me: "I would ask you to send for Dr. Babinski, Céleste, but I haven't seen him since Mother died, and what would it look like if I asked him to come now?"

Dr. Babinski came. It must have been about four o'clock. The three doctors conferred in the bedroom. M. Proust could hear it all—I was there, and I could see from his eyes. His brother suggested an intravenous injection of camphor, but Professor Babinski

358

said: "No, my dear Robert. Don't make him suffer. There is no point."

Dr. Bize went away, and soon afterward Professor Babinski shook hands with Professor Proust and left. I was in despair. Before I opened the door for him I said: "Professor, you *are* going to save him, aren't you?"

He was very moved. He took both my hands and answered: "Madame, I know all you have done for him. You must be brave. It is all over."

I went back into the room and stood beside Professor Proust. There were only the two of us there now.

M. Proust never took his eyes off us. It was terrible.

We stayed like that for about five minutes, and then the professor suddenly moved forward, and bent gently over his brother, and closed his eyes. They were still turned toward us.

I said: "Is he dead?"

"Yes, Céleste. It is over."

It was half-past four.

I couldn't stand upright for exhaustion and grief. But I couldn't believe it—he had died so nobly, without a shudder, without a gasp, without the life and the light of the soul even vanishing from the eyes looking on us to the end. His last words had been the last two exchanges with his brother. Despite what people have said—again for literature's sake, I suppose—he didn't say "Mother."

The professor and I tidied up the things on the bed, quietly, as if we were afraid of waking him. It was strange, for me; for the first time I was moving things about and putting them away in his presence. There were newspapers, various bits of paper, and a copy of the *NRF* with a note scribbled on it.

Then Professor Proust said: "Céleste, help me do him one last service. We'll lay him out."

I brought the things, and the professor dressed him in a clean nightshirt, and we changed the sheets and pillows. I was going to fold M. Proust's hands in the position I had seen on people's deathbeds in our village, and I was so upset I forgot his request that I should entwine his fingers with the rosary Lucie Faure had brought back for him from Jerusalem. If I hadn't forgotten, the professor would have let me do it. As it was, he said:

"No, Céleste. He died working, We will leave his hands as they were."

So he arranged the arms like that.

We switched off the little lamp and lit the light in the middle of the room. The professor asked me if M. Proust had expressed any wish about funeral arrangements. I said he had never mentioned the subject.

"Very well," he said. "I shall do what we did for our parents."

All I mentioned was M. Proust's wish that Abbé Mugnier be asked to come and pray at his deathbed. The Professor undertook to arrange this, but as I've already said, the abbé was ill and couldn't come.

The professor asked me to cut off one lock of hair for him and one for myself, and I did.

Later on Reynaldo Hahn came. It was he who telephoned the news to M. Proust's friends. He stayed all night. At first he sat up with me in the bedroom; then he went into another room and wrote some music. Every so often he would come in and meditate by the bed.

The next to come on the day M. Proust died was Léon Daudet, who wept for a long time. Professor Robert Proust said to him:

"Thank you for being so kind to Marcel, Léon."

"Don't thank me," he answered. "He was more than a century ahead of the rest of us. No one can do anything after him."

M. Proust died on Saturday. Professor Robert Proust thought he looked so "well"—his word—that he decided to delay the funeral to give friends a chance to pay their last respects. The body was put into a coffin on Tuesday, and the funeral was on Wednesday, November 22. Crowds of people had come during the three days before. I won't list the names, but I remember the Countess de Noailles, the poetess, who sobbed and kissed me and said:

"Dear Céleste—I know what you were to him."

On Sunday, November 19, Paul Morand came. Afterward, in the corridor outside the bedroom, he said to me:

"Sometimes when I came to see him he would say: 'Forgive me, Paul, if I shut my eyes for a little. I am tired. But go on talking, please, and I shall answer. I am only resting.' And he would shut his eyes," went on M. Morand, "but he would leave one eye just slightly open to watch. Well, I don't know if you have noticed it, Céleste, but he is doing that still even now: one lid is just slightly raised."

That same Sunday, at about two in the afternoon, at Professor Robert Proust's request, the painter Helleu, whom M. Proust had been so fond of, and who by then had had to give up painting because of his bad sight, came to do an etching. He told me he had meant to put his heart and soul into this portrait, but the electric light reflecting off his copper plate hampered him. I said I would open the shutters. But he said no, because if I opened the windows for a moment the air might affect the body, which, as Professor Proust had said, was in an amazingly good state of preservation.

Two proofs were made of this etching, and Helleu gave them to the professor, saying he was sorry they weren't better and that he was going to destroy the plate. The professor liked them and gave me one. Later on, Helleu heirs found the plate and had more copies made from it, though it had deteriorated and the prints were much less clear and satisfactory than the first two.

Going out, Helleu passed the great draftsman Dunoyer de Segonzac on his way in to make a charcoal sketch. Then it was the turn of the photographer Man Ray.

Reynaldo Hahn and Professor Robert Proust and I kept watch over him during these days, together with two nuns. I don't want to be nasty, but truth compels me to say I had to fight those two dragons to be allowed to stay in the room. I've always thought they wanted to keep me out because they couldn't go to sleep while I was there.

I was drunk with fatigue, but I didn't want to leave M. Proust. I remember looking at the body on the bed, the face hardly emaciated and as serene as I'd always known it, and begging in my heart, "Please, God, let him say something to me."

On Tuesday afternoon, before the body was put into the coffin, Professor Robert Proust stayed a long time alone in the room; then he let me go in to bid a last farewell. After that he told the undertakers to do what they had to as gently and quietly as possible.

On Wednesday, the day of the funeral, the professor asked me to sit in his car.

"You must come with the family, Céleste. No one was closer to him than you."

And he put the little cross of flowers I'd ordered in the middle of the coffin.

I only parted from M. Proust in the cemetery, and even then I didn't believe it.

And then one day a strange thing happened. Coming out of the apartment, where we had stayed—Odilon, my sister, and I—to finish putting things in order, I suddenly noticed the window of the bookshop nearby on rue Hamelin. It was all lit up, and behind the glass were the published works of M. Proust, arranged in threes.

Once again I was dazzled by his prescience and his certainty. I thought of the passage in his book in which he speaks of the death of the writer Bergotte: "They buried him. But throughout the night of the funeral, in the lighted windows, the books set out in threes kept watch like angels with outspread wings, as if they were, for him who was no more, a symbol of the resurrection."

EPILOGUE

There. It's finished. What more can I say?

During the weeks that followed his death my only desire was to die too. I couldn't bear it.

We stayed on at rue Hamelin until April 1923, until everything was in order. I stuck the last bits into the proofs of *La Prisonnière* as M. Proust had told me to do, and Professor Robert Proust helped me to tidy things up. Gradually it all went. The professor kept among other things his brother's bed. I kept the screen, the three little bedside tables, the little green lamp, the chairs and armchairs from the bedrooms of boulevard Haussmann and rue Hamelin, and the dressing table. I remember that on one of the little tables there was a deluxe edition of *A l'ombre des jeunes filles en fleurs,* left there because M. Proust had meant to inscribe it for me.

"I want your copy to have a beautiful dedication," he said.

I gave it to Reynaldo Hahn, who hadn't a copy and wanted one.

Then, after that, we had to tear ourselves away. I too went through a great uprooting. On the advice of Professor Robert Proust I went to Bagnoles-de-l'Orne for a rest.

In 1924, Odilon bought a hotel on rue des Canettes, near Saint-Sulpice in Paris. Our savings weren't enough, but we borrowed. I had lived in such a marvelous world, with a man so unique, that I couldn't get used to commonplace life. Even the ordinary daily schedule was a problem. I was like a night bird suddenly compelled to live in broad daylight. Secretly I took refuge in the memory of the magic nights.

As M. Proust had predicted, many people came to see me. Many others wrote. Also as he had predicted, I didn't answer. And there were some who didn't come. Gaston Gallimard wrote me a beautiful letter saying he couldn't do enough for me. But he didn't send me one of M. Proust's books.

I withdrew more and more into my memory. There I was alive. I had a few things, a few books and papers and photographs that used to belong to M. Proust. He had often said, "Céleste, when I am dead, you must take anything here you want. It is yours." I had never thought he would die, and I had never thought of taking anything. The day after the funeral Professor Proust came to see me at rue Hamelin. He asked me if there was any paper with M. Proust's wishes about me. "If there is I'll do what it says," he told me.

I said that there wasn't one as far as I knew. It was true; he had died without leaving a will.

The professor insisted gently: Had I any idea of what his brother would have wished for me?

"Nothing, monsieur. Thank you. And I don't want anything."

Horace Finaly and Mme. Straus also wanted to know what they could do for me. I thanked them very much too but said, "Nothing."

Then the years went by. We sold the hotel on rue des Canettes. Odilon died. For a few years I looked after the Ravel Museum at Montfort-l'Amaury, near Paris. People came to see me, and I reproach myself for having talked to the visitors much more about M. Proust than about Ravel.

Odilon and I had a daughter, Odile, the only other person in the world beside M. Proust to whom I'd have given the moon if she asked for it.

One day she fell very ill—as ill luck would have it, at a time when we had just started to build a little house for my sister Marie and me to retire to. I had to sell many of the souvenirs of M. Proust that I still had left. I didn't think he would have blamed me. But it was a terrible pang.

The picture I have of him in my heart is the most beautiful possible, and the loveliest of memories. He is as magnificent as he always was. A prince among men and a prince of souls.

He has never left me. Whenever I've had some problem, I've always found some admirer of M. Proust's ready to smooth the way for me. It was as if he still went on looking after me even in death. And as I said at the beginning, whenever I've had some personal problems I've consulted his memory and found the solution.

Let me tell you about a strange thing that happened quite recently.

One night when I was with M. Proust at boulevard Haussmann he was showing me some things he'd asked me to fetch from the chest, including some pretty pendant earrings made of coral which used to belong to his mother.

"I think they would suit my niece Suzy," he said. "Put them away, Céleste."

Then, when I came back: "Ah, here is my opal tie pin. Unfortunately I stepped on it and broke it. A pity. But the opal's all right and very pretty. Would you like it? Take it."

I had it mounted as a ring, and it never left my finger. Later, much later, I wanted to give it to Odile, but she was afraid she might lose it and, knowing how fond I was of it, preferred I keep it. I wore it night and day. Then one day I lost it. In despair I did as my mother used to do and prayed to St. Anthony. Mother used to say he always helped her find things. But nothing happened.

That same day my daughter had brought in some greens which I picked over and washed, cooked and chopped up. While we were at the table—Odile, my sister Marie, and I—Odile suddenly stopped eating.

"What's the matter?" I asked. "Did you break a tooth?"

It was M. Proust's opal.

He hadn't forgotten me any more than I could forget him.

SOME OTHER SOUVENIRS

SOME OTHER SOUVENIRS

I thought it might be of interest to append a few other souvenirs of Marcel Proust. None of them has been previously published; some belong to Mme. Albaret and the others to relatives of hers. These letters and telegrams are further proof of their author's "kindness"—the elegant courtesy and goodness, the affectionate and often anxious kindness, which Proust himself intended to convey and which were the qualities that touched him most in others.

—G.B.

The following two telegrams, referred to in Chapter 10, were sent by Marcel Proust to Mme. Albaret when she went back for a brief visit to Auxillac at the time of her mother's death.

Paris, 21/4/1915   18.50

> My affectionate thoughts are with you in your sorrow. Please convey to your sister and brothers the condolences of a friend. Marcel Proust.

Paris, 21/4/1915   18.50

> My poor dear Céleste I have sad news of your brother-in-law Jean reported wounded at Vasquois perhaps taken prisoner or killed. Forgive this blow but I promised to wire you the truth let us hope he is still alive affectionately Marcel.

The following letter is from Marcel Proust to Marcelle Larivière, daughter of Adèle Larivière, one of Mme. Albaret's sisters-in-law, then at La Canourgue, near Auxillac. It belongs to the same period as the two telegrams above.

Mademoiselle,

> I write to commend Céleste to your care. Unfortunately no one can do anything about her state of mind—she is bound to weep and be sad. But at least we mustn't let her become ill. You know how delicate she is and how little thought she gives to herself. She'll take less care even than usual now that she's thinking only of her terrible sorrow. Please think for her, and when you see she's hot, don't let her take anything off or sit in a draft. Make her stay as quiet as possible. We can't do anything about her mental suffering—all we can do is see that her poor body bears up as well as possible under this worst of blows. It is because I see her from up close every day and have come to know something about her health that I take the liberty of making these small suggestions—they are trivial and commonplace enough in such circumstances. But I know you are very fond of Céleste, and nothing is trivial or indifferent where those we love are concerned, especially when we are helpless about the big things and it is only the little things we can do anything about.

> Yours faithfully

> Marcel Proust

To this same period (spring 1915) belongs a letter from Proust to Adèle Rivière, Odilon Albaret's sister, concerning their brother Jean, who had been reported missing. Proust had asked his friend Reynaldo Hahn to use his contacts on the general staff to try to find out what had happened to him.

> As I wrote to Monsieur Hahn, I have been weeping all morning at the thought of you two, whose husband, whose beloved brother, whom you loved and idolized like a child, now wounded heaven knows where. Why is it always the best who fall? I know how

clever and good your Jean is. And why must it always be the tenderest hearts like yours, so marvelous a wife and sister, that are afflicted with pangs that many a hard heart could easily endure? Perhaps we shall have to wait till the end of the war to know what has really happened to him. I think of you with such sadness and sympathy. And poor Odilon. I don't think I am a coward, but I tremble at the thought of writing to him—I know the pain I'm going to cause him. It would be better if you wrote—your tenderness would soften the blow.

Very sadly yours,

Marcel Proust

A letter from Proust to Adèle Rivière, belonging to 1916. She had written to him to thank him for bringing her some sugar, which was then scarce because of the war.

102 boulevard Haussman

Dear Madame

My eyes are so bad I trust you will forgive a short reply to your charming and undeserved letter. What I did was quite natural, and I only wish it had been more. And when you say you didn't properly express—I won't say your gratitude, for you don't owe me any!—but the gracious feelings inspired by your delicacy and goodness of heart, you are even more unfair to yourself. It is I who am embarrassed at having been so warmly welcomed and thanked a thousand times too much. But I hope to be able to say all this in person soon, and to have the pleasure of making the acquaintance of Monsieur Larivière, the only member of the family I don't yet know. Meanwhile, if my eyes don't plague me too much I hope to write a few lines to your son—Céleste doesn't write to him as often as she should. I was sorry to hear that your nephew Lucien was so ill but am glad to hear that he is recovering. Please give my respects to Madame Jean Albaret and Mademoiselle Marcelle, and believe me to be your and Monsieur Larivière's devoted

Marcel Proust

A letter from Proust to Adèle Rivière. Mme. Albaret thinks the anniversary mass referred to was probably to commemorate the death of Alfred Agostinelli, who plunged into the sea in his airplane on May 30, 1914. This would mean that the letter belongs to the spring of 1916 or 1917.

Wednesday 17

Madame,

Thank you with all my heart for having been so kind as to make the arrangements at the Eglise Saint-Pierre. I could only ask someone who would do it with intelligence and tact—in other words, I couldn't have applied to a better messenger than you. I was glad, too, when Céleste told me you were able to attend the anniversary mass for the death of my poor friend. But I was even more pleased at another piece of news she gave me: I gather Monsieur Larivière got forty-eight hours' leave and that though he's tired from his long stint of service he's adapting himself bravely to his new life. Alas, you especially are the one we must wish the courage we all need at present, and I know it is difficult to find it when half your heart is in Neuilly and the other half on the firing line. That is a division unknown to surgery—but war finds a way to wound to the heart even of those who stay at home. I hope to be strong enough one day to come and tell you how much I think about you in your anxiety and how much for your sake I hope the war will soon end. Meanwhile, all my thanks. Please give my best wishes to your dear soldiers. My best wishes to Mademoiselle your daughter and to yourself.

Marcel Proust

Letter from Proust to Marcelle Larivière, Adèle Rivière's daughter and Mme. Albaret's niece by marriage.

31 January 1916

Mademoiselle,

> I owe you many thanks, but few of them give me more pleasure to express than those for your two "plays" for an essay. I was very much struck by the little summaries you were good enough to take the trouble to send me. And there is not only goodness and trouble but talent as well. They're perfect. No need to talk of the writing and the syntax—for someone as cultivated as I can see you are, these things are only secondary. But you show such knowledge and such intelligence, both in the form and in the content. There are few male scholars, even among the élite, who could have done nearly as well. I hope soon to express my congratulations and thanks in person. Meanwhile, my best respects to you and your parents.

> Marcel Proust

Letter from Proust to André Larivière on the death of his sister Marcelle. She had married and become Mme. Labit and died of puerperal fever in 1920, a year after her marriage.

My dear friend,

> I can't say at the moment whether I shall be well enough to go to pay my last respects to your dear sister, for whom you were everything, just as you loved no one more dearly than you loved her. How dreadful it is when there are so many cold hearts in the world that death should strike just where the living are as much

to be pitied as the dead, so great was the love between them. My dear friend, I hope you will find the strength to bear your sorrow in your efforts to lessen the suffering of your dear parents. Try to make them patient. Of course neither you nor they can forget the sweet person who has been taken away from them. But though they can't imagine it now, when they are enduring the awful suffering of their loss, a day will come when their hearts will be filled with a sorrow that is sweet, and the memory of Marcelle, as dear as ever, will only be all the sweeter to them, and their constant and loving companion. Help your mother and father to bear the time until that day comes, a day that will be a blessed one for you all, for having been perfect parents just as you were a perfect brother, they will have the happiness of never having done their daughter anything but good, of having cherished her as no other parents ever cherished a daughter. I didn't want to intrude on their grief by writing directly, but as soon as you can, please tell them I commiserate with all my heart. Please give my profound condolences to Monsieur Labit also. I won't ask you to come to see me just now—you are needed where you are. The only thing I could do would be to try to distract you for a moment from your grief, and I couldn't do that now that nothing could distract you, and I wouldn't want to do it now that nothing should distract you. But later, when though your memories as a brother will be as bright as ever your sorrow will be a little eased, be sure that when you come to see me you will find a heartfelt friend.

With all sympathy and affection,

Marcel Proust

Proust's transcription of the words of "Le temps des Lilas" (Lilac Time):

Ici bas tous les lilas
meurent
Tous les chants des oiseaux.
Je rêve aux étés qui demeurent
sont courts
Toujours !
Ici bas les lèvres effleurent
Sans rien laisser de leur velours
Je rêve aux baisers qui demeurent
Toujours !

Ici bas tous les hommes pleurent
Leurs amitiés ou leurs amours
Je rêve aux couples qui demeurent
Toujours !

INDEX

Index

379

TITLES IN SERIES

J.R. ACKERLEY Hindoo Holiday
J.R. ACKERLEY My Dog Tulip
J.R. ACKERLEY My Father and Myself
J.R. ACKERLEY We Think the World of You
HENRY ADAMS The Jeffersonian Transformation
CÉLESTE ALBARET Monsieur Proust
DANTE ALIGHIERI The Inferno
DANTE ALIGHIERI The New Life
WILLIAM ATTAWAY Blood on the Forge
W.H. AUDEN (EDITOR) The Living Thoughts of Kierkegaard
W.H. AUDEN W. H. Auden's Book of Light Verse
ERICH AUERBACH Dante: Poet of the Secular World
DOROTHY BAKER Cassandra at the Wedding
J.A. BAKER The Peregrine
HONORÉ DE BALZAC The Unknown Masterpiece *and* Gambara
MAX BEERBOHM Seven Men
ALEXANDER BERKMAN Prison Memoirs of an Anarchist
GEORGES BERNANOS Mouchette
ADOLFO BIOY CASARES Asleep in the Sun
ADOLFO BIOY CASARES The Invention of Morel
CAROLINE BLACKWOOD Corrigan
CAROLINE BLACKWOOD Great Granny Webster
MALCOLM BRALY On the Yard
JOHN HORNE BURNS The Gallery
ROBERT BURTON The Anatomy of Melancholy
CAMARA LAYE The Radiance of the King
GIROLAMO CARDANO The Book of My Life
J.L. CARR A Month in the Country
BLAISE CENDRARS Moravagine
EILEEN CHANG Love in a Fallen City
UPAMANYU CHATTERJEE English, August: An Indian Story
NIRAD C. CHAUDHURI The Autobiography of an Unknown Indian
ANTON CHEKHOV Peasants and Other Stories
RICHARD COBB Paris and Elsewhere
COLETTE The Pure and the Impure
JOHN COLLIER Fancies and Goodnights
CARLO COLLODI The Adventures of Pinocchio
IVY COMPTON-BURNETT A House and Its Head
IVY COMPTON-BURNETT Manservant and Maidservant
BARBARA COMYNS The Vet's Daughter
EVAN S. CONNELL The Diary of a Rapist
HAROLD CRUSE The Crisis of the Negro Intellectual
ASTOLPHE DE CUSTINE Letters from Russia
LORENZO DA PONTE Memoirs
ELIZABETH DAVID A Book of Mediterranean Food
ELIZABETH DAVID Summer Cooking
MARIA DERMOÛT The Ten Thousand Things
DER NISTER The Family Mashber
ARTHUR CONAN DOYLE The Exploits and Adventures of Brigadier Gerard
CHARLES DUFF A Handbook on Hanging
DAPHNE DU MAURIER Don't Look Now: Stories